THE ILLUSTRATED ENCYCLOPEDIA OF
ANCIENT EARTH MYSTERIES

THE ILLUSTRATED ENCYCLOPEDIA OF
ANCIENT EARTH MYSTERIES

Paul Devereux

CASSELL&CO

First published in the United Kingdom in 2000 by Blandford

Text copyright © Paul Devereux, 2000
Design and layout copyright © Blandford, 2000

Distributed in the United States of America by Sterling Publishing Co. Inc.
387 Park Avenue South, New York, NY 10016–8810

A CIP catalogue record for this book is available from the British Library

ISBN 0-7137-2764-0

Designed by Richard Carr
Edited by Sarah Widdicombe

Printed by Colorcraft Ltd, Hong Kong

Cassell & Co
Wellington House
125 Strand
London WC2R OBB

CONTENTS

INTRODUCTION

The primary purpose of this book is to help the reader navigate the 'grey zone' that exists between what we could call mainstream archaeology and anthropology, and the wild shores of pseudo-archaeology. Misinformation, myths and misunderstanding on the part of both scholars and New Age enthusiasts usually crowd out genuine understanding in this zone. For example, if one takes a topic such as 'leys', the scholar will dismiss it out of hand as a nonsense subject, while the New Ager will set out to vibe the energies of a supposed planetary grid of 'leylines'. Entries in this encyclopedia will provide a range of information that indicates another way entirely to approach the whole issue. I therefore hope both sceptic and enthusiast alike will find this book to be of benefit, for it brings a number of contentious areas up to date and provides a background network of information not all of which may have been hitherto readily available to the reader. By the same token, both sceptic and enthusiast might find material that challenges their prejudices, for without fear or favour some hoary old myths have been exposed for what they are, while challenging approaches to some subjects have been upheld or, at least, redefined.

The title 'ancient earth mysteries' is merely a popular label for the grey zone, the no-man's land where aspects of archaeology, ancient astronomy, folklore, ethnology, occultism, consciousness studies and many more topics come together without being any one of those disciplines. It is their juxtaposition and cross-boundary treatment that present problems for the orthodox mind. A further difficulty is that the ancient earth mysteries area ranges not only in subject matter but in mode as well, from the objective to the subjective. It is also true that considerable naivety and lack of factual knowledge are displayed by some earth mysteries proponents. It is these negative factors that colour the view of sceptics, causing a knee-jerk rejection that is simply the other side of the coin to the nonsense element within earth mysteries. To understand the value of some of the work and useful cross-disciplinary thinking coming out of the earth mysteries arena requires more discernment, and this encyclopedia has been produced in an effort to aid – or at least to encourage – that process.

The core term 'earth mysteries' seems to have first appeared in 1974 as a headline to an article in the *Whole Earth Catalog* that was trying to summarize aspects of the new wave of ancient mysteries writing and speculation. It was a time also when archaeology itself was in turmoil, especially with regard to the changes it was obliged to make to its dating systems – specifically, the recalibration of the radiocarbon dating method through correction by tree-ring dating – which made old monuments even older than had been thought until then. This was compounded by challenges from scholars outside archaeology, indicating that the megalith builders of western Europe and ancient societies elsewhere had possessed sophisticated astronomical skills, and by the breakdown of neat theories like diffusionism, which had purported to explain the circulation of technical knowledge and social development through the ancient world. Into this already disturbed situation blundered the refugees from various esoteric persuasions: the UFO buffs and ancient astronaut devotees, the ley hunters, the students of archaic and arcane systems of thought, and those who simply questioned the picture we had of the ancient mind. Certain themes emerged as the currency for ancient mysteries enquiry, and these are covered in the following pages, along with other thematic strands that have emerged subsequently.

The term 'earth mysteries' was picked up and used by the specialist journal *The Ley Hunter* in 1976, and from that time it has spread further through the work of researchers, writers and journalists, appearing in countless books and magazines and even becoming a category heading in some libraries and bookshops. Even so, 'earth mysteries' remains primarily a British term for what is more generally known as 'ancient mysteries' in North America. (At an early stage, some researchers on both sides of the Atlantic also used 'geomancy' to refer to the same general area of interest. But 'geomancy' has its own specific meanings, dealt with in the appropriate entries in this encyclopedia, and so is hardly an ideal alternative handle.) It would be best for all such labels to be quietly retired, for in many ways they hinder genuine discussion and even perception of useful work and ideas. But it is probably too late for that now, and because we always need convenient terminology, some new – and equally meaningless – phrase would almost certainly be invented to take its place and would merely add to the confusion. So this book seeks to balance the risk of putting the phrase 'earth mysteries' into circulation yet again by attempting to provide orderly, factual and updated information that will aid discernment between the valid and invalid, between lazy fantasizing and the genuinely conceptually exciting and intellectually challenging.

The end of a millennium is a particularly good time to look back over preceding millennia, to take stock of our understanding of the human adventure. Conceptual stock-taking is no different from any other kind: it is a process that requires the discarding of what is no longer of use and the re-ordering of what is.

ABOUT THIS BOOK

Of course, the subject area is so vast that entries in this encyclopedia have had to be kept relatively brief for purely practical reasons. There are bound to be topics not covered that some readers will feel should have been, but my concern has been to illuminate some of the deeper currents and themes that circulate within this diffuse field of interest rather than to notch up an endless alphabet of minutiae. Nevertheless, the main items are included, along with many minor ones. Those subjects I regard as being especially important – or particularly misunderstood – are given extended entries. I have not shied away from providing personal colouring to some of the entries, but I have tried to be balanced where this is called for in the case of topics that remain *genuinely* unresolved. A range of entries deals with specific ancient sites. As ancient monuments are legion, such entries could, of course, have been greatly multiplied, so while an element of personal choice has inevitably intruded, I have tried to select sites that I feel help to illuminate some of the thematic entries.

Despite these qualifications, I trust that this work is reasonably comprehensive and will provide a cognitive compass for newcomer and veteran alike. In the final analysis, the field of 'ancient earth mysteries' is probably not quite what any of us, whether sceptic or enthusiast, thinks it to be.

In compiling the book, I have attempted to keep the emphasis on the fact that this is an *illustrated* encyclopedia. However, it has not been our intention to produce a pretty but vacuous coffee-table book; rather, we have tried to provide illustrations that first and foremost perform an informative role.

Most of the photographs used in these pages are my own, taken during my extensive travels to ancient sites to study the various aspects of ancient earth mysteries. But I have also been greatly aided by additional visual material from others. Where this is the case, the source is indicated in the caption. To all these people and institutions, I offer my profound gratitude.

USING THE ENCYCLOPEDIA

Encyclopedic works are essentially designed to be dipped into or consulted as required. This encyclopedia can, of course, be used in that way, but it is also strongly recommended that in the first instance the *whole* is read through as if it were a narrative text. Why? Because by doing so the 'mirage' that is earth mysteries will be revealed. Although the entries jump from one subject to another, the underlying themes and connections will nevertheless gradually become apparent. This cannot be explained, only experienced.

In whatever way this book is read, it is most important to be alert to the internal referencing and cross-referencing that will be found in the entries. Such references are given in **bold** type, either within the main body of an entry or at the end, or both. It can be safely assumed that the fully rounded sense of a subject cannot be obtained without using the cross-references. Sometimes, a whole train of associations needs to be followed in order to build up the 'big picture' concerning a particular theme.

ACOUSTICS

Sound is so immediate that it does not readily present itself as a suitable tool with which to explore the mysteries of ancient sites. Today, however, both mainstream and earth mysteries archaeological investigators are pursuing various lines of acoustic enquiry in an attempt to eavesdrop on the ancient mind.

American researcher Steven Waller has conducted acoustic tests on Aboriginal rock paintings in Australia and the **Palaeolithic** painted caves of France and Spain. He has found that percussive sounds directed at the rock walls yield more echo decibels than unpainted surfaces nearby. Moreover, the echoes transform into sounds suggestive of galloping hooves that emanate from specific images such as herds of bison or horses, as if they had their own soundtrack. In 1996 preliminary acoustic investigations of another kind were undertaken by Professor Robert G. Jahn and myself under the aegis of the International Consciousness Research Laboratories (ICRL) group based at Princeton New Jersey. Tests were made of the acoustical resonances of various **Neolithic** chambered mounds in Britain and Ireland, including **Newgrange**. These sites were found to have resonant frequencies of 95–112Hz (Hertz or cycles per second), with most at 110Hz. This is in the male baritone range, raising the possibility that male ritual chanting took place in the chambers or that oracular pronouncements were made from them (a sound made at the resonant frequency of the chamber in which it occurs is amplified). Indeed, in 1973 Welsh archaeologist Frances Lynch had suggested that the entrance passages to Stone Age mounds might have been for acoustic communication. This challenges conservative opinion that such monuments were merely elaborate graves.

Subsequent to the ICRL work, investigators from Britain's Reading University announced the results of work they had been doing at the Easter Aquorthies stone circle and the Camster Round passage grave, both sites in Scotland. Their audio-recording equipment at the circle revealed that sound was bounced around its interior, reflecting off the inward-facing sides of the stones towards the centre of the circle. The sound was organized as effectively as in a theatre, and

Aboriginal rock art in the Kimberleys, Western Australia. Typically painted on the curved walls of rock shelters, these kinds of image have been shown to reflect percussive sounds in highly focused ways.

noises – even faint ones – varied in intensity at different places within the circle. Such acoustic effects would not have been audible to people outside the ring of stones. At Camster Round the Reading team found that moving a sound source around the chamber could affect the distribution of sound throughout the whole structure, and they were able to find the optimum spot where music, chanting or speech could be produced. In other words, they were able to determine where the religious officiant probably stood thousands of years ago. They also found that sound made within the chamber could change its nature when heard in different places and could be heard outside the mound in tightly defined locations.

In addition, the Reading researchers realized that the basic design of all prehistoric so-called passage graves – a cavity in the centre of the mound connected to the outside world by a narrow passage – forms a Helmholtz resonator. A simple demonstration of this resonator can be had by blowing air across the top of an empty, narrow-necked bottle, causing a humming noise due to the movement of the air in the body of the bottle and its interaction with that in the neck. A sound can be amplified significantly in this way, and this perhaps happened during rituals at the chambered mounds. The Helmholtz resonance of Camster Round turned out to be 4Hz, a very low bass frequency, which would be felt as a deep vibration rather than heard as a sound, like the sensation experienced when standing near a large bass speaker. Intriguingly, a 4Hz resonant frequency could be set up by rhythmic drumming. While the drumming would be heard in the chamber, everyone inside would also experience a peculiar physical sensation caused by the unheard resonance.

Such investigations are so far preliminary, but they hold great promise for producing a richer insight into the nature of what went on at the mysterious megalithic sites of western Europe. The same techniques could also be applied to Pueblo Indian **kivas** in the American southwest, and other sites elsewhere offer intriguing avenues for various kinds of acoustic research. The Mayan ruins, for instance, are rumoured to possess strange sound properties. A faint whisper can be heard all around certain Mayan ball courts, together with what is termed 'flutter echo', and investigators wonder if this played a part in some way in the little-understood activities conducted in them. (It is known that the Mayan ball game was more than merely a grim sport in which the loser lost his head – it was a ritual and ceremonial activity as well.)

At **Chichén Itzá,** on Mexico's Yucatán peninsula, a curious screeching echo reverberates from the north side of the stepped pyramid, El Castillo, in response to any percussive sound. The

Testing the resonant frequency of the chambers at Wayland's Smithy chambered mound in Oxfordshire. The white instrument is a sound generator.

sound is similar to the primary call of the quetzel bird, which was sacred to the **Maya**. At Tulum a 'whistle horn' sound is sometimes emitted by a temple. This seems to be due to a particular wind direction and may have been used as a storm warning. At the ancient Mayan site of Tikel there is a 'whispering gallery' effect in the Great Plaza, and there are tuned stone steps at a temple. At the major Mayan ceremonial city of Palenque normal conversation is possible between the tops of the three pyramids there, and there is a sound-enhancing effect through the slit in the 'oracle' pyramid. And there are other such examples – it is claimed that many Mayan buildings have 'acoustical signatures'. How much is coincidence or was genuinely engineered in the ancient past must await in-depth research. It also has to be borne in mind that some cultures, especially rainforest peoples such as the Maya, used their auditory sense much more than we do today. For people like the Umeda in Papua New Guinea, for example, hearing is the primary sense, followed by smell. Vision comes only third.

The amphitheatre at Epidaurus, Greece, capable of seating 1200 people. It is said that the sound of a coin dropped from knee height onto the base of the altar to Dionysius (still extant in the centre of the orchestra) can be clearly heard from the top seats. It is apparent that ancient Greek architects were aware of acoustics.

There are acoustic oddities at the sites of other ancient cultures, too. In Greece the so-called Tomb of Agamemnon at Mycenae is a tholos tomb, meaning it is beehive shaped. Such structures were designed literally to recall a beehive, as the bee symbolized death in ancient Greece. When one enters this tomb, an inexplicable buzzing – like a swarm of bees – can be heard near the great curved wall. This is balanced by an acoustically 'dead' spot in the centre. The Greeks also produced amphitheatres with acute acoustic properties. In Egypt for many years in Ptolomaic times the northernmost statue of the two so-called Colossi of Memnon in the Valley of the Kings issued weird sounds at sunrise from its earthquake-caused cracks and was used as an **oracle**. A tradition similarly states that the **Sphinx** sometimes produces a weird, piercing cry at sunrise. A granite rock in Riverside County, California, was sacred to the Cahuilla Indians, for it has prehistoric engravings on it and produces a bell-like sound when struck. In *The Mysteries of Chartres Cathedral* (1966) French author Louis Charpentier has even speculated that Gregorian plainchant was designed, or evolved, to penetrate Gothic space and cause the stone to resonate.

The psychological effects of sound at sites should also not be overlooked. Princeton psychologist Julian Jaynes has pointed out that oracle sites are often located near the sound of rushing water or the roar of wind through trees.

If the new trend towards acoustic research in archaeological contexts continues, the currently mute past might be given a voice. The old stones will speak.

See also **Loughcrew; Rock Art; Tiahuanaco**

ANASAZI

The Anasazi emerged in the last centuries BC out of bands of hunter-gatherers who roamed the American southwest. When they learned how to grow corn, they gradually adopted a more settled lifestyle, and horticulture and habitations developed. The early Anasazi lived in 'pit houses' – dwellings made of logs, brush and mud set into a circular or rectangular pit. They also wove fine baskets, which earned them the archaeological term 'Basketmaker' for this stage. Between AD 450 and 700 pottery made an appearance, and by the eighth century above-ground rectangular houses were preferred. Flat-roofed and made of mud, rock and timber posts and often built in terraces or groups, these 'pueblos' marked the beginning of the 'Pueblo Period' of Anasazi culture. The pit-house structure was converted to use in circular, semi-subterranean ritual chambers known as **kivas**.

The Anasazi culture reached its height between AD 900 and 1300. Its primary territory was the San Juan Basin, which is 400 miles (640km) wide, and the area around it, which is where present-day New Mexico, Utah, Arizona and Colorado meet, is now known as the Four Corners. The Anasazi stretched further afield than this, however, and there is even some evidence that over time they migrated from their key northern ceremonial centres such as Aztec, New Mexico, south to their major cult centre of **Chaco Canyon**, also in New Mexico, ending up at Casas Grandes in Chihuahua, northern Mexico. Aztec and Chaco Canyon were formerly linked by a wide, straight Anasazi road that runs due north–south. Archaeologist Stephen Lekson has used the satellite-based Global Positioning System to

Pueblo Bonito, built by the Anasazi in Chaco Canyon, New Mexico, is the largest prehistoric ruin in the United States. The main, dividing wall visible in the picture is an accurate meridian (aligned north–south). The circular depressions are kivas.

The so-called Sun Temple at Mesa Verde, which is thought to be the last Anasazi building to be constructed in the huge Mesa Verde complex. Work on this mysterious building ceased suddenly and inexplicably in AD 1276 , when the walls were between 12 and 15 feet (3.6–4.6m) high (their tops have been sealed with modern cement). Each stone in the walls was shaped and has a dimpled surface. There are unusual rooms and corridors in the 'temple', which also has a possible solstitial marker. There has been speculation that the 'temple' was being built to appease supernatural forces in order to prevent the disaster that was overtaking the Anasazi. The unfinished state of the structure suggests that they were too late.

calculate that Casas Grandes lies precisely on that meridian extended 390 miles (625km) south of Chaco Canyon.

The Anasazi culture seems to have collapsed suddenly during the fifteenth century, probably dispersing into what are now the various Pueblo peoples of the American southwest, such as the **Zuni** and the **Hopi**. The reason for this sudden decline is not known, although severe drought, evidenced in tree-ring records for the period, has been considered a prime candidate. Current opinion, however, favours the idea that political and religious changes and unrest may have been the deciding factors. There is said to be some evidence of cannibalism among the Anasazi, and this might possibly relate to troubled times near the end of the culture.

The Navajo moved into what had been Anasazi territory, and the name Anasazi is the Navajo term for 'Ancient Ones', although it can also be understood as 'Ancient Enemies'. The Navajo avoid Anasazi ruins, which are taboo to them, and if they do visit one, they have to undergo spiritual purification ceremonies afterwards.

The Anasazi were not only accomplished builders, basketmakers and potters, but they also engineered canals and remarkable, mysterious straight roads, even though they did not have the wheel or horses. Parts of this road system have been found throughout the San Juan Basin, and it is thought that the roads linked the kivas within the vast region. The roads are very difficult to trace today at ground level, and show up better in aerial views. Anasazi trade links extended to a huge geographical sphere. They were also adept at ceremonial astronomy and have left behind **rock art** and their intriguing ruined buildings, some of which are astronomically oriented. These are found scattered throughout the Four Corners area, including at **Hovenweep**, Utah, and the centres mentioned above.

For earth mysteries buffs, the Anasazi hold special interest because of their road system, which is so like earth mysteries ideas about **leys**, their religious beliefs, which probably included a form of shamanism, and their astronomical expertise.

See also **Archaeoastronomy**; **Hallucinogens**; **Shaman**

Roofing timber and ceiling inside a surviving room at Aztec, New Mexico.

ARCHAEOASTRONOMY

Occasionally referred to as 'astro-archaeology', archaeoastronomy is the modern study of the use of astronomy by ancient peoples. Its origins are in folk traditions. In Europe seasonal fairs and games were often held at ancient sacred places or local landmarks such as prominent hilltops. These festivities frequently related to important astronomical times of the year, such as the four solar divisions provided by the solstices (21 June and 21 December) and the equinoxes (21 March and 21 September), and the eight solar divisions when the cross-quarter days are added between. These latter are recalled in Celtic tradition as Imbolc (February), Beltane (May), Lughnassadh (August) and Samhain (November), and the Christian tradition remembers three of these as Candlemas, Lammas and All Saints. The May feast of Beltane was not given a Christian calendrical place, but the May Queen seems to have become associated with the Virgin Mary.

Stonehenge in Wiltshire was a classic location for such festivities, which were denounced as 'vile and indecorous' by the Bishop of Salisbury in 1223. These festivities and their locations caused antiquarians to start looking for possible astronomical aspects of ancient monuments, and Stonehenge was naturally a prime target. In 1740 William Stukeley noticed that its axis aligned to 'where abouts the sun rises when the days are longest', and in 1770 an antiquary documented that the Heel Stone at Stonehenge marked the summer solstice sunrise when viewed from the centre of the monument. In 1846 the Reverend E. Duke noted that the four Station Stone positions at Stonehenge, which form the corners of a near-rectangle on the site's groundplan, gave alignments to the summer solstice sunrise and midwinter sunset positions.

By the end of the nineteenth century ancient astronomy was firmly on the intellectual agenda in France, Germany, Ireland and Britain. Inspired by some German research, Sir Norman Lockyer, a well-known scientist of his day and editor of the prestigious journal *Nature*, gave the subject a major boost around the turn of the century when he undertook studies of Greek and Egyptian temples and found them to have solar and stellar orientations. He went on to make similar studies of Stonehenge. Taking account of precession (a 'wobble' in the Earth's rotational spin that causes specific rise and set points of heavenly bodies to shift noticeably over long periods of time), he calculated that the axis of Stonehenge had been directed at summer solstice sunrise between 1600 and 2000 BC. He also noted that a diagonal

The Heel Stone at Stonehenge in Wiltshire.

been worse 5000 years ago, due to precession. It could be that the midsummer sunrise connection with the Heel Stone is something of a coincidence, because when is seen the outlier from the centre of Stonehenge, it is at the mid-point between the furthest horizon positions north and south that the moon rises in its cycle.

At about the same time as Newham's Stonehenge inquiries, Gerald Hawkins, a British-born astronomer from America's Smithsonian Institution, was also becoming interested in the monument's astronomical possibilities, although it was some time before he became aware of Newham's work. Hawkins investigated the Station Stone rectangle, but he looked at other aspects of the site, too, in particular, the great sarsen stones that we most commonly think of as being Stonehenge. He found that the inner 'horseshoe' setting of the great trilithons yielded sightlines through the gaps between the uprights in the outer sarsen circle towards important solar and lunar rising and setting positions. The gaps between the trilithon uprights are narrow, and they act like gunsights to the wider gaps in the sarsen ring. These sightlines were too wide to be very accurate, but they would have provided 'windows' that framed astronomically significant sections of the horizon. This would probably have been sufficient for ceremonial purposes.

Hawkins also suggested that the ring of 56 pits known as the Aubrey Holes, just inside the circular ditch surrounding the stones of Stonehenge, was related to the 56-year lunar eclipse cycle. He felt the holes were the remains of an eclipse

Stone 91, one of four Station Stone positions set in a rectangular arrangement around the inner sarsens stones of Stonehenge, which belong to an early phase of the site and which yield some key solar and lunar alignments between them.

across the four Station Stones pointed to certain cross-quarter-day sunrises and sunsets. Lockyer's findings were resisted by the archaeologists of his day. He did make errors and some dubious claims, but ancient astronomy had definitely arrived as a subject worthy of study.

Over subsequent decades, a handful of other researchers conducted astronomical surveys of prehistoric sites, but it wasn't until new work at Stonehenge in the 1960s that the study began to mature fully. British researcher C.A. Newham looked closely at the positions of the Station Stones, and his careful measurements showed that the sides of the Station Stone rectangle gave alignments to key solar and lunar rise and set positions, confirming the suspicions of Duke over a century earlier. Newham went on to demonstrate the full extent of the alignments the Station Stones created, and his further studies convinced him that in its earliest stage Stonehenge was 'essentially a site for the investigation of lunar phenomena'. He felt that postholes, which archaeologists had discovered in the monument's entrance causeway, had been made by poles erected by the builders of Stonehenge to mark the passage of the moon's movements for over a century so that they could work out the skyline positions of the moon in the course of its complex cycle of 18.61 years, the so-called Metonic cycle.

Newham's conclusions are supported by today's researchers, who are now confident that Stonehenge was indeed originally laid out on a lunar axis. It seems that this was deliberately realigned by four degrees at a later date to form a solar one. But if Stonehenge was originally a lunar temple, why does the midsummer sun rise over the Heel Stone? In fact, this outlier, weighing 37 tons and rising to 16ft (5m), does not mark sunrise on the summer solstice. The sun rises just to the left (west) of the stone when viewed from the centre of Stonehenge, and this discrepancy would have

Looking through the narrow gap between two uprights of a trilithon towards a wider gap between sarsen stones on the outer ring of Stonehenge, along one of Hawkins's astronomical sightlines.

predictor or computer in which six rocks were used as markers, perhaps three of them light in colour and three dark, and moved by one Aubrey Hole per year, while a moon marker stone moved by one upright per day around Stonehenge's sarsen outer ring, their combinations telling of impending eclipses. Later, astronomer Fred Hoyle offered another version of the Aubrey Hole computer using a different system and fewer markers. Although neither idea has found favour with archaeologists, Hawkins's book, *Stonehenge Decoded* (with John B. White; published in 1965), put the idea of archaeoastronomy into the public domain. The notion of using modern computers to decode a Stone Age computer proved a potent and popular image.

In 1967 Scottish engineer and astronomer Alexander Thom published the findings of his decades of surveying prehistoric megalithic monuments in the British Isles. He deduced three things from his work: (i) many prehistoric monuments could have been used for precise astronomical observation; (ii) the groundplans of stone circles that were not truly circular were sophisticated geometrical configurations, and (iii) sites had been laid out to a standard of measure he dubbed 'the megalithic yard' (2.72ft/80cm). Thom's surveys were so detailed and accurate that his claims finally gave archaeoastronomy academic respectability. He and his son, Archibald, made a new, accurate survey of Stonehenge in 1973 and sought longer (and hence more accurate) alignments at the place than had hitherto been claimed. To do this, they came to a conclusion similar to Lockyer before them: that outlying landmarks in the landscape around Stonehenge were used, in conjunction with sighting posts, to mark important sun and moon rise and set positions.

The precision Thom felt he saw in megalithic astronomy and measure has subsequently been challenged, and it now appears that relatively few sites possess such exactitude. It seems that astronomy was used in ancient times more for ceremonial and magical purposes than for scientific enquiry as we would understand that today. Although calculation and accurate naked-eye astronomy were certainly conducted by the megalith builders, it was in the service of cosmology – more akin to what we understand as astrology and religion. As prehistorian Aubrey Burl put it in *The Stonehenge People* (1987): 'There are alignments, but they are not honed to the stiletto sharpness of a laser beam. They are diffused as bars of sunlight through stained glass.'

Astronomical awareness may, however, be even older than Stonehenge. Indeed, it may have been present as far back as the **Palaeolithic** era. Alexander Marshack discovered markings carved on bones thought to be 20,000 years old,

which can be interpreted as notations of lunar phases. Other researchers have pointed out that the Palaeolithic rock paintings in the so-called Hall of Bulls in the cave of Lascaux, France, could represent the prominent star groupings along the ecliptic because they were seen near the horizon at the summer solstice.

Although archaeoastronomy developed primarily in western Europe, it has now spread widely, especially in the Americas, as will be noted in other entries. Because of the survival of Native American lore and traditions or documentation regarding them, a measure of ethnological information has been available to American researchers that augments physical evidence found at sites. Anthropologists noted in the 1930s, for instance, that the **Hopi** Indians had sunwatcher priests who observed key agricultural or ceremonial dates by the sun's position relative to mountain peaks and notches. Other Pueblo Indians had special plates on the interior walls of their adobe homes that marked specific dates when the sun shone on them through carefully aligned window apertures. This ethnological dimension to archaeoastronomy is denied those studying the megalithic sites of European prehistory, as no recordable traditions survive from that period.

Archaeoastronomical studies in Europe now extend into the historic era, as research shows that astronomy was incorporated into medieval sacred sites. After the decline of Rome monastic orders of western Europe collated smatterings of astronomical knowledge from ancient Greece and Rome, and from Celtic and other native pagan sources. Elements of pagan solar and lunar calendars became Christianized, although detailed technical knowledge of how to observe the heavens and make astronomical calculations, which was present in ancient Greece if not before, seems to have been largely lost to Christian scholars for several centuries. They also brought in influences from outside Europe. For example, the fourth-century John Cassian governed his prayer schedule by observation of the stars, a practice he had learned in the monasteries of lower Egypt. Gregory of Tours strengthened the astronomical dimension of Christianity with his sixth-century treatise *On the Course of the Stars* (*De cursu stellarum*). The use of horizon calendars for ritual time-keeping, marking the risings and settings of stars and the sun against hills, skyline notches and roofs of monastery buildings, was routinely employed by medieval monks.

The assembly of astronomical knowledge in Europe was given a considerable fillip during the Carolingian Renaissance of the eight and ninth centuries. Charlemagne attracted scholars from around the known world to his court at Aachen, in order to staff an educational programme that included the teaching of astronomical calculation to the clergy. He also ensured that important ancient texts were identified, collected and copied. One of his key scholars was Alcuin of York (AD 730–804), who brought much astronomical knowledge with him.

These factors perhaps support observations made in the 1970s by German photographer Hermann Weisweiler in Charlemagne's octagonal palace chapel, which is the core of the present Aachen Cathedral. Weisweiler accidentally noticed that at noon on 21 June, the summer solstice, a sunbeam shone on a golden ball at the end of a chain on which hangs the Barbarossa chandelier, depicting the heavenly **Jerusalem**. Weisweiler went on to discover that on the same day a sunbeam would also have shone on the face (or crown) of whoever sat on Charlemagne's throne, which was used for coronations throughout the Middle Ages. The midwinter noon sun shines on a mosaic depicting Christ between the alpha and omega symbols. And, for good

The octagonal chapel at Aachen Cathedral, Germany.

measure, a sunbeam shines on the throne on 16 April – Charlemagne's birthday! These effects have been dismissed by some sceptics as merely coincidental, as they may be, but this judgement could be too hasty in the light of the Carolingian focus on astronomy.

The use of sacred or ceremonial astronomy is to be found at lesser known medieval churches, too. At St Lizier in France, for instance, researchers have found three solar alignments extending from it to other churches or landmarks. At Elm, a ski resort in the Swiss canton of Glarus, the Tschingelhorner mountain, which towers over the village to the southeast, is pierced by a natural rock tunnel 60ft (20m) in diameter known as St Martin's Hole. Every year, near to the equinoxes, the morning sun shines through this hole and for two minutes illuminates the tower of Elm church. The visible beam of sunlight is 3 miles (5km) long. This event obviously occurred long before Christianity, but it is telling that the church builders chose that spot, indicating that they were seeking astronomical associations. This is reinforced by the fact that there are four more such holes in the Alps through which sunlight strikes a church.

Medieval churches were supposed to be aligned to the point of sunrise on the day of the saint to whom they were dedicated. Very little is actually documented about this, but in the 1950s the Reverend Hugh Benson surveyed almost 300 medieval English churches and found that a significant proportion were indeed aligned accurately to sunrise on their patron saint's day. One example is the ancient St Piran's church in Cornwall, which is oriented towards a prehistoric earthwork over 2 miles (3km) away – the point where the sun would have risen on 15 August in the seventh century.

Evidence for ancient astronomy is found elsewhere than Europe and the Americas. It was brought to great sophistication by the ancient Chinese, for instance, for whom astronomy was linked to the emperor and his government. There were official court astronomers, one of whose titles was Inspectorate of the Spherical Sky. In the Tang dynasty (AD 618–907), there was a board of five 'star officers', each of whom had the responsibility for observing one of the then-known planets. Accuracy was a hallmark of ancient Chinese astronomy. For example, by AD 725 in the town of Gao cheng zhen (formerly Yang-cheng) a gnomon (shadow-throwing upright) 8ft (2.5m) tall, had been set up by the Buddhist monk I Hsing. It was one of a string of gnomons laid out on a single meridian (north–south line) almost 2200 miles (3500km) in length. Over such a distance, the shadows of the gnomons measured, say, when the sun was highest in the sky at noon on the summer solstice, would vary sufficiently for geographical distances (and, theoretically, the dimensions of the earth) to be calculated. This was a geodetic or earth-measuring use of astronomy.

An equally 'high-tech' measuring device was built at Gao cheng zhen by the astronomer Guo Shou jing in the thirteenth century. This consisted of a pyramidal tower, 40ft (12m) high, from the north face of which a low wall ran out for 120ft (35m). This wall, known as the Sky Measuring Scale, was water-levelled by means of narrow troughs and was calibrated. The shadow cast by the tower was precisely measured on the low wall at noon on the summer solstice and again when the sun was at its lowest, at midday on the winter solstice. Because of the height of the tower, the differences in the length of these shadows was great and could be measured with considerable precision, enabling Guo Shou jing to estimate the length of the year with great exactitude.

Looking at ancient astronomy as a whole, it is notable that there was remarkable variety in its application at sites. Usually, features at a site or its axis point to key rising or setting points of the sun, moon or other heavenly body, as at Stonehenge, **Ballochroy** in Scotland, Karnak in Egypt and many other sites around the world. But quite often it is the light of an astronomical body, usually the sun, that shines into an enclosed space at a site and is 'captured' there. This

The summer solstice sun setting behind the Anasazi site known as Hovenweep Castle in Utah. Slit-like apertures in this edifice align to the solstitial sunsets, and its doors are oriented on the equinoctial sunsets.

happens at sites such as **Newgrange** and **Loughcrew** in Ireland, Maes Howe in Orkney, Scotland, at Native American sites such as **Hovenweep**, at the **Externsteine** rocks in Germany, and at **Gavrinis** in Brittany, among many others. Occasionally, a stone or other feature at a monument can cast a shadow in a significant way, such as at Stonehenge (*see* page 169), Castlerigg in the English Lake District, or the serrated shadow cast by a corner of the stepped pyramid known as El Castillo in **Chichén Itzá**, Mexico, which simulates the moving body of a serpent at the equinoxes. Sometimes the astronomical involvement at a site is more culturally complex, as at Simloki (Soldier Mountain) in northern California. At solstitial and equinoctial sunsets, this prominent peak, sacred to the Ajumawi people, throws a shadow that touches various sacred sites in the landscape around its base. The shadow relates to Ajumawi myths and was considered to be a spirit in its own right. Braves would try to outrun the shadow as it spread across the valley floor in order to gain magical power.

It is clear that the ancient builders and skywatchers could use astronomical events as celestial lightshows and shadowplays in bravura performances of ceremonial showmanship, as well as for simply maintaining ceremonial and agricultural calendars. While there is much that is technical and cerebral about archaeoastronomy, there is no doubt that the actual effect on-site of ancient astronomy can be a visually and emotionally powerful experience.

See also **Cahokia**; **Casa Grande**; **Chaco Canyon**; **Rock Art**; **St Michael Line**

ARCHAEOLOGY

Archaeology is the organized study of the material remains of past peoples, cultures or societies. Such remains can include monuments, inscriptions, pottery, tools and other small artefacts, burial sites and even ancient refuse heaps (middens). Excavations or 'digs' using trenches are conducted with extreme care, with the stratification of ground materials revealed by the walls of trenches helping to ascertain the chronology of any artefacts found, and with the painstaking mapping and cleaning of objects that are uncovered.

When prehistoric remains are involved there are no written records to guide the archaeologist, so the *interpretation* of the remains becomes an essential skill. Such interpretative work is usually aided by cross-reference to the circumstances of similar finds, computer modelling, a growing battery of scientific dating methods and detailed chemical analysis. In recent years, some archaeologists have extended the interpretative process to such an extent that models of ancient thinking can be attempted – this is called **cognitive archaeology**.

There is a traditional enmity between archaeologists and earth mysteries enthusiasts, but the latter are often more dependent on the findings of archaeology than they care to admit, and archaeologists are often slow to appreciate the useful and intelligent thinking and observations that take place beyond the immediate bounds of their discipline. In recent years, however, especially with the advent of cognitive archaeology, allied with the natural roll-over of generations, a few archaeologists and earth mysteries researchers have started to find some common ground.

See also **Rock Art**

ARK (of the Covenant)

The Ark of the Covenant was a chest made from wood overlaid with gold plate in which were deposited the Tablets of the Law – the Ten Commandments. It was not to be touched by ordinary folk, but during the desert wanderings of the Israelites under the leadership of Moses, a man did so and was struck dead. Ancient **astronaut** theorist Erich von Daniken claims that the fellow was electrocuted because the Ark was essentially a condenser and that two gold cherubim on top were antennae that allowed Moses to communicate with a spaceship – with the 'Lord'. But in *Crash Go the Chariots* (1972) biblical archaeologist and electronics expert Clifford Wilson gave technical details of why none of this could be true. More recently journalist Graham Hancock has claimed that the Ark was a radioactive weapon (*The Sign and the Seal*, 1992). Conducting a detailed analysis, Mike Heiser, a biblical scholar and Hebrew and Semitic language expert, concluded that Hancock had selectively manipulated or misunderstood the actual historical data and literature (*The Anomalist* 6, 1998). In passing, Heiser notes that the Old Testament does not represent the Ark as a weapon and that the lethal force associated with it came not from the object itself, but externally, from Yahweh.

The Ark is said to have been lodged in Solomon's Temple and to have disappeared from there when Jerusalem was sacked by the Babylonians in 586 BC. Graham Hancock thinks it now lies under guardianship in a monastery in Ethiopia, while others fancy that they can trace it to Babylon, Egypt or Constantinople (modern Istanbul) or that it is still buried near the site of the Temple in **Jerusalem**. Texan scholar Dr Vendyl Jones, who was the model for the film character Indiana Jones, is convinced it is sealed in a

The Ark of the Covenant. *(Fortean Picture Library)*

cave in a cliff-face near Qumran, Israel, slightly north of where the Dead Sea Scrolls were found by an Arab shepherd in 1947. He is conducting excavations, confident that the contents of the more recently discovered Copper Scroll, along with electronic ground-penetrating methods, support his theory.

See also **Energies**

ARTHUR

The Arthurian legend is a shifting phenomenon, resembling a dream or a coiling mist, and the image of Arthur is multidimensional. It operates at three basic levels. The historical Arthur was probably a British warlord or chieftain of the sixth century AD who led successful campaigns against invading Saxon armies. On another level, Arthur was a legendary hero, a romantic figure surrounded by the noble knights and enchanting women who inhabited his glittering court at Camelot, riding out on great adventures against a background of sex, violence and intrigue. In short, he was a character in a richly tapestried medieval soap opera. On the deeper mythic level, Arthur is a semi-divine, solar hero, to some extent an expression of the same archetype as represented by the Greek Herakles (the Roman Hercules). At this level he is indeed a 'once and future king', biding his timelessness in an archetypal fairyland deep within our collective psyche.

The story of Arthur and the 'Matter of Britain' developed layer upon layer over centuries. Gildas, in his *Book of Complaints* (c.540), cites the battle of Mount Badon, where there was a great Saxon defeat. Although Gildas omits to mention Arthur, many think that he was the victor of Mount

Ancient castle ruins merge with the rocks of the rugged headland at Tintagel in Cornwall.

Badon, as is stated in the tenth-century *Cambrian Annals*. Also, in his ninth-century *History of the Britons*, Nennius says that Arthur was indeed the war chief (*dux bellorum*) of the Britons at the battle of Mount Badon. The legendary Arthur appears in late Cornish and Welsh Celtic poems and stories, which may have been written versions of earlier oral tales. He is a great hero, ridding the land of evil and strange beings. In 'The Spoils of Annwn', a tenth-century Welsh poem in the *Book of Taliesin*, Arthur takes a magical, diamond-studded cauldron from Annwn, the Celtic otherworld. The cauldron, which was made to boil by the breath of nine virgins and would not cook food for a coward, is probably a pagan Celtic prototype of the **Grail**. In the Celtic poems and tales the names of various characters are identifiable as the knights in the later Arthurian Romances. Thus Cei Wynn became Sir Kay, Bedwyr was Sir Bedevere, Llenlleawc was Sir Lancelot and so on. By 1100 the Arthurian stories had travelled far beyond Wales and Cornwall, being known in Brittany (and spreading to the whole of France) and as far afield as Italy and Poland.

The story of Arthur was first shaped into something resembling a coherent whole by Geoffrey of Monmouth in his twelfth-century *The History of the Kings of Britain*. Although Geoffrey claimed special access to an ancient source-book, his work is regarded as fiction by scholars, and it is probably a mix of inventive storytelling, early accounts and traditional stories. In Geoffrey's telling, British king Uther Pendragon fell in love with Igerna, wife of Gorlois, Duke of Cornwall. While Igerna's husband was under siege elsewhere, Uther persuaded his court wizard, Merlin, to use his magic arts to transform him into the likeness of Gorlois, so that he was able to gain access to the duke's home, Tintagel Castle, and Igerna's arms. The child who resulted from that union was Arthur. Later, when Uther (as himself) married Igerna after the death of Gorlois, they had another child, Anna. Uther Pendragon died when Arthur was 15 years old. The young man was of 'outstanding courage and generosity'. Wearing a golden helmet bearing a dragon crest and wielding the 'peerless sword' Caliburn, forged in the Isle of Avalon, he undertook many successful battles and drove back invading Saxons with great slaughter. He fought the Icelanders, the Scots and the Irish. When the country was finally peaceful, he married Guinevere, the most beautiful woman in Britain. Arthur's sister, Anna, married and had two children, Gawain and Mordred. But soon Arthur was off again, conducting battles in other countries. Nine years later he returned and was crowned king. He founded a fabulous City of the Legions, which Geoffrey places at Caerleon, Wales, and which became a centre for learning, religion and 'pleasant things' and to which important leaders were invited so as to secure peace pacts.

At this point in Geoffrey's account the first hints of chivalry become apparent, for he tells us that the inhabitants of the famed city were courteous and that the knights wore livery and arms showing distinctive colours, which were displayed by 'women of fashion'. The knights would hold mock battles and games while the flirtatious womenfolk watched. But eventually these idle pastimes were interrupted when Rome challenged Arthur for witholding Britain's tribute. Annoyed, Arthur commenced a military campaign on the Continent against the Romans and their allies. Although successful, his adventures cost the lives of his knights Bedevere and Kay. Taking Gawain with him, he had left Guinevere and his other nephew, Mordred, to rule in his absence. Before Arthur could march on Rome itself, he received word that Mordred had claimed the crown of Britain for himself and was living adulterously with Guinevere. The traitorous fellow had surrounded himself with an army of all those with reason to hate Arthur, including Saxons, Scots and Irish. Arthur returned to Britain at once and landed only with great difficulty, fending off the attacks of Morded's hordes. Remorselessly, however, the true king forced Mordred back to the river Camel in Cornwall, although Gawain was killed in the process. A final great battle took place (referred to in the *Cambrian Annals* as the battle of Camlann). Although Mordred was killed, Arthur suffered a mortal wound. Geoffrey states that after handing over the crown of Britain to his cousin, Constantine, he was carried off to Avalon, the Isle of Apples, so that his wound might be attended to.

Geoffrey's account became very popular among the Celtic peoples of Britain and Brittany as well as among the Normans. In 1155 Robert Wace translated the Latin of Geoffrey's *History* into French, making some modifications, including the introduction of the Round Table. By 1200 Layamon translated this version into English, with his own embellishments, such as the claim that a fairy boat had taken the dying Arthur to Avalon. Inspired by this material and also by Arthurian tales being propagated by Breton storytellers, Chrétien de Troyes in France began seriously to embroider the Arthurian legend. He developed Geoffrey's idea of a fabulous Arthurian court, and Camelot made its debut. He increased the emphasis on chivalry. It is in Chrétien's works that the romance between Lancelot and Guinevere and the cuckolding of Arthur are introduced into the literature.

Various other additions were made by other writers in following years. In the thirteenth century, for instance, Robert de Borron brought in the element of Arthur assuming rightful kingship by being the only one able to draw a sword from a stone. Other staple elements of the legend, such as Arthur's sword, Excalibur, being thrown into a lake when he was taken to Avalon, also appeared in the same century, as did the idea that Mordred was born as a consequence of an incestuous union by Arthur. Morgan Le Fay (Morgan the Fairy), probably a version of an ancient pagan goddess, appeared as the leader of a group of sisters – effectively, the Fates or **Wyrd** Sisters – on Avalon, the Isle of Apples, where the dying Arthur was taken and tended to.

A grand synthesis of selected Arthurian themes, and arguably their greatest literary expression, came in the fifteenth century with Sir Thomas Malory's *Le Morte D'Arthur*. Malory re-told the core story that had evolved, picking and choosing among the many embellishments that were on offer, as well as adding a few spins of his own. In his version, Arthur was brought up by Sir Ector, the father of Kay, ignorant of his true parentage. Merlin presided over the sword-in-the-stone incident, now specifically located in London. Merlin accompanied Arthur to a magical lake, where the spirit of the place, the Lady of the Lake, appearing as an arm in white samite protruding from the water, gave Excalibur to Arthur. The incest theme was maintained in Malory's version: according to him, Arthur was the father of

Mordred as a result of unwittingly making incestuous love to his sister Morgause (a figure who seems mixed up with Geoffrey of Monmouth's Anna). Mordred was thus both his son and nephew. Merlin prophesied that this incest would bring destruction to Arthur and the Round Table. Lancelot's passion for Guinevere was kept in, as were accounts of chivalrous quests by the knights of the Round Table, especially their adventures as they searched for the Grail. In the last book of *Le Morte D'Arthur*, Arthur again became the central character. Being obliged to face up to Lancelot's adultery with Guinevere, he pursued him to France but returned to England when he learned of Mordred's treachery. In his final battle, Arthur killed Mordred with a spear-thrust and was himself gravely wounded by the dying Mordred's last wielding of his sword. In this version, Bedevere outlived Arthur and was instructed by the dying king to cast Excalibur back into the lake. Arthur was then taken across the water to Avalon, the land of the immortals, in a fairy barge containing Morgan.

For those immersed in ancient earth mysteries, the Arthurian theme resolves primarily into questions to do with **mythic geography**. A key matter in this regard is Glastonbury in Somerset. Geoffrey of Monmouth did not identify this place with Avalon, the Isle of Apples, in either his *History* or his later *Life of Merlin*, but it was seemingly so identified in the thirteenth-century French prose romance *Perlesvaus* and Malory associated Glastonbury and 'Avilion'. There was also an early reference in 'The Spoils of Annwn' to the City of Glass. The traditional association of Arthur with Glastonbury has long been aided and abetted by what some have argued was a public relations exercise by Glastonbury monks, who in 1191 claimed that they had unearthed Arthur's grave. A stone slab and lead cross were found 7ft (2.2m) underground. On the cross, in Latin, were the words: 'Here lies buried the renowned King Arthur in the Isle of Avalon'. About 9ft (3m) below this was a coffin dug out of an oak log, containing the bones of a tall man with damage to his skull. This was the presumed skeleton of Arthur, and an accompanying group of smaller bones, together with a tuft of yellow hair, were taken to be the remains of Guinevere. The site of this exhumation is marked in the grounds of Glastonbury Abbey. The cross became lost, but in recent years a fellow claimed to have found it but re-buried it. Although the renowned Arthurian scholar Geoffrey Ashe has given reasons why the grave may actually have been an authentic find by the monks, such claims are contentious among those who delve into Arthuriana. For instance, in various works Alan Wilson and Baram Blackett have stated that their researches indicate that the site in the Arthurian legend usually identified as Glastonbury is, in fact, that

The site of King Arthur's tomb in the ruins of Glastonbury Abbey in Somerset. The contentious bones were said to have been found on the south side of the Lady Chapel. In 1278 they were placed in a black marble tomb on the site shown here. The tomb was destroyed in the Dissolution of the Abbey in 1539.

claimed that the Arthurian Romance was, in fact, a cryptic literary reflection of a mystery laid out in the countryside around Glastonbury. She decided that the Round Table was a **terrestrial zodiac**, but this has failed to convince as a real physical feature. John Michell, in his *New Light on the Ancient Mysteries of Glastonbury* (1990), has made a different kind of celestial proposal. He has noted that the ecclesiastical territory known as the Twelve Hides surrounding Glastonbury Abbey contains seven hills, which were islands many centuries ago, as was Glastonbury Tor. These happen to fall into a configuration in the landscape reminiscent of the pattern of stars in the Great Bear constellation, Ursa Major (commonly known as the Plough or Big Dipper). He further notes that some scholars claim that Arthur's name derives from the Welsh Arth Fawr, the Great Bear. Also, the last two stars in the tail of the Great Bear point to the bright star Arcturus, called Arturo in Spanish – Arthur. Furthermore, Ursa Major was sometimes called Arthur's Wain or Wagon. This could all be a mare's nest, a collection of coincidences, but it is at least intriguing.

Anciently named sites supposedly relating to incidents in the Arthurian tales are to be found in many parts of Britain, but Wales and southwest England are particularly rich in such places, and argument ensues with regard to some key locations. The battle of Camlann, for instance, is claimed by some to have taken place near Slaughter Bridge over Cornwall's River Camel, while Camlan, a site in Wales, is argued for by others. The original whereabouts of Camelot is another hot topic. There have been numerous claims for the site, including Cadbury Castle, an **Iron Age** earthworked hill in Somerset, Dinas Powys in Wales, Winchester in Hampshire, and Tintagel in Cornwall. In July 1998 an archaeological discovery gave the last the edge. Tintagel is now a ruined castle site perched precipitously on a rocky peninsula on Cornwall's northern coast. It has had a long

occupied by the remains of a Romano-British town near Wall, north of Lichfield in Staffordshire. They also argue that there was an earlier, fourth-century Arthur, of whom the sixth-century Arthur was a descendant, who was buried in a cave in South Wales.

Whatever the truth of the matter, Glastonbury Tor does stand like a mysterious, conical fairy hill above the flat Somerset levels, which were once a shallow sea that would indeed have rendered Glastonbury an island in Arthur's time and before. Furthermore, legend has it that the Tor was the abode of the **fairies** until they were banished by St Collen and that it contains the entrance to Annwn, the Celtic otherworld.

Glastonbury was given a further major push as a key Arthurian site in the 1920s, when Katherine Maltwood

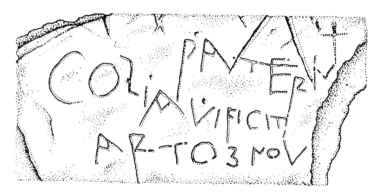

The lettering incised on a slate found at Tintagel, in 1998, which might give evidence of Arthur's presence there.

association with Arthur locally and was, of course, identified by Geoffrey of Monmouth as Arthur's place of conception and birth. The present castle is much more recent than Arthurian times, but several years of archaeological investigations have revealed that the site and its environs had been occupied from at least the early Christian era and that there had been an important and rich settlement there in the Dark Ages. During the 1998 excavations a broken piece of slate was uncovered beneath layers of shattered pottery and glass, which had lain undisturbed since the late sixth or seventh century. Faint incisions on the thin slab were deciphered as being sixth-century Latin script that read: *Pater Coliavificit Artognou* ('Artognou, father of a descendant of Coll, has made this'). Artognou was probably pronounced Arthnou. Serious discussion commenced as to whether this was a reference to King Arthur. As one archaeologist remarked, the inscribed stone may represent at long last the meeting of myth with history. This remains highly contentious, however. The Arthurian enigma prevails.

See also **Celts**; **Druids**

ASTRONAUTS (Ancient)

Those subscribing to the ancient astronaut school of thought call on biblical writings and other ancient texts or point to unexplained features in the archaeological record to argue that Earth was visited in remote antiquity by extraterrestrials or that there was some great, technically advanced civilization on Earth that has long since disappeared – or a hybrid of both ideas. Some proponents claim that the ancient extraterrestrials interbred with humans; others are more cautious and merely ascribe achievements such as the building of great megalithic structures in South America, the Great Pyramid and the megaliths of Europe to the technological guidance of the ancient space visitors. Otherworldly cultural heroes, such as the Mayan Kukulcan ('Feathered Serpent', **Quetzalcoatl** of the **Aztecs**), who brought and taught the skills of civilization, are interpreted as extraterrestrials enlightening a benighted humanity. Yet most cultures have such legends, and they can equally be seen as a mythological coding of the rise of knowledge within a society and also, perhaps, of foreign influences. The ancient astronaut thesis therefore pays scant regard to human skill and genius and tends to diminish human heritage.

A typical biblical account for those supporting ideas about ancient spacemen is the destruction of Sodom and Gomorrah. The story tells that two angels appeared to Lot in Sodom and warned him to leave with his family, as the city was about to be destroyed. As brimstone and fire rained down on Sodom and Gomorrah behind the fleeing family, Lot's wife looked back and was turned to a pillar of salt. To Erich von Daniken, the most famous (or infamous) exponent of ancient astronaut thinking, this is the account of a nuclear explosion, and the angels were space beings. The actual evidence, however, favours a natural cataclysm. The former cities were near the Dead Sea, which lies on major geological faults. The southern Dead Sea is much shallower than in the north and is known to cover archaeological remains. Here also is Jebel Usdum (Mount Sodom), which displays clear evidence of a violent eruption. For miles around its base there are salt deposits 150ft (45m) deep. There are deposits of sulphur and bitumen in the area, too, and 'brimstone' is a bituminous material. It seems the biblical account is a cautionary moral tale based on an actual earthquake and associated volcanic eruption.

Various ufological writers have championed the ancient astronaut theme. Among numerous others, there have been George Hunt Williamson (who claimed to accompany contactee George Adamski on a desert encounter with a spaceship), W. Raymond Drake, T.C. Lethbridge and Desmond Leslie. Leslie co-wrote the widely read *Flying Saucers Have Landed* with Adamski in 1953 and was, therefore, particularly influential. He delved into the ancient Vedic literature of India for references to the mysterious vimanas or 'air-boats' said to have been used by the elite and the military in that remote society. Whether these are literal descriptions of flying craft, mythological imagery or symbolic accounts of social class or mental states and apocalyptic visions is not clear at this distance in time and culture, but Leslie opted for their being Atlantean technology, for reasons he never quite explained. The flying saucer is 'only an interplanetary, more advanced, model of the ancient vimana', he claimed. Leslie sought other evidence in the Celtic myths, analysing in 1950s terms what he perceived as the super-weaponry of culture heroes such as Chuchulain of Ireland and Siegfried of Germany. It was obvious, Leslie maintained, that Chuchulain had use of heavy tanks and missiles, powered in some unknown way.

Erich von Daniken's book *Chariots of the Gods?* (1968) was a world-wide best-seller. His method is to take a random selection of unconnected archaeological mysteries to fuel his ancient astronaut speculations. There is no doubt that there are unexplained features in the archaeological record, but that does not necessarily make them anything to do with prehistoric extraterrestrials. To be genuine and effective, this technique requires a deep knowledge of archaeological and anthropological research, but von Daniken seems to scorn

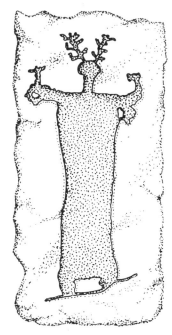

A rock art motif from Val Camonica in Italy. To von Daniken, the antler headgear was an aerial.

this. A few examples of his approach must suffice here.

Von Daniken suggests that the headgear worn by a figure carved in prehistory on the rocks of Val Camonica in Italy is 'very much like some kind of aerial'. He wonders if this means that it is the representation of a cosmonaut. In fact, the figure is obviously wearing deer antlers, the standard 'crown' of that universal tribal religious figure, the **shaman**. Similarly, von Daniken considers the radiating lines around the heads of other figures in prehistoric **rock art** to be possible antennae, whereas such depictions are known to symbolize cross-culturally the 'solarization' of tribal religious figures – that is, the enlightenment of high states of consciousness (the halo in medieval European art may be a descendent of this depiction). Von Daniken looks at rock paintings left in rock shelters by the Chumash Indians of California and similar prehistoric rock art and argues that rather than being depictions of gods, they look 'more technical than divine'. In fact, it is now widely agreed that such rock art was associated with the influence of native **hallucinogens** and consists of figures containing abstract imagery known as **entoptic patterns** – effects produced in the visual cortex during trance states. Von Daniken argues that forms sprouting from the outlines of a masked figure in the rock art of Tassili in the Algerian Sahara are 'antenna-like excrescences'. Yet they look much more like mushrooms than antennae, and it has been suggested that that is exactly what they are (the use of hallucinogenic mushrooms and other plants was widespread in antiquity). Another Tassili figure, probably showing a ritualist in ceremonial garb, was nicknamed 'the Martian' by archaeologists, and, von Daniken, of course, took that literally. It is noteworthy that he never seems to explain why his space visitors needed to wear space helmets or suits on Earth. If they did, our planet was hardly a home from home for them, and their bulky life-support clothing would presumably have interfered with their procreational activities with the 'daughters of men'.

In his rummage through the artefacts of the ancient world, von Daniken sees Egyptian effigies of the human soul, *ba*, as models of aircraft; Native American ritual costumes as copies of spacesuits; ornate or military headgear in any culture as space helmets; a ceramic Aztec incense burner as 'a bad copy of a jet engine' and so forth. His approach tends to eclipse the spiritual and ritual life of prehistoric humanity. Sometimes, in his quest for evidence of spacemen in the past, von Daniken does alight on truly intriguing objects such as the Baghdad Battery, a ceramic vase with copper inserts that could, indeed, have worked as a simple battery. There is no reason to suppose such knowledge was not available at times in the past, and there is nothing about such objects to suggest anything other than the technological capabilities of the day.

Two of the worst of Daniken's misinterpretations and yet probably among his better known pieces of 'evidence', relate to a carved Mayan slab and the **Nazca lines** of Peru. The slab is a tomb lid beneath a pyramid in the ancient Mayan city of

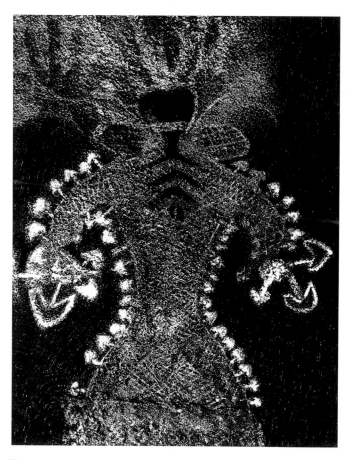

The prehistoric rock art depiction of a ceremonially dressed figure with headdress at Tassili in the Sahara Desert. What ancient astronaut theorists see as antennae, other researchers see as more likely representing ritual hallucinogenic mushrooms.

Palenque, and on it is carved the image of a human figure surrounded by complex designs, all depicted in the characteristic flowing Mayan style. This assemblage of imagery looks to von Daniken like a helmeted spaceman piloting a rocket ship from a reclining seat, in the manner of our own astronauts. To archaeologists, it is the image of the Mayan shaman-king Pakal, shown between the worlds of the living and dead, falling into the otherworld atop the deified plate of sacrifice. His 'helmet' is a smoking axe, a standard Mayan symbol of great spiritual power.

The imagery on the stone tomb lid in the Mayan city of Palenque.

Regarding the Nazca lines, von Daniken's well-known assertion is that the mysterious desert markings were landing strips for ancient spacecraft. In *Von Daniken's Proof* (1977), he notes, correctly, that no astronomical alignments have been confirmed among the lines, which he says are of Inca origin, so any idea of their being a kind of ancient calendar must be wrong. He jumps from this to the conclusion that they had to be a landing ground for the extraterrestrials. This leap of logic seems to be based on the fact that the markings are best seen from the air. The Nazca lines are, in fact, a thousand years older than the Inca and form only one example out of many groups of mysterious straight-line markings and 'roads' to be found throughout the ancient Americas (*see* **Shamanic Landscapes**). Any marks, even footprints and tyre tracks made on the delicate surface of the Nazca desert, remain visible, so any craft that landed or blasted off from this place would have left indelible traces. There aren't any. The best research to date indicates that the Nazca lines were religious and ceremonial features.

Von Daniken often points to examples of astonishing masonry in Inca architecture and the massive weight of huge stone blocks in megalithic monuments world-wide as evidence of alien or Atlantean technology, but there is no reason to suppose that human beings did not themselves develop the necessary skills, which later became dormant as cultures changed or declined. Indeed, modern experiments by Peter Hodges, a British master builder, have successfully shown how the **pyramids** could have been built with clever human engineering rather than alien help (*see* page 141). In

our automated age, we can too easily underestimate the basic practical genius of human beings.

A more thoughtful and scholarly version of the ancient extraterrestrial idea has been put forward by Robert Temple. In his *The Sirius Mystery* (1976, updated in 1997), Temple expands on the findings of two French anthropologists who had studied the Dogon people of the west African country of Mali. The Dogon believe that their culture derived from the Nommo, amphibious creatures from Sirius who landed in 'arks' in the region of Egypt and the Middle East long ago. Every 50 years the Dogon perform a ceremony, the Sigui, which involves the belief that a small and heavy star traces an elliptical orbit around Sirius, the Dog Star, every 50 Earth years. Remarkably, a small star near Sirius, invisible to the naked eye, was first observed by astronomers only in 1926, barely five years before the anthropologists first contacted the Dogon. This small star, Sirius B, is indeed a very dense 'white dwarf'.

Temple argues that the Dogon could have obtained such information only from the Nommo. It is true that an Assyrian god, Oannes, is shown as being a man-fish, but that could be to do with myths we know nothing about. It is also true that Sirius was central to ancient Egyptian cosmology. But then, it is the brightest star in the sky, and its first dawn rising each year coincided with the Nile flood. Critics have also pointed out that the Dogon have been exposed to Western education since 1906 and that there is an Islamic university in Timbuktu, 300 miles (500km) from the present Dogon homeland, where astronomy has been taught since the sixteenth

A desert marking near Nazca, Peru. A landing strip for ancient spacecraft? (*Peruvian Embassy*)

century. They could easily have incorporated modern knowledge into their existing myths and cosmologies, as is known to have happened with tribespeople elsewhere. Moreover, their knowledge about Sirius B is not entirely correct – it orbits Sirius every 60 years, not every 50 – and no evidence has been found for the Dogon belief in a third star and planets they say also revolve around Sirius. Further, Temple reproduces a sand drawing of Sirius B's orbit, but this is apparently only part of a cosmological diagram that in its entirety depicts eight more symbolical worlds. The Dogon case remains interesting, but the argument is not watertight.

The ancient astronaut theme was very much intertwined with the emergence of earth mysteries in the 1960s, leading to observations that from the air **Stonehenge** resembles a flying saucer. Could it have been a cult representation of a spacecraft, similar to the cargo plane cults of New Guinea? The ancient spacemen belief even coloured the **ley** revival. *See also* **Ark**; **Atlantis**; **Celts**; **Death Roads**; **Easter Island**; **Energies**; **Hollow Earth**; **Maya**; **Shaman**; **Trance**

ATLANTIS

The myth of Atlantis started with an elaborate friend-of-a-friend tale that was included in two of Plato's dialogues, *Timaeus* and *Critias*. At the invitation of Plato, Critias tells what he heard as a child from his octogenarian grandfather, Critias the Elder, who, in turn, heard it from his father, Dropides, who heard it from his friend and relative, the great Athenian sage and lawgiver, Solon, who heard it from Egyptian priests, who themselves spoke of events some 9000 years earlier. (Critias claimed that he saw fragments of an original account written by Solon, and there is an implication that this was still in his possession, but if so, it never surfaced as tangible evidence.) The tale told of a large and wonderful island that once existed beyond the Pillars of Herakles (the Straits of Gibraltar) and that was the homeland of a powerful and technologically advanced race of people but was destroyed after a series of earthquakes and floods in a final cataclysmic event lasting one day and night. It was said that the sea god Poseidon founded the city of Atlantis on a low hill near a level and fertile plain extending through the middle of the island. It was oblong in shape and well watered by rivers. The city was laid out in the form of concentric circles, two of land and three of seawater, centred on a citadel containing a temple. Some walls and ornamentation were covered in gold, tin or a substance called orichalcum (possibly red gold). The concentric rings of land and water were eventually transected by a canal equipped with bridges to provide access to the south and the open sea. The Atlanteans were superb sailors and conquered peoples in the Mediterranean region, resisted only by the gallant (and mythic) Athenians of old, until their army, too, was destroyed in the terrible cataclysm.

The tale as written down by Plato contained remarkable detail about Atlantis, including descriptions of its buildings, government, military organization and ritual practices. Diodorus Siculus, writing between 60 and 30 BC, about three centuries after Plato, mentions Atlanteans, 'the most civilized men', but his geography is vague, and it is thought that he may well have been referring to a North African people. The philosopher Proclus (AD 412–485) cited other sources than Plato for the Atlantis story, but direct knowledge of these does not survive, if they existed at all. He refers to three islands in the Atlantic, the inhabitants of which preserved a memory of a great island that had once existed there.

These are the basic Classical sources that give rise to later writings and speculation about a lost continent called Atlantis. In 1627 Sir Francis Bacon's utopian romance *New Atlantis* was published, but this was primarily influenced by discoveries relating to the Americas – the New World. Atlantis was a theme for European intellectuals and poets thoughout the seventeenth and eighteenth centuries. Even some respected scientific figures, such as Alexander von Humboldt, were sympathetic to the idea of a lost Atlantic continent, but this was largely due to the need to explain scientific conundrums that the later continental drift (plate tectonics) discoveries were able to unravel. One of the greatest popular exponents of Atlantis as a sunken land in the central Atlantic was Ignatius Donnelly, a one-time US Congressman, who wrote what is doubtless the most influential work of Atlantean fantasy, *Atlantis: The Antedeluvian World* (1882). He felt that the cultures in the Old and New Worlds had derived from the common source of Atlantis, citing the **pyramids** in central America and Egypt, and common legends of a Flood among his evidence. Many authors have followed in his footsteps, notable among them being British author Lewis Spence. It has been estimated that over the years more than 5000 books have been written on the subject in various languages.

Like virtually all supposed long-lost lands, Atlantis was embraced by the occultists. Madam Blavatsky, the main founder of **Theosophy**, considered that the fourth of the world's 'root races' had lived there. Theosophist W. Scott-Elliot used astral clairvoyance to travel back in time to visit Atlantis and so was able to describe in great detail what happened there. There were inhabitants of great stature, he said, but the rulers were the people whom we now know as

The Neolithic passage grave of Gavrinis is now situated on a tiny island just off the coast of Brittany, but when it was built well over 5000 years ago it was on a hilltop that could be approached on foot.

the Toltecs, one of the pre-Hispanic civilizations of Mexico. He said that it was the use of Black Magic by the rulers of Atlantis that led to the destruction of the great island. Probably the most famous of this type of occult account were those by the 'sleeping prophet' Edgar Cayce, the American clairvoyant and faith-healer who died in 1945. He pieced together a view of Atlantis that allowed him to claim that its civilization had been at least the technological equal of our own and that it had finally blown itself up. He prophesied that part of Atlantis would rise again in the latter years of the twentieth century off the island of Bimini in the Bahamas. This has proved to be a no-show, but an underwater archaeological expedition off Bimini in the 1970s led by David Zink did find a curious J-shaped, road-like feature made of great stone blocks, which was at first thought to be part of a submerged jetty. Later opinion however, has relegated this to being a natural feature.

There are two fundamental problems with the Atlantis myth for those seeking a physical reality behind it. The first is that if there ever was such an island, it did not exist in the central Atlantic, as that ocean floor has now been well mapped. There is no sunken continent there. Furthermore, the facts of plate tectonics do not allow for such a feature having been there. The second is that the account in Plato simply cannot be taken at face value. There is no way that an essentially oral account survived for over 9600 years in the

kind of detail provided in *Timaeus* and *Critias*. Indeed, Plato's pupil Aristotle was of the opinion that Plato had invented the whole thing in order to illustrate his philosophy. But none of this has stopped people trying to provide a geographical fix for Atlantis. Starting with Pliny, who positioned it on the west coast of Africa, suggestions have been legion, including the Azores, the Caribbean, the coast of Denmark and even the North Sea.

Another candidate that crops up quite often is Antarctica. Authors Rand and Rose Flem-Ath argue for an Antarctic Atlantis, drawing on ideas to do with the crustal displacement of the Earth. A reason some people feel that a land existed long ago that is now covered by Antarctic ice is the observation that certain ancient maps show a land there. The one most cited in popular writings is the Piri Reis map of 1513. Piri Reis, a Turkish navigator and chart maker, drew on numerous earlier sources, including nine Arab maps, and Atlantis enthusiasts following this line of enquiry wonder if these earlier maps contained handed-down information reaching back to the remotest times, when an ice-free land did exist where Antarctica is now located – perhaps before some catastrophic flip of the Earth's poles. In actuality, there is no mystery about

The roof-box above the entrance to Newgrange in County Meath, Ireland. Note the rock art engraved on its underside.

early maps showing a great southern continent: there was a belief in a Terra Australis from the second century, when the father of all cartographers, Ptolemy, expressed the feeling that there should be such a continent. Some subsequent map makers included a purely fictitious land mass for the sake of completion and to conform with this belief.

It could nevertheless prove to be unwise to dismiss completely the possibility of some form of physical reality in the Atlantis myth. One can (and should) ignore the literal chronology and size of Atlantis as given in the Plato accounts yet still be prepared to accept that there may be some germ of truth in the story. There are two serious contenders for a physical Atlantis. The theory currently favoured by scholars posits that the Mediterranean caldera of Santorini (Thera), 70 miles (110km) north of Crete, was the site of the real, **Bronze Age** Atlantis. This was originally a single volcanic island that exploded with terrific, awesome force c.1550 BC. The three present-day islands surround a flooded volcanic crater covering an area of 32 sq miles (80 sq km). It has been estimated that the destruction of Santorini involved about five times the force that destroyed Krakatoa in Indonesia in 1883. (To give a hint of what this means, the Krakatoa explosion could be heard almost 3000 miles (5000km) away and sent tidal waves across the entire Pacific Ocean that were still powerful when they hit the coast of South America.) The destruction of Santorini signalled the effective demise of the **Bronze Age** Minoan civilization of Crete and caused havoc throughout the eastern Mediterranean. Proponents of this theory state that Plato was drawing on surviving tradition that carried the memory of this catastrophic event.

A more obscure theory is that proposed by Paul Dunbavin, and expounded in his *The Atlantis Researches* (1992). Put at its simplest, the Dunbavin hypothesis suggests that there was a cataclysmic event triggered by a small excitation of the Earth's rotational axis some time in the period 3300–2900 BC, the greatest probability being the years around 3100 BC. This sounds at first hearing like any other ancient catastrophy theory, but Dunbavin has drawn together detailed scientific evidence in a way no one has before, resulting in a picture that some would consider to be more satisfying than the Santorini explanation. In his book, Dunbavin explains how the Earth bulges at the equator because of the centrifugal force caused by its spinning. Both the land mass and the oceans swell out due to the dynamics of the motion, creating a specific crustal form all over the world. If the axis were changed by only a small amount, the curvature of the crust and the displacement of ocean waters would have to change and be redistributed in order to accommodate the new axial dynamics. These effects would be relatively minor for the planet as a whole but would be of serious proportions for human beings affected by them. The most likely candidate for causing this shift of the rotational axis would be the glancing impact from some object from outer space, such as cometary material. (A smaller version of this type of event is the best explanation to account for a bizarre explosion and large damaged area that occurred in Tunguska, Siberia, in 1908.) This would result both in raising land on the one hand and the inundation of coastal regions on the other.

There is considerable geological data on both raised and submerged beaches around the world, showing varying tilts that can be explained only by changes in the curvature of the earth at those places and proving that changes in sea level have occurred. Some of these are the result of melting ice at the end of the Ice Age and events far back in geological time, but Dunbavin has correlated this mass of material and dated it as best the evidence allows. As a result, he has been able to identify what he considers to be a distinct pattern of coastal change around the world that occurred during the **Neolithic** period of western Europe. He has also checked the pollen and other records that indicate weather changes for the period, which are also distinctive. He further notes that the archaeological record indicates a 'dark age' for the British Isles between 3100 and 2850 BC, as evidenced in a dearth of radiocarbon dates for that period. It certainly looks as if something momentous happened that interrupted human activity.

We also know that there has been inundation along the western coastline of Europe, for very ancient (pre-3300 BC) megalithic monuments are known to be submerged in the waters off the French and Irish coasts and around the Channel Islands and the Isles of Scilly near England's Cornish peninsula. In addition, submerged forests and other features have been studied off the coast of the British Isles, and all authorities agree that the continental shelf around Britain and Ireland has been drowned. Prior to this, when this now-submerged land was exposed, it would, of course, have created a bigger land mass than is now the case (although nothing like the mythic proportions in the Plato accounts), and Dunbavin observes that this would have fitted very well with the structural description of the island of Atlantis as given in Plato's dialogues. In particular, the bed of the shallow eastern part of the Irish Sea would have been a very level plain when exposed, and it is crossed by ancient river beds as well as being situated in the middle of the land mass. A hill nearby is marked today by the Isle of Man.

So, Dunbavin claims that it is a memory of the island that was pre-inundation Britain and Ireland that is contained in the accounts in Plato. As an aside, Dunbavin's theory explains oddball archaeological facts such as the **Maya** calendrical system being based on a specific date in 3113 BC – a curiosity for which no one else has been able to supply an explanation. He also feels that the obsession with astronomical observation apparent in many later Neolithic monuments resulted from the great consternation the cataclysmic events had caused among the population of western Europe. He pays particular attention to **Newgrange**, the great Irish chambered mound that allows in the beams of the rising midwinter sun through a roof-box aperture over the entrance passage. He notes that charcoal deposits found in the roof-box when it was opened by archaeologists provided a radio-carbon date of **c.**3150 BC and claims that the sunbeam at that

The famous triple-spiral rock carving in Newgrange. Could this be, in effect, a symbol of the cataclysm that gave rise to the Atlantis myth, as Paul Dunbavin suggests? (*Brenda Dunne*)

time would have shone on to a superb triple-spiral **rock art** motif carved on the back wall of the chamber. Dunbavin feels that the implication is that the building of Newgrange was triggered by the cataclysmic astronomical event that he proposes took place.

The Atlantis myth has a reality of a kind quite apart from any physical one, however. Like other 'lost land' motifs, it represents a yearning for a lost paradisaical golden age that persistently haunts the human psyche. This archetype gives rise to all kinds of romantic beliefs and notions, some more ludicrous than others, including off-Earth ideas about human forebears on Mars. In this sense, Atlantis is a metaphorical continent submerged in the deep collective ocean of the human unconscious.

See also **Archaeoastronomy**; **Lemuria**; **Mu**

AZTECS

The Aztec people dominated much of Mexico at the time of the Spanish Conquest in the sixteenth century AD. The Mexica Indians emerged out of tribes that inhabited the Valley of Mexico after the collapse of the Toltec empire, and in AD 1345 they founded Tenochtitlán, a city built on a lake island containing palaces, plazas and pyramids. (This now lies beneath modern Mexico City.) By the middle of the fifteenth century, Tenochtitlán had become an independent state, and its builders controlled the whole valley in an alliance with Texococo and Tlacopan, of which the Mexicas were pre-eminent. The Aztec or Triple Alliance empire covered Mexico from its northern desert as far south as Oaxaca, even partially extending to what is the present-day Guatemalan border. All the time, Tenochtitlán grew and developed and became a mighty imperial city, with a population of nearly 200,000, requiring tribute from the provinces the Triple Alliance had conquered. Unfortunately, this great city was razed by the Spanish in 1521.

The Aztecs were a militaristic people, and their chief deity was Huitzilopochtli, a war god who had to be offered the blood of sacrificial victims. This required the Aztecs to engage in almost constant warfare in order to maintain a steady supply of captives for use as sacrificial victims. The Aztecs were also fine masons, craftsmen and traders, and effective agriculturists. Their society had a hierarchical structure, with nobility, priests, administrators and professional warriors forming class tiers over the commoners. Their religion made sophisticated use of plant **hallucinogens** for sacramental purposes.

See also **Teotihuacán**; **Xochipilli**

B

BALLOCHROY

This late **Neolithic** or early **Bronze Age** site consists of three standing stones and a burial kist, situated on the western coast of Scotland's Kintyre peninsula. It was one of the many sites surveyed for archaeoastronomical significance by Professor Alexander Thom. He found that the alignment of the stones, continued over the burial kist (a box of stone slabs), pointed towards the midwinter sunset position and that the point where the sun settled down behind the horizon was exactly where a small island called Cara was located, 7 miles (11km) out to sea. It seems that the megalith builders had carefully positioned their stones so that Cara could act as a foresight.

Thom also noticed that the middle stone of the Ballochroy group has its flat side placed at right angles to the line of the stone row. At the latitude of Ballochroy, the points of the midwinter and midsummer sunsets are exactly 90 degrees apart on the horizon, so Thom realized that by looking along the flat face of this slab one would be looking generally at the midsummer sunset position. Doing this, he saw that the foresight used to make such an indication at all accurate was Corra Bheinn, the most northerly peak of the mountain range called the Paps of Jura, on the island of Jura some 19 miles (30km) distant across the sea. This marked where the midsummer sun would have set about 1800 BC, and with some precision, because the slope of the mountainside is almost the same as the apparent path of the setting sun, which would have taken about three minutes seemingly to slide down it. When the Smithsonian astronomer Gerald Hawkins examined Ballochroy, he noted that, when reversed, this alignment also indicates the extreme northerly position of the moon during the major standstill period. Ballochroy was, he exclaimed, an 'ingeniously neat combination of site selection and astronomical knowledge!'

It is very possible that symbolism as well as astronomy was intended by the builders of the site. The word 'paps' means breasts, and the Paps of Jura are so called because the central peaks do indeed look like two rounded breasts. Place-names can be of incredible antiquity, and we can imagine that the

The summer solstice sunset over the Paps of Jura as viewed from Ballochroy on the west coast of Scotland. (*John Glover*)

mountains looked like breasts to the megalith builders, too. When the midsummer sun sets behind the Paps of Jura as viewed from Ballochroy, a ribbon of sunlight dances across the intervening water, and can be thought of as looking like an umbilical cord connecting the viewer with the old Earth Mother **Goddess,** whose breasts stand out, starkly silhouetted against the majesty of the sunset.

See also **Archaeoastronomy**; **Simulacra**

BICAMERAL MIND

The hypothesis of the bicameral mind was put forward by Princeton psychologist Julian Jaynes in *The Origins of Consciousness in the Breakdown of the Bicameral Mind* (1976). The theory states that until a few thousand years ago, human beings had the 'software' of their brains configured in a different way from that of modern people. The (greatly simplified) essence of this proposal is that in prehistory the brain functioned as two halves rather than as one unified whole, as is the case today.

The human brain is divided into two hemispheres, separated by a band of over two million fibres called the corpus callosum. In each hemisphere is an area known as the temporal lobe, which seems to be related to dreaming, hallucinations or visions, language and other functions. These two are connected across the corpus callosum by a thin bundle of nerve fibres called the anterior commissure. In over-simplistic terms, the left brain or hemisphere handles speech, logical, analytical thought and stage-by-stage cognition, while the right hemisphere deals with patterns, connections, intuition and gestalt (*see* **Correspondences**). Most of our sensory functions 'cross over', so that the left eye, for example, sends its signals to the right hemisphere of the brain. When someone has a problem with their anterior commissure, defects are found in perception, although the person in general does not feel that anything is untoward. So, for instance, such a person could not describe the contents of a slide shown only to the left eye, and thus the right brain, because the right brain does not have speech – but the left hand could point to a matching picture. As only the left brain has articulate speech (although both hemispheres understand language), it tends to be the hemisphere that dominates in a culture like our own.

Jaynes argues that each hemisphere of the brains of prehistoric people operated on separate tracks, as it were, and right-brain thinking was 'heard' as voices. Like the voices heard by unmedicated schizophrenics today, these auditory hallucinations, which were taken to be the voices of the ancestors or the gods, had an aura of enormous authority. They gave instructions to the left hemisphere or waking, daily consciousness. Jaynes calls this condition 'the bicameral mind'. As with schizophrenics, these voices could seem to emanate from a point in the environment and were not necessarily heard as if 'in the head'. If Jaynes is correct, in the ancient, bicameral world auditory hallucination was highly organized, using the skulls of the dead as the 'sources' of the voices and providing contact with the spirits of the ancestors, with variations on this function being managed in later prehistory through the use of idols and statues. (It is the case that there were ancient ceremonies involving the mouth-washing of idols to keep their speech clear, and the Indians of Mexico told their Spanish conquerors that their statues spoke to them.)

Eventually, according to Jaynes, the bicameral condition began to break down, initially in the eastern Mediterranean region, it seems, due to both social and natural changes, and there was a twilight phase between it and the modern mind that was coped with by the use of **oracles**. Oracular functionaries were usually women (women are more 'lateralized' in brain function than men, their psychological functions being less tied to one hemisphere or the other), and the locations of oracles were often 'hallucinogenic' in that they had roaring water or wind at them, or dramatic, elemental settings where the presence of wild nature overpowered human sensibilities – **Delphi**, in Greece, is a classic example.

While the hypothesis is viewed as contentious by most of Jaynes's mainstream colleagues, many other people consider it to be persuasive. It can be said that whether or not the theory is correct, it is sufficiently original to spur creative thought about the ancient mind, which must have inhabited a significantly different mental world from that of present-day human beings. This is a factor all too easily overlooked when studying the material remains of past cultures.

See also **Cognitive Archaeology**

BLUE STONES

The most familiar use of the term 'bluestones' relates to the smaller and oldest standing stones at **Stonehenge**, but the lesser known Blue Stones of Europe belong to a medieval tradition of urban **geomancy** (using that term to mean sacred geography). They were usually geometrically shaped flat stones, embedded in the ground, and are probably better preserved in the Netherlands than in most other countries.

At Schoonhoven a flat, dark blue stone is set in a cobblestone mosaic on a thirteenth-century bridge at the centre of the old town. At Nijmegan, a rectangular stone replacing the original Blue Stone marks the main crossroads of the city, and funeral processions were conducted around this spot until the twentieth century. Leiden has a hexagonal Blue Stone at the intersection of two roads, one an ancient, narrow lane, at the exact centre of the medieval town. Dutch-based British artist John Palmer, who is a leading researcher into Blue Stones as well as their keen protector in the face of modern encroachments, has found the locations of two other geographical marker stones in Leiden, one 'White', the other 'Red'. In **folklore** the Leiden stones were considered magical and sacred until the seventeenth century. Blue Stones existed in other old Dutch towns, such as Delft, and in other countries, too, such as in Lier and Ghent in Belgium and in Zurich in Switzerland. There was a 'Blue Stane' in St Andrews, Scotland, said to have been touched for good luck by soldiers on their way to the battle of Culloden in 1746. There seems, therefore, to have been a widespread tradition of ceremonial urban geography in medieval Europe in which the 'Blue Stones' acted primarily as *omphaloi* (see **World Navel**).

In addition to their 'geomantic' role, Palmer's research indicates that Blue Stones had a judicial function, marking the meeting points of open-air courts, and may possibly have been a survival of associations belonging to earlier times than the medieval period. For example, one of the routes running from the intersection marked by the Leiden Blue Stone leads to a mound in the town associated with Lugh, the Celtic god of light, who gave his name to Leiden. Further, Palmer has

found that the preferred stone used for the Blue Stones – in the Low Countries, at least – was imported from the Ardennes region of France. The Ardennes are said to be named after Arduinna, a pagan goddess once worshipped there. But the full story of the Blue Stones has yet to be told, and a major work on the topic by Palmer has met with depressing indifference from publishers.

See also **Omphalos**

BOG BODIES

The waterlogged peat in bogland has anaerobic and chemical properties capable of preserving organic material sealed within it, including human bodies. In the last two centuries, approximately 700 bodies have been found in bogs in Denmark, Germany, Britain, Ireland and Holland. Many of these resulted from accidental drownings, suicides and possibly murders over the centuries, but some date back to the **Iron Age**, ranging from roughly 800 BC to AD 200. Some of these probably relate to ritual killings and sacrifices, for it is known from apparently votive deposits that bogs were viewed as spiritually significant to pagan **Celts**. These Iron Age bodies give us a rare and thrilling opportunity to see the faces of prehistoric people.

The level of preservation can be remarkable, as exemplified by one of the most famous of bog bodies, 'Tollund Man'. Found in Tollund Fen in Denmark, this body was radio-carbon dated to **c.**210 BC, and was naked except for a leather cap with a chin strap and a belt around the waist. The man had shaved a couple of days before his death, because there was stubble on his chin. A noose-like hide rope was around his neck, and he had been strangled or hanged (although the type of rope was not ideal for hanging). Another Danish bog body, Grauballe Man, seems to have been badly knocked about, displaying skull injuries and a cut throat. Lindow Man, the second of three bodies found in Lindow Moss, near Manchester in England, and naked except for a presumably symbolic fox-fur armband, had been poleaxed, garrotted and had his throat slit. An elderly man and a teenage girl in a bog at Windeby in northern Germany seem to have been deliberately drowned by being pressed down beneath the bog surface, possibly by a wicker frame. And other bodies display a range of similar evidence of having been strangled, hanged, drowned, struck or otherwise traumatized, or even of having being hacked so as to bleed to death. Needless to say, such hard facts do not often get into the 'golden age' Celtic literature of the more popular earth mysteries circles.

See also **Iceman**

The hexagonal Blue Stone at the junction of ancient ways in Leiden, the Netherlands.

BOROBUDUR

This great, multi-tiered Buddhist temple is located in Indonesia, virtually at the geographical centre of the island of Java. Volcanic peaks punctuate the skyline as viewed from Borobudur. It stands on an earlier Hindu site, and perhaps before that this powerful place was important to the indigenous Earth religion. A vast hilltop construction, the temple was built in the ninth century AD and fell into disuse sometime prior to AD 1500. It boasts nearly 2 miles (3km) of stoneworked panels, depicting Buddhist teachings and legends, and almost 1500 perforated stupas (which give a ragged effect to the temple's profile), and it contains over 500 life-sized, seated statues of the Buddha. The hands of each of these express various *mudra*, or sacred gestures.

The temple consists of nine superimposed terraces reducing in size upwards, creating the impression of an ornate, stepped **pyramid**. The whole is crowned by a huge, bell-shaped stupa. This tiered structure relates to the Buddhist cosmological model of the universe, rising though the sensual world to the realms of pure form and spirit. The visitor or pilgrim moving up through the temple is effectively journeying through different stages of consciousness. Borobudur is meditation made physical: with good reason has this fabulous holy place been called 'a prayer in stone'. Sir Thomas Stamford Raffles initiated the clearing of the site from its coverings of earth and rubbish in 1814, and the first attempt at restoration began in 1907 under the direction of Theo van Erp. Subsequent phases of restoration have continued up to recent years.

Such powerful places always attract today's students of ancient mysteries, and a feature relating to Borobudur that is of particular interest to them is that it stands on a perfect alignment with two other temples, Pawon and Mendut. In fact, the remains of at least one other temple also fall on the line. These monuments are the only Buddhistic temples within a 3-mile (5km) radius of Borobudur. Indonesian archaeologist Soekmono has indicated that this line might have been one of the factors contributing to the importance of Borobudur's site to its builders. To earth mysteries enthusiasts, it sounds remarkably similar to a **ley**.

See also **Omphalos**; **Simulacra**; **World Navel**

BRONZE AGE

This is the second broad chronological period in the Three Age System. In 1816 Christian Thomsen was appointed as the first curator of the National Museum of Denmark. He began sorting the mass of artefacts in the collection there on the basis of their

Part of the profile of Borobudur in Indonesia. (*Chris Ashton*)

material – stone, bronze and iron. In 1836 he published a book (translated into English ten years later) in which he proposed that prehistory in Europe had been first a stone age, then one of copper and finally iron, and that this indicated a chronology based on materials (bronze is, of course, an alloy of copper and tin). He was aware, however, that the various 'ages' overlapped and that there were no distinct boundaries between them. His assistant, Jens Jacob Asmussen Worsaae, was able to demonstrate the relevance of this Three Age System in excavations: by practising the careful 'peeling away' of layers at a site, he was able to show that artefacts made from the three basic materials did occur at different levels, with stone being the deepest buried and therefore deposited the longest ago. (This stratigraphic appraisal of a site has caused Worsaae to be dubbed the first professional archaeologist.)

This system is, however, an extremely general way of dividing up prehistory, and it is, moreover, only a technological classification and does not necessarily indicate social or cultural evolution. The Victorians believed in the evolutionary development of humanity, but modern archaeologists realize that such matters are far more complex than a simple set of universal evolutionary steps. In reality, there was much greater cultural diversity in prehistory than had been supposed. In Britain the Bronze Age relates very roughly to the period between 2000 and 900 BC, but it began earlier in Continental Europe. In Asia the advent of bronze technology coincides with written history, so the system is not relevant as a means of chronological classification. The system is not used in the Americas either, as bronze appears sporadically in American prehistory rather than as a wide technological development, and archaeology has been able to draw on anthropological data. There was no Bronze Age in Australia.

See also **Iron Age**; **Neolithic**; **Palaeolithic**

CAHOKIA

A Mississippian Indian city and ritual complex, Cahokia was occupied between AD 700 and 1500, and at its peak it covered some 6 sq miles (15 sq km) and had a population of 20,000 – the largest prehistoric community in what is now the United States. What remains of the site can be found in southern Illinois near Collinsville. Still impressive, these remnants cover 2,200 acres (890ha) and include 68 preserved mounds, including Monks Mound, the tallest earthwork in prehistoric North America.

There were three types of mound at the site. Platform mounds are so called because they have flat tops and supported buildings such as temples, charnel houses and dwellings for the elite. The less common conical mounds seem to have been mainly for burials. There are only eight ridge-topped mounds, and while burial seems to have been one of their functions, their primary role appears to have been as geographic markers: five of the eight ridge-tops fix the extreme limits of the mound area, and three of them align with Monks Mound to form a meridian, a north–south line – Cahokia was laid out to the cardinal points.

Monks Mound, which rises in four terraces to over 100ft (30m) in height, covering 14 acres (5.5ha) at its base, was the hub of the sacred geography of Cahokia's ceremonial landscape, the centre of the Four Directions (*see* **World Navel**. The remains of a temple or shrine were uncovered on the southwest corner of the first terrace, a position that is precisely on the course of the north–south line running through the Cahokia complex. This shrine would have presented itself as a meridional (north–south alignment) marker silhouetted against the sky when viewed from ground level. Running south from this position on Monks Mound, the meridian passes through a ridge-topped mound (mound 49 in the archaeological categorization used at Cahokia), between a great platform and conical mound pair nicknamed Twin Mounds, across the southeast end of ridge mound 72 and on to the southernmost ridge mound, the massive Rattlesnake Mound 66.

An artist's impression of Cahokia, Illinois, in its heyday, when it boasted over 120 mounds contained within a palisaded, D-shaped area. The general populace lived in pole-framed dwellings outside this boundary. (*William R. Iseminger/Cahokia Mounds State Historic Site*)

The remains of Monks Mound at Cahokia.

On the summit terrace of Monks Mound, the Mississippians erected a timber building 105ft (32m) in length, 48ft (14.5m) wide and perhaps 50ft (15m) high. This was presumably the king's or chieftain's dwelling. A massive pole was erected outside this building, forming a landmark visible from long distances away. The Cahokian chieftain may well have symbolized the sun, as is known to have been the case in other Indian tribes. Astronomical effects may have been used to reinforce this concept: in 1961 archaeologists found the remains of an incomplete ring of postholes about ¼ mile (0.5km) to the east of Monks Mound, just south of the east–west line (marked by ridge mound 2 and the now-destroyed ridge mound 86). Warren Wittry and his team uncovered fragments of cedar posts and evidence of earthen ramps within the holes that would have facilitated the raising of tall poles. It became clear that there had been a succession of five timber circles at the site – which they nicknamed Woodhenge – bracketing a period around AD 1000, according to the radiocarbon dating of organic material found in the excavations. The third circle in this sequence, 410ft (125m) across, has now been partially reconstructed. The site seems clearly to have had a ceremonial astronomical function, with various poles on the eastern circumference marking three key sunrise positions – midsummer, the equinoxes and midwinter. But the archaeologists discovered that the centre of this Sun Circle would not have given an accurate observation position: any sunwatcher priest would have had to have stood just off centre. They excavated in the appropriate spot and, sure enough, found a posthole. But as is often the case in ancient astronomy, the function of the Sun Circle had symbolic value as well as a calendrical one: not only did a perimeter pole mark the equinoctial sunrise as viewed from the sunwatcher's pole, but so did Monks Mound looming on the skyline. The sun would have appeared to rise out of the mound and out of the chieftain's temple or palace: the Royal Sun himself.

In 1994 what appeared to be the remnants of another Sun Circle were discovered, this time close to ridge mound 72. This prompts a wild speculation: was there a Sun Circle at each of the Four Directions at Cahokia? Whatever the answer to this ultimately proves to be, the Cahokia complex clearly presents a classic example of sacred or ceremonial geography and is of special interest to earth mysteries students because of that.

See also **Archaeoastronomy**; **Geomancy**; **Mythic Geography**; **Sacred Place**

CARNAC

This name is shorthand for an area of exceptional megalithic density around Carnac-Ville, on the north side of Quiberon Bay in Morbihan, Brittany, France. Much of Morbihan (and Brittany in general) is rich in megalithic sites, but the Carnac region is remarkable even in this context.

The most famous of the monuments of the Carnac area are the stone rows. The most important are Ménec, Kermario and Kerlescan, but there are other rows, too, and also other megalithic monuments, such as passage graves, isolated menhirs (individual standing stones), cromlechs and dolmens. In all, there are several thousand megaliths still standing in the region. The stone rows consist of multiple, roughly parallel alignments, which originally started or terminated at semi-circular arrangements of standing stones (cromlechs). Kermario, which is aligned roughly southwest–northeast,

Cruz-Moquen, Carnac, in Brittany. Although this Neolithic dolmen has been obviously – and crudely – Christianized, it was associated with pagan fertility traditions in local folklore until fairly recent times. The monument is also known as La Pierre Chaude.

has seven main lines of stones, of which over a thousand are still standing. Kerlescan has 13 lines of stones standing in a general southwest–northeast orientation, with the tallest stones to the west by a cromlech. Ménec has remnants of 12 stone rows oriented generally to the east. In fact, these break down into two joined groups rather than being a single complex. The stones rise in height towards the western end, the largest standing 12ft (4m) tall.

The purpose of the Carnac rows has puzzled archaeologists and researchers of all kinds. Astronomical orientations have been suggested, and a few of these might be valid, although with so many stone alignments and sites these could be accidental. The most startling suggestions have come from Belgian researcher Pierre Méreaux-Tanguy, who considers that the arrangement of the alignment complexes relates to the distribution of earth **energies**. He notes that the Carnac monuments lie on granite intrusions surrounded by geological faulting, and that the area has the most intense record of seismicity in France. He considers that the stones must be surrounded by piezo-electrical fields caused when seismic activity affects the quartz crystals in the granite landscape. Méreaux has also conducted measurements that he says show that some of the Carnac rows form a 'precise frontier' between zones of slight positive and negative gravity variations. The terrestrial magnetic field is more disturbed in the middle of the field of standing stones, with variations up to 250 gammas. In fact, he has found disturbances varying between -400 and +1100 gammas at Ménec, Kermario and Kerlescan. Méreaux feels that 'the fields of menhirs of this area were not planted there by chance and that their presence would be in direct relation to terrestrial magnetism'.
See also **Gavrinis**; **Leys/Leylines**; **Spirit Ways**; **Shamanic Landscapes**

CASA GRANDE

The main feature at this site is the Big House to which its name refers: a mysterious four-storey structure left standing in an otherwise almost vanished prehistoric Indian village in southern Arizona. The village had belonged to the Hohokam people (a name that means 'those who have gone'). They appeared in the area around 300 BC and were active until the fifteenth century AD, when their culture disappeared for unknown reasons. They were accomplished canal engineers, a skill that allowed them to farm in the desert, and fine jewellers, and they seem to have lived peacefully. Their culture reached its height between AD 1000 and 1400.

Casa Grande was abandoned by 1450, and it was not until

The ruins of the Big House, Casa Grande, in Arizona. Note the small, round (solar) aperture at upper left, and the square (lunar) opening at upper right.

1694 that it was first seen by a European. Although it is in something of a ruinous state (it has a protective metal roof over it now), the basic structure of the Big House is discernible. It is 35ft (11m) high, with a base measuring 60 × 40ft (18 × 12m). Its walls, which have deeply entrenched foundations and contain nearly 3000 tons of sunbaked caliche mud, are 5½ft (1.6m) thick at their bases, tapering to 2ft (60cm) thick at full height. It had over 600 timber roof beams, which must have been imported from over 50 miles (80km) away. The building as a whole contained 11 rooms, and the top storey consists of just one of those rooms, rising as a smaller unit above the lower storeys.

The Big House is a curious building, and archaeologists do not really know what to make of it. It clearly had special importance, hence the effort that went into its building. The most intriguing aspects are two apertures, one circular, the other square, on each of the upper corners of the west wall. It has been found that the southerly of these two, the square opening, gives a sightline to an extreme setting point of the moon during is 18.61-year Metonic cycle, while the round aperture opens to the midsummer sunset. The single-roomed top storey also has apertures in its fabric that align variously to significant sun and moon rises.

Because of these factors, it is generally agreed that the Big House was some kind of Hohokam observatory, but a clue to its deeper significance may lie in an 1887 observation by Frank Hamilton Cushing, an anthropologist who lived for five years with Pueblo Indians a little further north. He recognized the floorplan of the Big House as being like the pattern created during the ceremonies in which Hopi corn-fields were consecrated. Anthropologist David Wilcox has subsequently endorsed Cushing's view, and sees the astronomy of the site as possibly fitting in with concepts enshrined in the cornfield consecration ceremonies. In this view, Casa Grande is a three-dimensional concretization of the annual ceremonial pattern in which the central area of a cornfield represents the Hill of the Middle, with the surrounding areas of the field representing the Hills of the four cardinal directions. Wilcox suggests that at Casa Grande the central tier of rooms represents the two vertical directions of up and down (zenith and nadir), forming the Middle or **World Navel**, with the rooms around representing the Four Directions.

See also **Archaeoastronomy**

CELTS

A culture that can be identified as 'Celtic' started to appear in Europe c.900 BC, reaching its height in the mid- to late first millennium BC, when it stretched across non-Mediterranean Europe from Ireland and the Iberian peninsula in the west to the Black Sea in the east. The pagan Celtic heritage is recognized by a combination of linguistics, archaeological finds showing distinctive characteristics, contemporary descriptions in the works of the Mediterranean Classical writers (Herodotus, Julius Caesar and so forth) and early texts from Wales and Ireland – although even these were written down during the Christian era and probably give a somewhat distorted view of the pre-Christian Celtic world. But despite these varied sources, we still know only a limited amount about the pagan Celts.

The Classical descriptions indicate that 'the Celts' varied in appearance, so they were not one people who invaded Europe; rather, it seems that to some extent at least there was a Celtic cultural effect, which insinuated itself into existing cultures north of the Alps and which spread by a kind of Brownian motion, even if possibly instigated by physical incursions into eastern Europe by peoples from the steppes. Celtic origins must be found in the **Bronze Age** and even **Neolithic** peoples of Europe – indeed, Celtic scholar Anne Ross has commented that there was perhaps no real break in the traditions of those who built the great Neolithic monuments, such as **Newgrange** in Ireland. What came to be the Celtic culture we now recognize gradually emerged out of indigenous populations rather than being suddenly imposed from outside. It was symbiotic with the advent of the **Iron Age** in Europe.

The first hints of Celtic emergence can be traced to central Europe in the second millennium BC, when a funerary rite involving cremations in distinctive pots deposited in large, level fields appeared. This 'urnfield culture', which spread north of the Alps for many centuries, is technologically characterized by the innovative ability of its metalworkers to make thin sheets of bronze, which could be used for creating large containers, shields and body armour. Also, certain motifs, such as sun-wheels and bird-ship designs, appeared and were to recur in the later Celtic culture. By the eighth century BC the use of the horse as a steed had become widespread, indicated by the appearance of metal harness fittings and other equestrian accoutrements in the archaeological record, along with weaponry designed to be used from horseback, such as long iron swords. (The horse was a major Celtic passion, symbol and socio-religious icon.)

This period is termed the Hallstatt culture after a site near Salzburg in Austria, where late Bronze Age urnfield burials were superseded by full Iron Age graves containing remarkably preserved material due to the salt deposits there. This phase has produced some splendid archaeological material, such as rich burials, like those at Hochdorf in Germany, in which the corpse was interred on whole wagons surrounded by luxury goods. At Vix, in France (the Celtic Gaul), the body of a woman was placed in a wooden mortuary house within an earthen mound and accompanied by a dismantled four-wheel wagon with bronze fittings, bronze and silver bowls, brooches, a Greek cup and a bronze bowl some 5ft (1.5m) tall. The woman was wearing a heavy gold torc, and rich textiles were arranged in her tomb.

The centuries of full pagan Celtic flowering from c.500 BC to Roman domination are called the La Tène period

The Iron Age burial mound at Hochdorf in Germany. (*Sol Devereux*)

The Stone of Fal at the Hill of Tara, the royal seat of the pagan Celtic kings of Ireland. Tara is a multi-period site, with monuments dating from the Neolithic era to the Celtic Iron Age. The Stone of Fal, 6ft (2m) tall, was said to cry out when touched by the rightful king.

and are characterized by fine decoration in a range of materials, including metal and stone using flowing, abstract motifs based on plant forms and sometimes incorporating human and animal imagery. During this time, Celtic societies – viewed by the Mediterranean culture as being on the fringe of the known world – not only extended across central and northern Europe, including the British Isles, but also began to extend into Italy, Greece and Anatolia (in modern Turkey). In 387 BC they sacked Rome, and in 279 they ransacked the Greek oracle temple of **Delphi**. But by the later third century BC the Romans started to get the upper hand, aided and abetted by migratory Germans, and eventually the Celtic peoples

were absorbed into the Roman empire. During this time, Celtic languages based on archaic Indo-European elements were being spoken at many points throughout Europe; two groups of these survive today in the British Isles and Brittany – Goidelic in Irish, Scots Gaelic and Manx, and Brythonic in Welsh, Cornish and Breton. Celtic paganism survived within the Roman context, falling to Christian influence only after the Roman withdrawal, and even then not completely.

From the combined sources of evidence, we know that the Celts were proud and even cocky people, and fierce fighters. They were head-hunters, and there was possibly a Celtic head cult, although some scholars now cast doubt on this. They were elitist, having a strongly hierarchical society with a tripartite leadership (the number three and its multiples carried great significance for the Celts): an aristocracy formed by a king or ruling lawgivers and a warrior-knight class, together with a priesthood, called **druids** by Caesar. Craftsmen held high status, and there were also poets and bards, then the landowners, then what was virtually a serf class. Social structure was organized on a clan, tribal (*tuath*) basis. The Celts enjoyed feasting and drinking; we might picture them as a rather loud and boisterous lot. The use of iron tools allowed land to be cleared very effectively and a surplus agricultural economy to be maintained.

The Celts were supreme craftsman, producing artefacts, ranging from weapons and armour to chariots, utensils, vessels, jewellery and sculptures or votive effigies, variously in metals (including gold and silver), wood, stone, leather and glass, often decorated with fine, richly intricate designs or images. They also produced textiles. Men were clad in trousers and cloaks, and women in long tunics and capes. Well-preserved **Iron Age** male **bog bodies** found in Denmark and Britain had well-trimmed beards. Men might fight naked, but they also had armour, shields and helmets, many with animal or bird crests fashioned out of iron and bronze.

The Celts built earthworked settlements and forts, often on hills but sometimes on flat land. Their religion, as far as we can tell, involved a plethora of local, place-related spirits and deities, with relatively fewer general gods and goddesses (*see* **Druids**). Lakes, springs and wells seemed particularly favoured. The natural landscape that surrounded them was freighted with meaning for the Celts, and we have a relic of this consciousness in an old Irish Celtic text, the *Dinnshenchas* ('The Lore of Famous Places'), where topographical mythology is recorded. Small wonder, then, that the Celts had a penchant for spirits of place. When the Celts became Christianized after the Romans, they were able to change from this pantheistic religious worldview to a monotheistic one, because they could lodge many of their pagan deities in the identity of Christian saints. That is why, in Wales and Cornwall in particular, there are many Celtic holy wells that bear the name of a Christian saint.

The term 'Celtic' arouses much fascination in 'New Age' circles and is a major plank of the modern ancient mysteries arena in general, judging by the almost endless stream of books with the word in their titles.

See also **Arthur**; **Mythic Geography**; **Ogham**; **Sacred Place**

CHACO CANYON

This is a shallow sandstone gorge running east–west across arid mesa country in New Mexico. It lies at the heart of the San Juan Basin, which spreads across what is known as the Four Corners region, where New Mexico, Colorado, Utah and Arizona meet. The site holds a fascination in earth mysteries circles because it melds a number of intriguing elements: a mysterious lost people; hints of enigmatic ritual and religious practices; baffling ruins; ancient astronomy, and enigmatic straight, **ley**-like 'roads'. Chaco is believed to have been an **Anasazi** ceremonial focus a thousand and more years ago. Although people lived in the canyon, archaeologists now think it was primarily a ritual centre that attracted a much larger population from the vast landscape around at certain times of each year.

Along the canyon floor are the ruins of nine Great Houses, multi-storeyed complexes of pueblos (flat-roofed buildings made of sunbaked mud, rocks and timber) with walls, courtyards, storage pits and many **kivas** (semi-subterranean ceremonial chambers). Great Houses seem to have been essentially ceremonial buildings. The largest was Pueblo Bonito, said to be the greatest prehistoric ruin in the United States, covering 3 acres (1.2ha) and containing 800 rooms, two Great Kivas and 37 smaller ones. All the Chaco Great Houses were built between AD 900 and 1115. The tumbled ruins of a further 150 of them have been identified in the countryside for many miles around the canyon. Many of these are on mysterious straight 'roads', engineered features up to 30ft (10m) wide. Some of these have been traced running for up to 50 miles (80km) or more, passing through special gateways in walls alongside Great Houses and converging on the canyon. Some roads run in parallel sections, 30ft (10m) wide. Why a people who had neither horses nor wheeled vehicles wanted such features, which are now virtually invisible at ground level, is unknown. Where some of the roads reach the canyon rim, large staircases are to be found hewn out of the rock of the canyon walls. Many researchers think the roads had ceremonial rather than utilitarian functions or, at least, served multiple purposes.

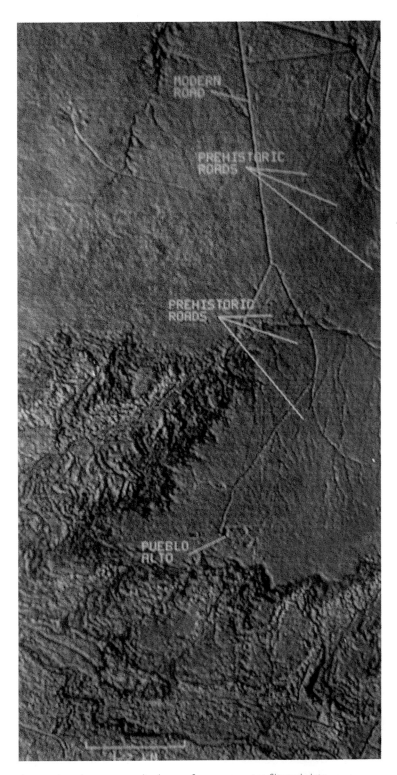

A pseudo-colour composite image from computer-filtered data, showing some of the straight Anasazi roads that radiate around Chaco Canyon in New Mexico. These are now subtle features, even with the high technology used here, and are virtually invisible with the naked eye at ground level. Chaco Canyon is at the bottom of the image, and the Great House of Pueblo Alto, on the northern rim of the canyon, is indicated. (*NASA*)

Part of Casa Rinconada in Chaco Canyon, New Mexico, showing one of the T-shaped doorways and the square aperture thought to align to the summer solstice sun.

A major feature within the canyon is Casa Rinconada, the largest kiva ever discovered at 63ft (19m) in diameter (its roof is now missing). This was the ritual gathering place, where rites would be performed and the 'long chants' or mnemonic stories told, holding the history of the people and the knowledge – especially the astronomical knowledge – of the elders. A 'secret' entrance leads into the kiva and emerges in the floor of the chamber; this was doubtless for the sudden, magical appearance of ceremonial characters in certain ritual dances and performances, vaguely akin to the medieval Christian mystery plays. Here, also, preparations of plant **hallucinogens** (probably *Datura* based) might have been drunk or smoked to aid direct access to the spirit world.

There is evidence of ceremonial astronomy at Chaco. At various locations along the canyon walls are rock paintings and carvings, some Navajo and others Anasazi. It is thought that some of these mark positions for sunwatcher priests. Near Wijiji Pueblo, the easternmost ruin in Chaco Canyon, is a white-painted symbol with depictions of rays emanating from four sides. A person standing near this probable sun symbol can witness the winter solstice sun rise from behind a natural sandstone pillar on the canyon rim rock opposite. Warning was given of this event. At a carved boulder nearby, an observer can see a V-shaped notch to the southwest. When the sun is seen to set in this notch, the winter solstice is just 16 days away. At the other, western, end of Chaco Canyon a rock overhang near the ruins of Penasco Blanco harbours a rock painting of a crescent, a hand and a star. Some researchers think this may represent the supernova that formed the Crab Nebula, which appeared next to the waning

moon on 4 July 1054 (the hand signifies a sacred place).

Ancient astronomy still functions at Chaco. On a high ledge near the summit of Fajada Butte, a 430ft (130m) sandstone outcrop at the southeastern entrance to the canyon, three fallen slabs lean against the rock wall. One late morning shortly after the summer solstice in 1977, artist Anna Sofaer was on the ledge looking for **rock art**. She suddenly observed a sliver of sunlight projecting through a gap between the slabs on to the shaded area of the rock wall behind. On that wall she found two spiral rock carvings, one about the size of a dinner plate, the other much smaller. The sliver of sunlight, the Sun Dagger, as Sofaer called it, was cutting almost through the centre of the larger spiral design. Subsequent study of this site showed that at noon on the

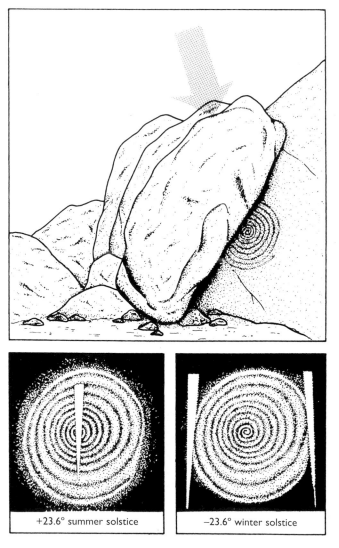

+23.6° summer solstice   −23.6° winter solstice

How the Fajada Sun Dagger calendar works. Sunlight is broken by the gaps between the slabs into slivers of light that interact with the petroglyphs on the rock behind.

winter solstice, when the sun shines at a lower angle in the sky, *two* Sun Daggers are projected between the slabs, framing the larger spiral carving perfectly. At the equinoxes, one long sliver of sunlight cuts the large spiral just to one side of its centre, while another, shorter Sun Dagger bisects the smaller carving. More recent research suggests the possibility that the rock calendar might also record the motions of the lunar cycle, as the moon shadow of one of the slabs cuts across the larger carving's centre and left-hand periphery at the minor and major lunar standstills respectively, and across the right-hand periphery of the petroglyph at the mid-point of the 18.61-year lunar cycle.

A more arguable solar effect occurs at Casa Rinconada. A short time after the summer solstice sun rises, it casts a beam of light through a curious, singular aperture in the northeastern wall of the Great Kiva. This shines across the circular chamber to strike one of six irregularly spaced wall niches. While this is interesting to see now, it would have been particularly dramatic when the kiva's roof was in place and the sunbeam would have stabbed its way through darkness. However, critics have wondered whether the kiva might have had an external structure built against it where the aperture is situated, so that the sun would not have been able to shine through it, or, if the sunbeam could enter the chamber, if it would not have been blocked by one of the thick posts supporting the roof. As these no longer exist, it is not possible to test this theory.

Casa Rinconada is also aligned to the four cardinal directions, with its two large, T-shaped entrances precisely aligned north–south. Moreover, this alignment also gives a sightline to Pueblo Alto, a ruined Great House high on the rim rock of the northern wall of the canyon, where one of the major Chacoan roads comes in off the desert. Pueblo Bonito, across the canyon floor from Rinconada, was similarly laid out on a cardinal plan, being divided into western and eastern halves by a low wall that is meridional – that is, it lies on a virtually exact north–south line.

See also **Archaeoastronomy; Shamanic Landscapes**

CHARTRES

This French place of worship, the epitome of Gothic cathedrals, was constructed between AD 1194 and 1220. It is probable that the site of the building had formerly been a major Celtic or druidic centre, on which the Romans subsequently erected a shrine. A well, 108ft (33m) deep, known as the Well of the Strong Saints, sinks into the floor of the

The west front of Chartres Cathedral. Note that the towers are slightly different heights, which has been explained as a distinction between solar and lunar symbolism (*see* Correspondences).

cathedral's crypt, which also houses a replacement sculpture for a wooden effigy of the Blessed Virgin and Child. The original had been a Black Virgin, destroyed in the French Revolution. This Notre Dame de Sous-Terre was a representation of a Celtic goddess, according to French author, Louis Charpentier. In *The Mysteries of Chartres Cathedral* (1966), he claims that it had been carved from the wood of a pear tree and had become blackened with age. Ean Begg, author of *The Cult of the Black Virgin* (1985), similarly believes that the original Chartres Madonna – and other curious Black Virgin images that are to be found scattered across Europe – had their origins in Celtic fertility idols, although a seventeenth-century replica of the lost Chartres effigy indicates that it was a depiction of the Madonna. Although conservative opinion dismisses the Black Madonnas by saying that they simply became darkened by candle smoke or general

between') times of the year, such as the eves of All Hallows and New Year, was deeply rooted in medieval Europe – and probably further afield – as evidenced by the widespread custom of erecting and placing **spirit traps** and the **sweeping** of old paths and crossroads to clear them of spirits. The champions of this 'spirit line' approach to the ley concept suggest that it is likely that such notions reached much further back than the medieval period, as all pre-industrial societies (and traditional peoples today) tended to populate the physical landscape with spirits. Critics, however, put a tight frame of reference around the death roads and see them simply as old-fashioned ways of carrying the rural dead to rest and deny or ignore the possibility that the physical features themselves act like a kind of topographic litmus to reveal a spirit lore much older than the paths themselves. Whatever the truth of this argument, the new ley hunters are finding that the retracing, rediscovering and mapping of old corpse ways in the British countryside can be just as romantic and exciting an outdoor pursuit as the older Watkinsian notion of ley hunting. In addition, it has the added satisfaction of helping to rescue a particular chapter of human heritage from oblivion.

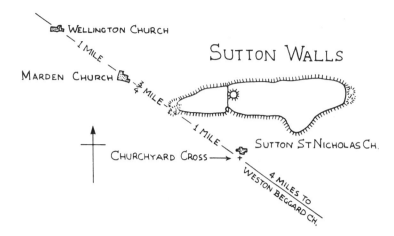

A likely example of a Watkins ley being the remnant of a medieval church way is this alignment of churches (or, more accurately, church-yards) discovered by Alfred Watkins. It passes through one end of Sutton Walls (a prehistoric earthworked hill) in Herefordshire. A farmer later told Watkins that during ploughing in a field on the course of the alignment, a dark linear marking showed up, revealing the existence of a former old straight track falling on the alignment. (After *Alfred Watkins*)

Medieval paving and steps mark the course of this church way or corpse road near Lower Brailes in Warwickshire.

In Old Europe, the various forms of death roads may have carried ancient ideas to do with spirit ways through the medieval period and almost certainly account for some of Alfred Watkins's 'ley' alignments. While these funerary features are visible in the landscape, there are other 'paths' that are invisible, though in the folk mind they had definite physical locations (*see* **Spirit Ways**). These are spirit lines by definition, and the very fact that they were believed to exist does tend to support the ideas of the the new ley hunters and to support their suspicions about the physical death roads. *See also* **Entopic Patterns; Nazca Lines; Shaman; Shamanic Landscapes; Trance**

DELPHI

This powerful atmospheric site on the lower slopes of Mount Parnassus was considered a **World Navel** by the ancient Greeks. Plutarch, a Classical writer and a priest of Apollo at Delphi, recorded a legend that stated that Zeus sent out two eagles (the birds associated with Zeus) from the extremities of the Earth. Where their flights crossed, at Delphi, was the centre of the world. In another legend the **oracle** of Delphi was discovered accidentally by a herdsman, Koretas, who happened across a chasm or fissure at the site of what became the temple. Fumes issuing from it put him into a trance in

The ruins of the Temple of Apollo at Delphi, Greece, viewed from the top of the amphitheatre.

which he saw visions of the future. A timber oracle house dedicated to the Earth Goddess, **Gaia**, was built there. A further legend states that when the young god Apollo came across the place, then called Pytho, he encountered and killed the she-dragon, the Python, that dwelt there. The Pythian Games were instituted to commemorate this mythic event, which seems to encode the memory of the usurpation of a **Bronze Age** goddess shrine by a later Apollo cult. The oracle of Delphi was active for over a thousand years, and kings, generals and regular folk came from far and wide to consult it.

The prophetess, or Pythia, issued the oracular pronouncements in the Temple of Apollo, and the ruins standing there today date from the fourth century BC, on the site of earlier stone and timber shrines. The Delphi prophetesses were originally young peasant women, but after one of them had been abducted and raped older women were instituted in the role. The woman would purify herself before an oracular session by bathing in and drinking from the Castalian spring (created in myth by the hooves of the flying horse, Pegasus) at the foot of the mountain and also drink the waters from the Kassotis spring, which ran into the temple itself. The Pythia would then burn laurel leaves (as tradition has it) with barley on an altar before entering the oracle chamber, the *manteion*, where she was attended by priests. No other woman was allowed there. The client would go into a room adjoining the oracle chamber and write his question on a lead tablet. The Pythia seated herself on a tripod – a tall, three-legged metal stool

with a bowl-like seat – and held a laurel leaf in one hand, which she occasionally shook. She would go into **trance** and utter the oracular response to the question asked.

Within the sacred precinct at Delphi are the remnants of many shrines and temples, a theatre and other buildings, with a Sacred Way winding through them. Being a **World Navel** site in legend, it is not surprising that the classic Greek navel stone or **omphalos** has been found there. Indeed, three versions still survive. One is a plain, grey rock shaped like the nose cone of a missile, now standing alongside the Sacred Way. The second is an altogether larger and more fancy affair, carved with a curious lattice pattern (*see* **Omphalos** for more information). The third omphalos is a holed stone over which the prophetess may have been suspended on her tripod. A stadium above the precinct was where the Pythian Games were held. They took place every eight years originally, but every four years at a later date.

The fame of the Delphic oracle surpassed all others in Greece, and pilgrims came from all over the ancient world, paying a fee to the city of Krisa (or Kira), which had taken on the administration of the oracle temple. This fee became extortionate, and Delphi complained to the Amphictyonic Council, a consortium of the region's 12 tribes. This league of city states declared the first Sacred War (595–586 BC). Krisa was destroyed and its territories confiscated, and Delphi came to enjoy autonomy under the wing of the

An omphalos stone by the Sacred Way at Delphi.

The anti-seismic platform beneath the temple of Apollo.

Amphictyonic Council and was the religious centre of the 12-tribe federation. Over the Delphic oracle's thousand years of activity, various other Sacred Wars were fought, and sporadic attempts were made to destroy the sanctuary or corrupt the officiants there. The Romans took over in 189 BC; they generally had less faith in the oracular pronouncements that emerged from the temple than those who had gone before, and in AD 385 Theodosius destroyed it.

The overriding impression that strikes many visitors to Delphi is its sheer physical presence. Its situation on a precipitous valley side is dramatic, and this is quite often aided and abetted by electrical storms in the area, when it can seem as if Zeus is throwing his thunderbolts through the valley alongside the precinct. Such storms can give the temple a brooding and elemental aspect. Further to this, the locale is also subject to fairly regular earthquake activity – so much so, indeed, that the ancient Greeks built the Temple of Apollo on a great 'anti-seismic' platform of polygonal stones, which can rock and roll, thus absorbing the force of a tremor or quake. The forces of the Earth acted as protectors of the temple in the third century BC, when a quake caused rocks to crash down on approaching Celtic Gauls who were intent on attack. The Soteria festival was inaugurated in celebration of this apparently divine act. Despite the presumption of Apollo, it would seem that Delphi remains a place of the Earth Goddess, Gaia.

The true nature of the actual mantic, prophetic session at Delphi has long remained a vexed question among scholars.

Did the Pythia really go into a prophetic trance or was it all simply an act for the gullible? There have been protagonists for both views. Some of those arguing for a genuine trance point to the tradition of the burning of laurel leaves by the Pythia (she was also said to have chewed them). It had been supposed that this smoke might have been psychoactive, but Albert Hofmann, the Swiss chemist who first synthesized LSD, was unable to find any chemically active principles in laurel that could induce altered mind states. This has been supported in self-experimentation by Princeton psychologist Julian Jaynes, who crushed laurel leaves and smoked quantities of them in a pipe. He felt somewhat sick 'but no more inspired than usual'.

Other suggestions have been made for a plant source of the (assumed) trance-inducing smoke at Delphi. The strongest contender is the psychoactive herb henbane (*Hyoscyamus niger*), which contains the tropane alkaloids hyoscyamine, scopolamine and atropine. This suggestion is particularly championed by the German cultural anthropologist Christian Rätsch. He points out that the Greeks consecrated henbane to Apollo, which would certainly have made it appropriate, and it has been used for trance induction or for its medicinal properties from the times of Sumeria through to medieval western Europe.

The prime candidate for a trance-inducing agent at Delphi, however, has been the belief that the Temple of Apollo was situated over the fuming fissure discovered by Koretas, and that the tripod was designed to suspend the prophetess over it in order that she would be able to breathe in the fumes and thus enter into the prophetic trance. But scholar Joseph Fontenrose, who spent some 40 years investigating this idea, found no evidence for a fissure and concluded that the whole concept of a toxic vapour was a romantic myth.

Nevertheless, this scepticism has subsequently been challenged by Jelle de Boer, a geologist at Wesleyan University, Connecticut. He has claimed that he has identified an active geological fault exposed to the east and west of the Temple of Apollo, presumably passing beneath the temple. The faulting was exposed by roadworks, which de Boer feels explains why earlier researchers had not detected it. De Boer also found another, smaller, fault running approximately north–south, connecting with the main fault at the temple. This faulting has created cracks in the rocks that could open and close during periods of seismic activity. In the rock strata below Delphi is a limestone layer rich in hydrocarbons, and it is feasible that gases such as ethylene, methane and hydrogen sulphide could be sporadically released, especially during tectonic stress and strain, and vented out through the rock fissures into the open air. De Boer suggests that such gases could have intoxicated the Pythia. If these observations are true, the Delphi prophetesses were, in effect, the ancient forerunners of today's glue sniffers! The old legend of Koretas may therefore contain more than a whiff of truth.

See also **Bicameral Mind; Hallucinogens; Sibyls**

DIVINATION

Divination is the structured use of intuition for purposes of prophecy, insight and healing. Virtually all cultures through all recorded time have used divination, and techniques are legion. There are relatively simple tribal and folk systems of divination, such as tea-leaf reading, bubble-watching, reading the cracks of burnt shells, casting bones, finger prickling and thumb-sucking, interpreting the snorting and neighing of horses, reading the moles on a person's face – or even facial tics! More complex methods were developed in certain cultures over long periods of time, such as the Chinese systems of the *I Ching* (yarrow-stalk divination) and **feng shui** (landscape divination). Etruscan augury (the observation of bird flight), the Egyptian tarot and Norse **runes** are other examples of highly structured divinatory methods.

Two forms of divination have developed into particularly important traditions – dreaming and the study of the stars and planets. Pictographic records of dreams go back to the Sumerians of the fourth millennium BC, and the ancient Egyptians felt that dreams could contain messages from the gods. The earliest collection of Egyptian dream material dates to between 2040 and 1786 BC (Middle Kingdom). Known as the Chester Beatty Papyrus, it tables 143 good dreams, partially indicated in black, and 91 bad ones, shown in red. The interpretations display a familiarity with the symbolic aspects of dreams. In India and China, too, organized dream study goes back to before 1000 BC. In ancient Greece dream divination (*psychomanteia*) involved a structured form of temple sleep primarily for the purposes of receiving healing information. Other cultures and societies throughout the Old and New Worlds similarly developed their own methods of dream divination.

Astrology, too, must have been a world-wide phenomenon. In the Andes the Indians studied the dark patches of the Milky Way; in ancient China the movements of the stars were observed and measured, and the constellations told of the fortunes of men. We will never know the details of the astrological systems of the skywatchers who built the great megalithic monuments like **Stonehenge**, but we can be sure they had them. Zodiac-based astrology as we know it emerged and developed in the Middle East, especially Mesopotamia and Egypt, and eventually passed to Europe around the twelfth century AD via the Arabic world.

In more recent times the pendulum has become a fairly common divinatory tool. It was was introduced by Spiritualists for spirit divination (contact with the dead), but has subsequently become one of the devices used in **dowsing** for the finding of water, lost objects and other purposes.

Although divination is supposedly alien to mainstream contemporary Western culture, many millions of people still assiduously scan their horoscopes in their daily newspapers. While the popular horoscope is certainly a degraded form of astrology, divination as a whole need not be dismissed as worthless superstition; it can be seen as a way of achieving insights that may not be apparent to the waking, rational mind. It can be considered as a way of augmenting one's awareness without fearing that it may supplant the basic logical norms we are used to. A divinatory method is a structured procedure for reaching the unconscious mind and by-passing the interfering intellect, yet allowing the waking mind to decode the unconscious information through the medium of that system (its symbology, terminology and so forth). All that distinguishes the 'higher' or more complex forms is that they have more intricate and sophisticated mechanisms for finely decoding the divinatory information; they provide a better scaffold for the intuition to build on, using layers of processing, archetypal images and so on.

Divination need not be just for obtaining specific information: it can be a form of general openess or 'reaching out' for insight. Sometimes we don't know what it is we need to know.

See also **Archaeoastronomy; Correspondences; Druids; Geomancy**

An ancient Egyptian temple at Dendera where divinatory dreaming is said to have taken place.

DOWSING

Also known as 'water divining' or 'water witching', this is a form of **divination** that uses a suitable hand-held implement to amplify minor muscle twitches that are said to occur when the dowser locates whatever it is he or she is looking for. The method is primarily used on-site for finding water sources, metal deposits and lost objects, although it has other claimed applications as well.

The traditional dowsing tool is a flexible forked branch or twig – typically hazel, but not necessarily so – which bends up or down when a target has been reached. Towards the end of the nineteenth century the pendulum (any small, suitably weighty object tied to a length of thread) started to be used as well. Nowadays, there are all kinds of dowsing gadgets, probably the most popular being angle rods, pieces of metal rod or wire (such as from wire coathangers), which are bent in a right angle, with one end held lightly or inserted in a sleeve that is held in the hand. Some dowsers do not use devices at all, holding their hands in such a way that they can feel the slight reactions in them when they pass over a target location.

The direct ancestor of the dowsing pendulum was the Spiritualist's 'ring and disc' method of obtaining 'yes' or 'no'

A nineteenth-century illustration showing a German miner using the traditional forked stick for dowsing. (C. Stern)

answers to questions directed at supposed discarnate spirits. The spread of the use of the dowsing pendulum in the nineteeth century was due largely to the German physicist, Johann Ritter. He was impressed by the ability of the Italian dowser Francesco Campetti, who was already working with scientists. Campetti taught Ritter how to use the pendulum for dowsing.

It is possible that dowsing in some form or other has been practised since early times, but apart from some debatable evidence for it in ancient China, one of the first securely documented historical accounts of the method being used was in a sixteenth-century German book on mining called *De Re Metallica*. Although the book's author, Georgius Agricola, expressed scepticism about the method, something made the Germans into the best miners and mineralogists of their day. This and other early historical references are to dowsing as a means of prospecting for minerals. One of the first mentions of water dowsing was provided by the antiquarian John Aubrey in the latter part of the seventeenth century, when he reported that in Wiltshire 'water may be found by a divining rod made of willowe'.

The Dauphine region of France produced many dowsers, but none more famous than Jacques Aymar. He could dowse for water and minerals, but came into national prominence when he used his ability successfully to assist police with a murder inquiry. This aroused intellectual interest in dowsing. Aymar carried out experiments with the Abbé de Vallemont, who wrote an important dowsing treatise called *Occult Physics* in 1693. A famous French dowser of the following century was Barthelemy Bleton, who was subjected to various tests by the court physician, Pierre Thouvenel. They joined forces and carried out numerous surveys, which included the discovery of the mineral waters near Contrexeville in the Vosges mountains.

In the early twentieth century Henri Mager arranged a series of tests with dowsers to see if they could find lost mines under Paris. The dowsers did this with notable success and the experiment aroused considerable public interest. After World War I there was a great deal of active research into dowsing in France.

Dowsing has had an association with earth mysteries that goes back to the 1930s, when French dowsers claimed that standing stones were positioned over the crossing of subterranean streams. This was noted in England just before World War II by dowser and archaeologist Reginald A. Smith. Around the same time, German dowsers began reporting that they could detect harmful radiations coming from the ground, and some claimed there were grids of such energy spread over the entire globe. After the war Guy Underwood

The Crickhowell Stone in Wales. Dowser Bill Lewis dowsed what he called energy nodes on this 14ft (4.5m) monolith and marked them with chalk. Scientists then ran a magnetometer down the stone and magnetic anomalies were duly recorded at the marked spots.

underground streams of water. He found the stones of the Rollright circle near Oxford in England to be connected with such a beam or thread of energy, with lines shooting off into the surrounding landscape. Graves wondered if these could be 'the non-physical reality' behind Alfred Watkins's **leys.** He was not the first to suggest this: Arthur Lawton in 1939 had proposed that there were **energies** linking ancient sacred sites that were dowsable, and he associated these with Watkins's leys.

In the wave of interest in ancient mysteries and occult matters that had emerged from the 1960s, the New Age assumption that leys were lines of dowsable energy criss-crossing the ancient landscapes of old England and, indeed, the world became fixed. Over the years, this basic idea has expanded to include fantasy claims that dowsers can detect interplanetary (and even intergalactic) energy lines, lines of yin and yang energy linking ancient sites, energy ley lines consisting of multiple channels of energy, and other notions.

Separating the wheat from the chaff in dowsing is a tricky business. The fantasy claims have certainly been a burden for legitimate earth mysteries enquiry, making it appear truly lunatic fringe. The truth is that most people cannot dowse very well, if they are effective at all, and nearly all dowsing techniques make self-deception rather easy. Even dowsers who have a successful track record in finding, say, water, can be prone to exaggerated opinions as to what is happening and what 'energies' they may think they are finding. But all the fantasizing aside, there does seem reason to accept that there is limited validity to basic dowsing when conducted by gifted dowsers – a rare breed. Some people do dowse for water repeatedly and successfully. Dowsers have been used on authentic archaeological digs and have found hidden foundations of old buildings and buried deposits, impressing the archaeolgists involved. In 1976 Bill Lewis's claim that there were 'energy nodes' on standing stones was even validated to some extent in an experiment designed and directed by scientists at a Welsh standing stone. There were no unknown exotic forces, but it did seem that Lewis was able to pick up magnetic variations in the stone. Occasional other experiments have also indicated that good dowsers can detect changes in electrical and magnetic fields.

Care clearly has to be taken not dismiss the whole subject out of hand, even though modern dowsing is afloat with highly questionable claims. Randi, the American stage magician who has been the scourge of those making claims that have challenged mainstream science, appeared not to take such care when dealing with dowsing on one of his shows for British television. He had several dowsers on the programme, and he put them through a range of tests. All of them failed

picked up on Smith's rendering of the French work and proceeded to develop a complex theory that involved underground streams beneath megalithic sites and old churches. He felt that dowsing had been part of 'prehistoric religions'. When his book, *The Pattern of the Past*, was published posthumously in 1969, it had a great impact on the new generation of ley hunters and other ancient mysteries enthusiasts, helping to cement the already prevalent notion that underground water, dowsing and the siting of megalithic structures were connected – although no one seems to have asked what the significance of such a connection could have been.

In 1976 Tom Graves wrote an influential book explicitly associating dowsing with the new surge of interest in earth mysteries. Graves had interviewed Welsh master dowser Bill Lewis, who informed him that he found standing stones to have force-fields of some kind around them and that there were energy points or 'nodes' on the stones that a dowser could detect. Graves himself claimed to be able to dowse overground lines of energy linking megalithic sites as well as miserably except one, who passed every test. In his summing up, in which he in effect damned dowsing, Randi failed to dwell on the remarkable success of the one dowser. Dowsing may sit uneasily between fact and fantasy, but it deserves more scientific attention than it currently receives. What can be said, though, is that dowsing has little directly to do with ancient earth mysteries, despite its reputation to the contrary.

See also **Dragon Project**

DRAGON

Dragon lore is held in great affection by ancient mysteries aficiandos. **Folklore** has it that dragons are scaly, reptilian beasts that can fly, emit fiery or noxious breath, sit atop hills and squeeze spiral contours into them with their mighty tails (thus explaining the appearance of prehistoric earthworked hills), devour cattle, sheep and the occasional maiden, and terrorize villages and whole districts. They are usually killed by local heroes.

The dragon image is extremely complex. Some commentators think of it as a symbol of the chthonic forces within the earth, and it is this that makes it so popular with earth mysteries enthusiasts. The image of St Michael spearing the dragon is also seen by many earth mysteries people as not only being a symbol of Christianity putting down that old serpent, Satan, but also suppressing **paganism**. In China the dragon is associated with royalty and divinity and with electrical storms. Various researchers over the years have noticed a curious recurrence of certain numbers in dragon tales, both British and Chinese, especially three and its multiple, nine. Author Paul Screeton has commented on this in the folktale of the Lambton Worm of Northumberland ('worm' being an old English term for dragon or serpent), in which it is stated that the creature had nine holes on each side of its head, encircled Worm Hill three times and drank the milk of nine cows at a sitting. Some British dragon stories have an almost documentary quality about them, suggesting that the dragon is a metaphor for *something* real happening in the specified countryside: one suggestion has been that this might have been invasions and was perhaps an oblique reference to dragon images emblazoned on the sails of Viking boats.

A popular notion in 'mysteries' circles is that the dragon was an old way of describing what we would call **UFOs.** This is more factual than it seems at first, especially if one dispenses with the idea of unidentified aerial lights being extraterrestrial spacecraft, but instead are unusual natural phenomena (*see* **Earth Lights**). There is ample documentation

that people in former times actually did refer to unusual lights seen in the sky as dragons. In November 1792 a Scottish pastor wrote in his diary that 'many of the country people observed very uncommon phenomena in the air (which they called dragons) of a red fiery colour, appearing in the north, and flying rapidly towards the east'. For centuries before that people had muttered darkly about *Draco volans* (flying dragon) with regard to strange things seen in the skies. In the thirteenth century Albertus Magnus wrote: 'Some people say they have seen dragons flying in the air and breathing sheets of fire. This I think impossible.' He argued that they were 'Meteors', which people mistook for a flying dragon breathing out fire because of clouds of smoke flying out on either side of the object. In 1590 Thomas Hill similarly argued that the flying, luminous dragon was simply 'a fume kindled' that just looked like the mythical beast to the superstitious eye.

As with many other folklore motifs, it is probable that the dragon image had multiple sources.

DRAGON PROJECT

The Dragon Project, latterly the Dragon Project Trust (DPT), was founded in 1977 in order to mount an interdisciplinary investigation into the rumour (existing in both **folklore** and modern anecdote) that certain prehistoric sites had unusual forces or **energies** associated with them. The DPT, a loose and shifting consortium of volunteers from various disciplines, conducted many years of physical monitoring at sites in Britain and other countries. In the end it was concluded that most stories about 'energies' were likely to have no foundation in fact and in a few cases might be due to mind states and psychological effects produced by certain locations. But hard evidence of magnetic and radiation anomalies was found at some sites, as well as some questionable evidence of infrared and ultrasonic effects. In addition, it was found that the kind of locations favoured by megalith builders tended to have a higher-than-average incidence of unusual lightball phenomena or **earth lights**. (*See* **Energies** for more details of the findings of the DPT and other research efforts in these areas.)

Some initial on-site studies were conducted with dowsers and psychics, but the results of this work were not published as the research remained incomplete. In 1990 the DPT, with its limited resources, decided to shift the main focus of its work to the study of the interaction between human consciousness and ancient site environments. It has started this broad area of enquiry with a research programme

Infrared measurements being taken at the King Stone, Rollright in Oxfordshire, during an early Dragon Project session.

watch while he or she is asleep. When the helper notes a rocking and rolling action beneath the volunteer's closed eyelids, a motion called Rapid Eye Movements (REM), which denotes dreaming sleep, the sleeper is awoken and a report of any dreams being experienced at that time are tape-recorded *in situ*. These are later transcribed and sent, along with control 'home' dreams from each subject, to the Saybrook Institute in San Francisco under the consultancy of Dr Stanley Krippner. There the dreams are subjected to long and painstaking analysis, breaking each one down into a set of designated elements, and coded. They will ultimately be presented for double-blind judging under scientifically accepted protocols.

The aim is to test whether dreams experienced at these places reveal *site-specific* components: will there be a statistically significant number of the coded dreams that, in effect, could be identified as relating to the sites at which they took place? Is there something about the physical nature of the places that influences dreams experienced at them? For instance, do the geophysical anomalies of the places affect the dreaming mind? (The DPT had already noted that places with high background radiation can trigger brief, vivid hallucinatory episodes in some subjects; *see* **Energies**.) Even more exotically, do these ancient and long-used magico-religious locations have a 'memory field' that could be picked up by the dreaming mind? (If so, this might speak to such ideas as Rupert Sheldrake's 'morphic resonance'.)

But the research programme *is* an experiment, and there may be negative answers to all such questions. The point is to test and see. Even if the experiment does produce a negative result, the DPT will be able to console itself that a unique and important body of dream data has been brought into existence that can be used for other, future research.

DREAMTIME

The term 'dreamtime' was coined in 1927 by Europeans, not by the Australian Aborigines themselves. Nevertheless, the Aborigines felt that it well enough described the timeless time of the *tjukuba* (one of its many Aboriginal names).

Once, the Earth was flat and uninhabited. Then, during the Dreaming, giant totemic beings emerged from within the ground – or from some vague portion of the sky in some traditions – and they walked the land, the country. In the course of their meanderings they created the topography, the landscape that now exists. They left their tracks across the surface of the landscape, they camped, made fire, defecated, dug for water, fought, copulated, conducted rituals and so forth. Everything they did left on the country a mark that

investigating dreaming at selected ancient sacred places. This programme, which is being conducted jointly with the Saybrook Institute in San Francisco and is still ongoing at the time of writing, is a kind of modern re-visiting of the ancient practice of temple sleep (*see* **Divination**).

The basic aim of the programme is to run many dream sessions at just four selected ancient sites: a holy hill in the Preseli range in Wales and three Cornish sites – a **Neolithic** dolmen, a Celtic holy well and an **Iron Age** underground passage and chamber (called a *fogou* in Cornish dialect and a souterrain by archaeologists). Each of these places possesses an interesting geophysical anomaly. The sleep volunteers are drawn from as wide a range of the public as possible. Ages have ranged from teenagers to 70-year-olds. Women volunteers have so far slightly outnumbered men. Work at the Welsh site and the Cornish souterrain has now been completed, although dreams are still being collected at the other two sites. Each volunteer is accompanied by a least one helper who keeps

EARTH LIGHTS

This is a nickname given to anomalous light phenomena belonging to the same family as earthquake lights and ball lightning but possessing their own characteristics. They have been reliably and scientifically observed and to some extent instrumentally monitored. It is a subject that impinges on ancient earth mysteries interests not only because it would seem to be a genuine earth mystery in its own right, but more specifically because the existence of strange lights has been encoded into the lore of some traditional and tribal societies and because there are reports of such lights being seen at ancient sacred places. In addition, some temples are known to have been erected because mysterious lights were frequently seen at certain locations and were assumed to be manifestations of spirits or deities (*see* **Energies** for more on lights and sites). Earth lights have also, inevitably, become entwined with the vexed matter of **UFOs**.

The history and nature of earth lights is discussed in depth in my own *Earth Lights Revelation* (1989).

See also **Corpse Lights**; **Fairies**

EASTER ISLAND

The giant stone statues or *moai* on this remote island far out in the Pacific provide an evergreen megalithic mystery. Thought to date to AD 1000–1500, some stand on stone platforms, others are placed in the ground, and still others are half-buried in the quarries where they originated. The finished statues on the platforms range from 6ft (2m) to 33ft (10.5m) in height and weigh between 4 and 82 tons. They seem to represent ancestral figures belonging to the ancient Easter Islanders. The main quarry at the volcanic crater of Rano Raraku is littered with the remains of picks made from compacted basalt capable of working the hard-surfaced but internally spongy tuff from which the statues are formed.

Because Easter Island has no trees, it has long been a mystery as to how the statues were transported from the quarries to the platforms (*ahus*) and raised there. However, it has

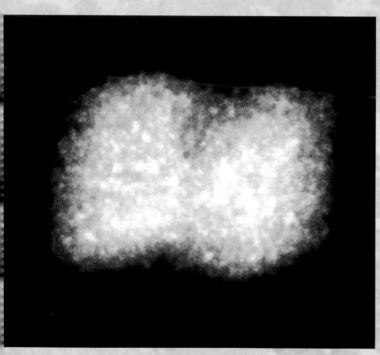

This (enlarged) photograph of a mystery light was taken in 1981 near Grimstad, Norway. It is just one of dozens of pictures obtained during an outbreak of anomalous light phenomena in Norway during the 1980s, notably in the remote valley of Hessdalen, where automatic monitoring stations are currently under construction. *(Project Hessdalen)*

Stone statue or *moai* at the Rano Raraku crater, Easter Island, where statues were quarried. (*Klaus Aarsleff/ Fortean Picture Library*)

EFFIGY MOUNDS

Huge terrestrial effigies are to be found on prehistoric landscapes scattered throughout the Americas (*see* **Shamanic Landscapes**). These ancient ground markings or 'geoglyphs' can depict animals, human beings and strange creatures that are half-human, half-animal. One form of these terrestrial images is the earthworks in the United States produced by what archaeologists call the Effigy Mound Culture. They are to be found in an area spanning parts of Iowa, Minnesota and Wisconsin. Between AD 300 and 1300 as many as 10,000 earthen effigies were built, and the 1000 or so that survive are profoundly enigmatic. Usually rising 3–4ft (1–1.2m) above ground level, many of these terrestrial sculptures have not yielded any burials. Many are conical or cigar-shaped, but some are in the form of animals, humans or strange beings. The greatest surviving concentration of such features is to be found at Effigy Mounds National Monument, near Marquette, Iowa, which covers 1475 acres (590ha) and contains some 200 mounds. There are 26 animal figures, the largest being Great Bear Mound, which is 70ft (22m) across at the shoulders and 137ft (42m) in length. One group of monuments forms a cluster of 13 effigies of birds and marching bears in a huge arc. All animal effigies are accompanied by geometric mounds.

now been shown by pollen analysis that the island was once forested. It was almost certainly the exhaustion of timber supplies that helped lead to the cessation of statue-making. Indeed, some are left unfinished in the quarries. Researchers tried to reproduce possible transportation methods, but they achieved only mixed results until they took note of the islanders' own belief that wooden sledges were used. It was found that sledges made from green wood running over short rolling logs could move a statue so speedily and effectively that the biggest problem lay in slowing it down! Traces of prehistoric roads leading out from Rano Raraku have been located.

There is some evidence that stone ramps may have been used to raise the figures on to the platforms, and in 1955 Thor Heyerdahl's Norwegian expedition was able to raise the fallen 25-ton statue at Anakena in 18 days, using two levers and gradually building a ramp beneath the statue using small stones. Despite this achievement, though, it is thought that wooden scaffolds were probably often used as well, as postholes have been found at some platform sites.

Whatever methods were used, strong ropes would have been essential, and the only real sources of rope material were from the inner bark of the *Triumfetta* shrub and the crowns of the now-extinct palm. The eventual loss of ropemaking resources must also have contributed strongly to the decline in statue-making. The preoccupation with their megalithic ancestor cult eventually robbed the ancient Easter Islanders of their supportive habitat.

Ancient **astronaut** writer Erich von Daniken has fantasized that the *moai* were the work of temporarily stranded ancient astronauts, whereas they were in fact the product of human beliefs and obsessions. It is an old, earthbound story.

Just some of the effigy and geometric mounds at Effigy Mounds National Monument, Iowa. (*US National Parks Service*)

Perhaps the most famous of the earthen effigies is Serpent Mound in Adams County, Ohio, which stretches for about ¼ mile (0.5km). It was probably built by the Adena people approximately 2000 years ago. The earthen effigy stands 4–5ft (1.2–1.5m) high and does not contain any burials.
See also **Hopewell Indians**; **Shaman**; **Trance**

ELEUSIS

This temple, situated 12 miles (19km) west of Athens, was the focus of a Greek Mystery cult that lasted for nearly two thousand years. In myth, Eleusis was where Persephone (Kore) was abducted by the king of the underworld, Hades. Persephone's mother, Demeter, wandered the Earth looking for her daughter and vowed never to return to Olympus nor allow crops to grow on the Earth until Persephone was delivered back to her. Eventually, Zeus was obliged to send Hermes to the underworld to retrieve Persephone, but before she escaped Hades tricked

Eleusis, near Athens in Greece, looking towards the ruins of the Plouton and the cave-like entrance to the otherworld beyond.

her into eating pomegranate seeds, which meant that she would have to return annually for a third of each year to his realm. Thus was the cycle of the seasons mythically presented to the ancient Greeks. Reunited with her daughter, Demeter gave Triptolemos, the son of a nearby king, seeds of wheat and a magical chariot in which he could roam around the world teaching agriculture and the use of the plough. Demeter taught humans the rites that were to be carried out at Eleusis.

A settlement arose at Eleusis between 1580 and 1500 BC, but the area now occupied by the ruins of the Eleusian precinct was left empty, suggesting that an early form of the Mysteries may have been in operation, even at this early date. The first stone structure on the site, known to archaeologists as Megaron B, dates from the fifteenth century BC. Over the following thousand years various structures came and went, and buildings were enlarged and added. The Mysteries themselves were a ten-day event, held in September each year, and were open to almost anyone. The climax was the procession from Athens to the temple for the Mystery Night, where the revelation of the Mystery, the *epopteia*, to the initiatory candidates, the *mystai*, would take place. After initial preparation, involving a period of fasting, the *mystai* were led by the *mystagogos* in joyful procession along the Sacred Way from Athens to Eleusis. This took all day, because observances were made at various shrines along the route. As they proceeded, the *mystai* imbibed a sacred drink, the *kykeon*. They arrived at Eleusis by nightfall, in flickering torchlight. They danced and conducted rites at various points around and within the temple complex, including the Plouton, a temple connected to a cave, which can still be seen in the hillock forming the acropolis around which the whole temple complex was arranged. This was considered to be one of the entrances to the underworld.

Eventually, the *mystai* assembled at the Telesterion (*teleo*, 'to initiate'), a vast building unlike other Greek temple architecture in that it had a plain exterior. Inside there was a forest of columns and an inner enclosure known as the Anaktoron. Although the Telesterion had been rebuilt and enlarged numerous times, this central structure remained. In the great, final revelation of the Mysteries, under the control of the Hierophant ('he who makes the holy things appear'), flames erupted from the only door in the Anaktoron, and there was a manifestation of Persephone. Exactly what this was no one has been able to determine, for it was kept secret on pain of death or banishment, but those who saw it – and this included many notable names of ancient and Classical Greece, such as Plato, Aristotle and Sophocles – felt their lives to have been changed by the experience; it was said that after it, death could hold no more fears. The revelation seems to have been some kind of powerful theatrical event unleashed on the *mystai*, who by now would have been in a highly suggestible state. The flames, the Great Fire, could be seen issuing out of a special opening in the roof of the Telesterion, a signal to those outside that the *epopteia* had taken place. The Hierophant closed the event by wordlessly showing an ear of corn to the congregation within the Telesterion.

There has been much speculation as to whether the sacred drink, the *kykeon*, was some form of hallucinogen. We know that the beverage was carried in metal or pottery containers, some of them fixed to the heads of priestesses and initiatory candidates by cords or thin straps. It wasn't wine, for wine was not permitted. Ingredients of the potion, of which a definite dose had to be taken, were said to have been water, barley and fresh leaves of some variety of pennyroyal – probably the mint *Mentha pulegium*. The principle constituent of pennyroyal is poley oil (*Oleum pulegii*), large doses of which can induce delirium, unconsciousness and convulsions. Jungian scholar Carl Kerènyi noted that a plant of the same family, *Salvia divinorum*, was found in use among the Mazatec Indians of Mexico in a divinatory context, and may have been the Aztec magic plant Pipiltzintzintli. It contains non-alkaloidal constituents called Divinorin A and Divinorin B, whose psychoactive effects have been experimentally verified. Kerènyi implied that this may indicate a psychoactive quality to the *kykeon*, but Swiss chemist Albert Hofmann felt that Kerènyi had 'overstated' the possibility. Instead, Hofmann joined with other researchers into **hallucinogens**, Gordon Wasson and Carl Ruck, who had their eyes on the barley. They pointed out that a water solution of *Claviceps purpurea*, or ergot, a parasitic fungus found on wheat and barley, could easily have been made, and ergot contains alkaloids from which LSD can be produced. This possibility of the *kykeon* having been a hallucinogenic ergotized beer is supported by the fact that Demeter could be referred to as Erysibe, 'ergot', and her symbolic colour was purple, the colour of ergot at certain stages of its growth cycle (hence *purpurea*). This hypothesis remains the most persuasive suggestion so far, but the poet Robert Graves felt that hallucinogenic mushrooms were involved with the Eleusian Mystery.

See also **Mythic Geography**

ENERGIES

The idea of unusual energies or strange forces being present at ancient sacred places has long been a major belief within earth mysteries circles, and, indeed, it is implicit in certain **folklore** motifs, so the notion clearly goes back generations. In the

One of the stones at the Long Meg and Her Daughters site, Cumbria, which exhibits localized points of radiation and near which a witness went into an involuntary trance-like state.

twentieth century, the idea developed further from work at prehistoric monuments by psychic mediums between the two World Wars, who claimed to be able to see with their inner eye the use of various types of 'cosmic forces' by the builders of the sites (*see* **Psychic Archaeology** for examples of this). These people were heavily influenced by **Theosophy,** a powerful occult movement that developed towards the end of the nineteenth century. Along with other occultists, their ideas allowed Theosophical ideas to colour the fledgling 1960s ancient earth mysteries movement. **Dowsing**, too, provided a channel for exotic beliefs and ideas about unknown energies to influence powerfully the earth mysteries field, especially in the United States, where it was primarily dowsers who imported the new interest in **leys** and 'alternative archaeology'. By the 1970s the belief in ancient energies was barely questioned within earth mysteries circles. The **Dragon Project** (DP) was called into being in 1977 to try to determine what substance, if any, there was to all the rumours.

The DP confined itself primarily to checking for physical, measurable energies, although some on-site testing of psychics and dowsers was attempted. (These latter efforts remain unfinished, although the results obtained did not augur well for there being a great deal of objectivity in dowsing and psychic claims at ancient places.) The sites monitored mainly involved British prehistoric monuments, but a few sporadic sessions were conducted at ancient sacred locations in France, Greece, Egypt and the United States. Anecdotal material was also collected from further afield. The shifting, volunteer personnel of DP members decided to search for energies that might be expected to be present at megalithic monuments, linking these where possible to reports of people's experiences at specific sites.

Radioactivity was one obvious candidate, for this occurs naturally in various forms, being emitted by rocks, especially granite, and streaming down from the sky as a result of cosmic ray bombardment of the upper atmosphere. The DP was looking for anomalies in this background radiation around prehistoric monuments, but for any to be identifed required a great deal of monitoring to be conducted, both at the site and in its environment. Over time, however, it became apparent that some standing stones did emit notable amounts of gamma radiation. The Long Meg and Her Daughters site in Cumbria was measured because of a report from a reliable witness who experienced an involuntary light **trance** in the vicinity of the stones in the northwest quadrant of the stone circle. The DP found that these stones had localized patches emitting levels of radiation stronger than those recorded on the surfaces of the other stones, all of which were granitic.

The DP discovered heightened natural radiation in other sacred sites contexts. The waters of various healing wells and

Hot spring water at Bath in Avon, issuing through an old Roman conduit.

springs, for instance, proved to be radioactive. A notable example was the hot springs of Bath in Avon. These were resorted to at least 7000 years ago, and later, in the **Iron Age**, they became a Celtic shrine. The Romans made the site into one of their temple and bathing complexes, and it was still a renowned spa over a millennium after the Romans had left Britain. The thermal waters rising at Bath contain appreciable amounts of radium, and when the DP monitored water feeding beneath the Great Bath, a noteworthy level of natural radioactivity was confirmed. The DP found that various Celtic Christian holy wells in Cornwall also had mildly radioactive water.

The third situation in which the DP found radiation to prove significant was inside the **Neolithic** and Iron Age stone chambers it measured. Typically, the radiation levels there would be up to four times the average open-air background count. This was due to a build-up of radon within the granite structures. Interestingly, the DP found that the interior of the King's Chamber inside the Great Pyramid at Giza yielded virtually identical radiation counts to the British monuments. Although the Great Pyramid is constructed from limestone, the King's Chamber is clad in Aswan granite, a stone the ancient Egyptians considered to represent, or even contain, 'spirit'.

Naturally occurring magnetism was another obvious target for the DP's energy survey. The DP found two forms of magnetic anomaly at ancient sacred places. The first of these was extremely low-level magnetic fluctuations in standing stones, measurable with magnetometers. These types of effect could last up to one or two hours, and then the stone reverted to a stable state. The DP was unable to carry out a sufficiently long-term survey to find out just how common this effect was – although indications were that it was very occasional and apparently random – nor was it able to determine the cause of the fluctuations. The other effect was more robust and less mysterious, though striking nonetheless: some stones at megalithic sites were discovered to be sufficiently magnetic to deflect a compass needle held close to them. This magnetism was caused by the iron content in the stones in question and a field being 'set' within the rock when it was formed that is at variance with today's magnetic field. Although there was nothing mysterious about this effect, the DP felt that the presence of such stones at specific sites, and often in key locations within those monuments, had possibly been intended by the megalith builders.

Outside the British Isles, magnetic anomalies have been noted at other sacred places. At the Namoratunga II standing stone complex in Kenya, for example, an American university team found that magnetic fields around the megaliths were affecting their instrumentation.

ENTOP⌐

These are spec
during early s
resulted from
Klüver with
fascinated no
provoked by
studied the d
subjects and
less points of
ings', 'living
'cobweb-like
on. Someti
objects like
sometimes
glow', 'gorg
iridescent,
oriental
buttresses
or 'a kale
prisms,
uniformi
similar r
projecte
     Klüve
hallucir
these
lattice.
design'
consta
specia
vessel
from
of-bo
parti
whe
patt
visi
ima
is f
wo
ba
tia

g
i
s
s

A magnetometer monitors subtle changes of magnetism in a standing stone.

A third broad category identified by the DP as a candidate for possible energy effects at ancient sites is definitely exotic – anomalous light phenomena or **earth lights**. A whole strand of anecdotes related to them seem to involve ancient sacred places. The sacred Chinese mountains, of Wu Tai shan, for example, apparently had large golden-orange light-balls that frequented its peak at night. These were interpreted as Bodhisattva Lights. A tower was specially erected at a summit temple on Wu Tai shan for viewing these holy lights. In India two pilgrimage shrines dedicated to the Goddess Bhagbatti on the Purnagiri Mountain were likewise founded because of local light phenomena. The most sacred of the two shrines is situated on a fault. The distinguished German-born Tibetan Buddhist, the late Lama Anagarika Govinda, also saw lights in the mountains of India. While he was staying at Dilkusha, he noticed lights moving rapidly on distant slopes. The local maharaja told him that the lights were often seen and he had once witnessed them moving through his palace grounds towards a temple. That spot had always been considered a sanctified place, he said.

In Britain there have been numerous reports from people seeing strange lights over or near prehistoric monuments, and there are even some accounts of this in folklore. In 1919 two hill walkers in the Lake District reported seeing numerous large, softly glowing white globes floating lazily hither and thither above the Castlerigg stone circle. One of the witnesses later suggested in a magazine article that these lights could be unknown natural phenomena that occurred at that place from time to time, and the megalith builders, taking them to be spirits, erected their stone circle there because of that. This certainly appears to be the case with the Chinese and Indian temples referred to above.

Whatever the nature of such lights, their connection with ancient sites may, in fact, be related to a common factor: it is thought by a number of authorities that geological fault lines are part of the apparatus that produces earth lights, and the DP found that the locations of, specifically, stone circles and stone chambers in Britain correlated with the distribution of surface faults and associated intrusions. This may have been because stone was more accessible in such regions, in which case the association may have been coincidental, or it may have been because lights were seen relatively often in such areas and were regarded as 'spirits'.

There is also some evidence that pre-industrial people could deliberately relate to faulting. The ancient Icelandic ceremonial centre, the Althing, was deliberately sited in a rift valley, Thingvellir, by the Scandinavian settlers. In Arizona the Indians who built **Wupatki** apparently recognized the vast fault system lying beneath the pueblo site (*see* page 183). The Greek oracle site of **Delphi** is not only related to faulting in its founding myth, but that faulting has now been scientifically claimed as a physical fact at the place. Moreover, the faulting was considered integral to the divinatory procedure at the temple. Then there are less definite associations, such as the astounding coincidence that the remarkable 2000-year-old serpent mound in Ohio (*see* **Shamanic Landscapes**) is located over a crypto-volcanic zone riddled with faulting, said to be unique in the United States. Again, the Belgian researcher Pierre Mereaux has mapped the **Carnac** stone rows in Brittany against geological information and reports that their positioning relates closely to the distribution of the fault lines in the region.

The nort
opposite
Preseli h
to see v

The
ancier
film a
sunri:
odd
into
T
199(
gati
rese
ma
DI
M
tis
ri
ir
n
u

kinds of mental illness, the influence of mind-altering drugs, nitrous oxide (laughing gas), dreaming sleep and hypnogogia, fever and hallucinatory states arising from hunger and thirst. He also suspected, well in advance of his time, that it was processes within the brain that provided the sensory impressions underlying visions and auditory hallucinations. In 1888 P. Max Simon studied the imagery of schizophrenic hallucinations in his patients. He observed the repeated occurrence of spider webs, ropes, meshes and balls. These images were always in flux, changing from one to another, and displayed specific movement patterns.

In 1924 Louis Lewin, author of the seminal *Phantastica: Narcotic and Stimulating Drugs, Their Use and Abuse*, noted, like Moreau, the similarity of imagery elicited by several drugs. Marijuana, he observed, frequently produced hallucinations such as 'fireworks, rockets, and many-coloured stars', while mescalin produced forms such as 'coloured arabesques', 'carpets', 'filigree lacework', 'stars', 'crystals' and 'geometrical forms of all kinds'. Following this observational trend, Siegel and Jarvik noted that 'surprisingly similar imagery' had been observed for a variety of other trance-inducing agents, including alcohol (in delirium tremens), **fly agaric**, antihistamines, numerous anaesthetics, the South American 'soul vine' or *Banisteriopsis, Datura stramonium*, harmela alkaloids, ketamine, psilocybin ('magic') mushrooms and tobacco in heavy doses. They remarked that entoptic-style imagery can also be provoked by some chemicals used in chemotherapy. To all of which they add conditions such as psychotic states, fevers arising from illnesses, such as measles and malaria, epilepsy and half-sleep states.

So it now seems clear that the basis of hallucinatory imagery lies in the actual structure of, or processes within, the human visual system, whether optical, cellular or electrical – or probably a combination of all these. These can underlie more complex imagery, to some extent in the manner that the dots of a newspaper photograph can 'carry' a photographic image. In addition, the geometric patterns can be accompanied by or precede convincing haptic (bodily) feelings of movement, such as if the soul were flying out from the body and down a long tunnel, avenue, road or similar image. Further, **hallucinogens** can cause changes in body-image perception that can even extend to a sense of becoming another creature entirely. A graphic example of this occurred when a friend of psychologist William James took a large dose of hashish, in which entoptic imagery developed into a full-blown sensation of being transformed into a fox. He felt as if he had long ears and a bushy tail and his eyes seemed placed at the back of a long snout. Such sensations probably account for the half-man, half-animal or

'therianthropic' imagery in prehistoric **rock art**, the animal costumes in shamanic cultures and the ceremonial association of specific creatures or familiars with shamans.

While all this can be only inferred from iconographic material in archaeological remains, it becomes pretty certain when specific hallucinogenic plants are depicted, when items of drug-taking equipment are uncovered at ancient sites, and when physical data are allied with anthropological information. For instance, anthropologists have observed the social use of entoptic patterns with the Tukano Indians of the Colombian Amazon. These people take a number of hallucinogens related to their ritual life, which itself is closely tied to their everyday existence. In particular, they use ayahuasaca mixtures based on *Banisteriopsis*. They clearly distinguish entoptic patterns from figurative hallucinations, and each form constant holds a specific meaning for the Tukano that revolved largely around sexual themes – so patterns variously represent the uterus, the male organ, the female organ, drops of semen and so forth. They use the entoptic images as a basis for their decorative art, and this serves an underlying purpose of regularly reminding tribal members of the threat of incest.

To understand the full impact of entoptic imagery on a wide range of archaeological and earth mysteries themes, it is important to refer to the entries listed below.
See also **Chavín de Huantar**; **Cognitive Archaeology**; **Effigy Mounds**; **Gavrinis**; **Leys/Leylines**; **Loughcrew**; **Nazca Lines**; **Newgrange**; **Shaman**; **Shamanic Landscapes**; **Tiahuanaco**

EXTERNSTEINE

The Externsteine is a group of weathered natural sandstone towers, each around 100ft (30m) tall, located in the Teutoberger Wald district near Detmold in Germany. Apart from a few finds suggesting the presence of reindeer hunters c.10,000 BC, there is scant archaeological evidence to demonstrate the presence of people at the rocks during prehistory. Some researchers have maintained that the place was a centre for pagan worship until Christianization by Charlemagne in 772. It is claimed that he destroyed a representation of the Irminsul, the pagan Tree of Life, situated on top of one of the rocks. Other scholars have maintained that early Christian worship took place at the site. Whatever the truth of these conflicting claims, the site presents a bizarre appearance today: steps carved out of some of the sandstone pillars lead to shrines or platforms that have disappeared, an apparent sarcophagus is hewn out of a giant boulder, and caves or 'rooms' honeycomb the lower reaches of some of the pillars. (These may have been used by anchorites at some remote period.) Foundations of medieval fortifications have also been uncovered. A slightly enhanced natural projection on one rock looks like a man with his arms raised, and there has been debate as to whether this was supposed to represent Odin or Christ (see **Simulacra**).

Even if it was originally used as a pagan shrine, the Externsteine was Christianized at some point, because on another of the rocks is a large bas-relief showing Christ's descent from the cross. Interestingly, one of the figures in this is standing on a bent Irminsul (World Tree), as if indicating the victory of Christianity over paganism.

Probably the most striking feature of the site is a rock-hewn chapel high on one of the central pillars known as Tower Rock. At some point it has suffered damage, as its roof and outer wall are now missing. It can be accessed only by means of a bridge from an adjoining rock. It could have been a pagan chapel, partially destroyed in the process of Christianization, or it could have been an ancient Christian chapel, but no one knows for sure. Its main surviving point of interest is an alcove on its northeastern side, which contains a small, altar-like plinth, behind which is a circular window. It has long been noted that the rising midsummer sun shines through this aperture when viewed from a niche in the opposite wall. Nowadays the effect is lost, but when the whole chapel was enclosed, this would have been a dramatic sight from inside the darkened building. On top of the altar-plinth there is a slot, and perhaps a crystal or a gnomon (shadow-throwing device) was fitted into this to throw rainbow lightbeams or a shadow into the niche. It is also thought that the window framed a view of the moon at its northerly extreme rising position. The German antiquarian Wilhelm Teudt conducted studies at the chapel in 1925 and concluded that on looking through the chapel's window distant landmarks could be seen on the skyline marking the solar and lunar events. Teudt had been tracing such alignments, or *heilige Linien* ('holy lines') as he called them, across the German landscape in support of his theories of a superior German high culture of antiquity. He was sure the Externsteine chapel was an ancient Germanic solar temple. By 1933 his ideas were taken up by the cultural propaganda of the Third Reich, and the Externsteine rocks became a Nazi cult centre. Even today one can see where the eagle emblem of the Third Reich was positioned.

The rocks continue to attract visitors, including apparently only women bent on suicide by jumping from the bridge leading to the chapel and other high points. As a consequence of this curious phenomenon, at the time of writing access to Tower Rock is partially restricted.

See also **Archaeoastronomy**; **Leys/Leylines**; **World Navel**

Some of the pillars at Externsteine, Germany, from the west, showing the little bridge leading to the tall Tower Rock.

The altar-plinth and recess in the now-roofless chapel at Externsteine. The circular window is oriented towards the midsummer morning sun.

FAIRIES

Fairy lore is the classic example that has come down to us today of the pre-industrial worldview in which the visible world was considered to be inhabited by spirits. You might not be able to see the fairies, or not very often, but they were there all right, thick in the air, shimmering but a few light vibrations beyond the spectrum of normal mortal sight. (Some people were believed to be gifted with 'second sight', because they were able to see on these rarified frequencies of supernormal vision.) There was also a parallel dimension or realm – fairyland – where time passed at a different rate and to which mortals could sometimes be whisked away.

Fairies took many forms in different traditions – and even within the same cultural context. Almost always basically anthropomorphic in form (although there were a few shape-less horrors), they appear in the folk record variously as humanoid beings over 7ft (2.2m) tall and known as the Gentry in Ireland; as little entities, from a few to several inches in height, ranging in appearance from delicate, exquisitely formed aristocratic and beautiful creatures to wizened or even grotesque beings; as dwarf-like creatures; and as elemental spirits. There were also human-sized fairies appearing either as beautiful women or as hags. Fairy beings had many names, covering the whole spectrum of types: sprites, piskies (often misspelled as pixies), elementals such as sylphs, undines and dryads, the Shee (Dana o'Shee) of Ireland, the beautiful and bewitching glaistigs of the Scottish Highlands, the Welsh Tylwyth Teg in their white or striped and multi-coloured clothes, the wailing banshees of Ireland, and brownies, boggarts, goblins, elves and many more.

Despite their variety, fairies displayed some fairly common traits. All of them could be tricksters, ready to play more or less harmless pranks on mortals, while many were able and willing to punish human beings who annoyed them with quite serious ailments, to cause cattle and domestic animals to become sick or even die or to spoil milk or food. Certain types of fairy beings were downright dangerous and evil, and these counted among their ranks entities like water kelpies, which sought to devour humans, the Redcaps of the Scottish border (their

Glastonbury Tor in Somerset, home of the fairy king until he was evicted by a Christian saint.

headgear coloured by the blood of travellers they had killed), the child-eating Black Annis of the English Midlands, the ugly Yarthkins of the Lincolnshire fens and the troublesome trolls of Scandinavia. Fairies were eminently clean and tidy, and they profoundly disliked human beings who interfered with their orderly ways. They hated to be spied on by mortals. They would pilfer human-owned items, such as milk, cattle and anything else they needed, although woe betide the mortal who stole from them! But they respected and rewarded acts of generosity towards them. Indeed, they sometimes disguised themselves in order to test a mortal's kindness.

It was considered sensible for humans to observe special rules of etiquette when they dealt with fairies. It was generally unlucky to speak of them but if one had to it was wise to make only complimentary comments. If they were encountered, one had to be courteous towards them and be sure to thank them if they performed some service or kind act, although one did not thank certain types of fairies. It was thought advisable to leave the house tidy at night, with the hearth swept and the fire made up, and a container of water left nearby in case the house was visited by a fairy overnight to bathe its baby. A variant on this was to leave a fire burning at night so that any fairy happening by might be able to roast a frog for its evening meal. It was also a good idea to leave a piece of cake or other morsel overnight to keep the fairies happy, and a suit of clothes should be left to repay a helpful fairy such as a brownie. A human always had to avoid partaking of fairy food or drink – failure to observe this would result in enchantment.

There are recurring motifs in fairy lore. The 'fairy wife' is one of them, the basic storyline being that a mortal man and a beautiful fairy girl meet accidentally and fall in love; the fairy lives with the man in the human world, but there are certain taboos the man must observe. Inevitably, one of these taboos gets broken, and the fairy woman has to return to fairyland, leaving the man alone and desolate. Another theme relates to 'fairy processions', which are preserved in folk beliefs such as the Fairy Ride and Trooping Fairies. Sometimes, such processions were part of a fairy wedding, itself another key motif.

Then there was fairy abduction: fairies were often on the lookout for young men with special skills and abilities and for young girls, especially if they had golden hair. They would be taken off to fairyland or tricked or tempted into leaving the mortal world. In Cornwall this was referred to as being 'pisky-led'. Such abducted humans were generally happy in fairyland for a time, but would eventually pine to get back to the world of humans. This motif is closely related to another, that of 'enchantment' – the Rip Van Winkle effect – in which a mortal spending a seemingly short time in fairyland

Remains of the Fairy Stone, Shropshire. A farmer passing by one evening saw small lights shining steadily on the grass around this stone. He kicked at some of them, and one or two became stuck to his trouser leg. Alarmed, the man rushed home, by which time he found that holes had appeared in his trousers where the lights had clung to the fabric.

will find on returning to the world of mortals that many years, usually centuries, have passed. All friends and relatives have died or grown very old. In some stories using this theme, the mortal returns from fairyland on horseback and on dismounting and touching the ground, turns to dust.

An especially grim motif is that of the 'changeling'. In this, the fairies leave a strange, ugly fairy child in place of a bonny human baby. This belief probably led to considerable child abuse in the past, for a way to get the fairies to return the abducted child was supposedly to beat the changeling mercilessly. If a human child was returned, though, it would never be normal again.

Yet another motif is that of 'fairy ointment'. A typical version of this is the Cornish story of the unfortunate Pee Tregeer. She furtively tried out a greenish ointment while at the house of a woman believed by locals to be a witch. Some of the ointment got dabbed on to one of her eyes. Later, when she was at Penzance market, she saw the witch's husband stealing from a stall. He noticed Pee Tregeer looking at him. 'Can you see me?' he asked. Pee nodded. 'Which eye can you see me with?' the man enquired further. She pointed to the eye that had been dabbed with the ointment. The witch's husband, a fairy fellow, immediately poked his finger into the eye, blinding it. As this tale indicates, there are connections between fairy lore and witch lore, and a particularly close match occurs in the 'flying' motif. Fairies, like witches, can fly

The first effects of *Amanita muscaria* intoxication are generally reported as a feeling of pleasant invigoration, and the individual may break into song, dance and laughter. This is accompanied by a marked increase in physical strength. In the next stage of intoxication, hallucinations set in. In the 1790s a Polish soldier called Joseph Kopec unwillingly ate part of a fly agaric for medicinal purposes. He fell into a sleep in which he had visions of fabulous gardens 'where only pleasure and beauty seemed to rule'. Beautiful, white-clad women fed him fruits and berries and offered him flowers. When he awoke he was so distressed to return to mundane reality that he consumed an entire mushroom and fell back into his visions.

Amanita muscaria intoxication typically produces macropsia, in which small objects can look many times their actual size; the complementary effect, micropsia, can also occur. The mushroom-taker is likely to hear voices telling him or her to perform bizarre actions, or the spirits of the mushrooms might appear and converse with the taker directly. The mushroom spirits tend to wear wide hats on heads that sit on stout cylindrical bodies without an intervening neck, and the number seen depends on the number of mushrooms eaten. Bemushroomed people will run after the spirits, who tell them things as they lead them on a merry chase along paths known only to them, that seem interminably intricate to the mushroom-takers and often lead past places where the dead reside. The mushroom eaters are likely to become unconscious of their surroundings by this stage.

The reindeer of these remote wastes love fly agaric. If one is killed after consuming some of the mushrooms, its meat will pass on their intoxicating effects to anyone eating it. Its urine will do likewise. The Siberian reindeer-herders must have noted this long ago, for as well as mushrooms, reindeer also like certain mosses and lichen that cause them to develop an insatiable desire for urine-soaked snow. When that urine was from a reindeer that had eaten some fly agaric mushrooms, the beast ingesting it would be seen to stagger around as if drunk. This doubtless caused the tribespeople generations ago to realize that the urine of a human being who had eaten the magic mushroom likewise retained its intoxicating effects. A Swedish prisoner of war in the early eighteenth century reported seeing Koryak tribespeople waiting outside huts where mushroom sessions were taking place for people to come out and urinate. When they did, the steaming golden nectar was collected in wooden bowls and greedily gulped down. The *Amanita muscaria* effect could apparently be recycled up to five times in this manner and, remarkably, was less likely to cause the vomiting often associated with the direct ingestion of the mushroom itself. (The important

psychoactive compounds of fly agaric are two isoxazoles, ibotenic acid and the alkaloid muscimole. Muscimole is an unsaturated cyclic hydroxamic acid, which passes through the kidneys in an essentially unaltered form, and this is the secret of the mushroom's remarkable ability to retain its effects in urine. Ibotenic acid converts to muscimole when the mushrooms are dried, the preferred method of preparation by the Siberian tribes.) Psychologist and anthropologist Rogan Taylor has commented that it is hardly surprising that the tribes viewed reindeer as great spirits, considering that the animals could satisfy simultaneously both hunger and the desire for ecstatic experience. This conspiracy between mushroom, deer and human being is quite possibly at the root of the archaic, virtually universal shamanic emblem of the deer-antlered headgear and skin robe of the shaman.

The antiquity of the association between the fly agaric mushroom and shamanic practice in the vast Siberian region was underlined by the discovery in the 1960s of **Bronze Age** engravings on a rock surface alongside the Pegtymel River near the northeastern coast of Siberia, in Chukchi country. These petroglyphs depict various animals and also many mushrooms of the *Amanita* type, together with human–mushroom forms probably portraying mushroom spirits. Also, in many Finno-Ugric languages (that is, the family of tribal languages spanning eastern Europe and western Siberia) words meaning 'ecstasy', 'intoxication' and 'drunkenness' can be traced to names meaning fungus or fly agaric, and evidence for a Bronze Age mushroom cult in Scandinavia exists in matching mushroom-shaped motifs engraved on bronze, wide-bladed razors found in Bronze Age burials in Denmark and on rock surfaces in Sweden.

The most amusing hint of the memory of *Amanita*-based shamanism may well be enshrined by accident in the contemporary image of Santa Claus, according to Rogan Taylor. The figure of Father Christmas evolved over centuries out of pagan traditions, but the modern image of Santa owes most to the elements cobbled together in the 1820s by Professor Clement Clark Moore of Albany, New York, along with illustrators Thomas Nast and Moritz von Schwind, both of Germanic descent. Taylor feels that some traditional elements got pasted into their version, perhaps from the professor's wide reading, or from the illustrators' Old World links, or both. He points out that Santa's robe of red edged with white is in the colours of fly agaric, that the idea of Santa clambering down the chimney evokes the entry via the smoke-hole into Siberian yurts during winter and that the reindeer-drawn sleigh links to the reindeer-herder tribes who were the ones who took the magic mushroom, along with all the reindeer connections noted above. And the magic flight of Santa Claus through the midwinter night sky is a superb expression of the basis of all shamanism – ecstasy or the out-of-body flight of the spirit.

See also **Hallucinogens**; **Rock Art**; **Trance**

FLYING SAUCER

See **UFOs**

FOLKLORE

Students of earth mysteries treat folklore as a thread that can lead them back into the thinking and beliefs of ancient peoples. Unfortunately, most folklore that is studied in Europe comes from written versions of legends that date back only a few centuries, and the tease is to try to determine which elements, if any, may reach back farther into undocumented, oral tradition. It is quite possible to speculate that some folk survivals take us back perhaps to prehistoric times, because even though the mainstream culture in a country may evolve, causing changes to religion and political leadership, rural communities tend to be conservative, whatever the macro developments around them might be. After all, crops have to be tended and animals fed despite any social or religious upheavals, not to mention the fact that the peasantry rarely has the means to migrate significant distances. Even in places like Britain, which experienced massive demographic displacement due to the Industrial Revolution,

The 'Oss is led by a Teaser who waves a shield-shaped bat at it, encouraging it to dance. If the 'Oss snares a woman beneath its skirt, it is said she will become pregnant. Periodically, the rhythm slows and the 'Oss dies, then leaps back to life with a roll of drums in the merry morning of May.

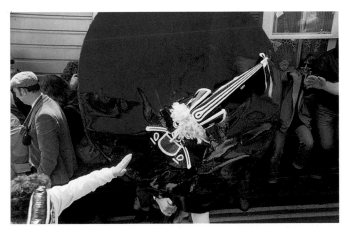

The wheeling and dancing of the 'Obby 'Oss in Padstow, Cornwall, can sometimes be mildly dangerous for onlookers. This, along with the drumming, singing and extensive ale drinking that accompany it on its many hours of parading through the narrow village streets, which are decorated with greenery, conspire to provide a powerful experience.

a few pockets of fairly undisturbed rural continuity stretching back for considerable periods of time can still be found, evinced by the survival of ancient dialects, and a curious experiment at Cheddar in Somerset, where scientists compared the DNA of 20 local volunteers with that removed from the molars of a prehistoric skeleton found at the turn of the century in one of the famed Cheddar caves. Amazingly, the DNA of one of the volunteers, local schoolteacher Adrian Targett, was found to match the caveman sample. If DNA can survive within a specific community, indicating extreme conservatism, it can reasonably be argued that so can folklore motifs.

Nevertheless, the matter is fraught with difficulties. Certain annual festivities have been widely touted as indicating vestigial pagan survivals. The May Day parade of the original 'Obby 'Oss at Padstow in Cornwall, as just one better known example, has been claimed as a folk relic passed down from generation to generation, possibly from the **Iron Age**. It is said to be so old that the meaning behind the design of the 'Oss has become lost. Folk historian Ronald Hutton, however, casts doubt on an Iron Age origin for the Padstow folk ritual. In *The Pagan Religions of the Ancient British Isles* (1991) Hutton points out that the earliest documented record of it occurred in 1803 and that none of the seventeenth- and eighteenth-century descriptions of Cornwall mentions it. He does not see anything especially Celtic about the 'Obby 'Oss festival. While such observations do not necessarily disprove the possibility that a strand of tradition has passed down the centuries and even the millennia at Padstow – some things do not leave the paper trails that academics demand for their purposes – they do sound a note of caution.

A surviving folk ritual that seems more securely linked to Iron Age times, however, was discovered by Celtic scholar Anne Ross. She heard a rumour about a strange, miniature 'house' at the head of Glen Lyon, beyond Loch Lyon, deep in the Grampian mountains of central Perthshire, Scotland. This is a wild area, and the top of the glen is nowadays uninhabited. Ross learned of a Celtic legend about the site, which told that long ago, during fierce snows on 1 May (Beltane in the Celtic calendar) a man and woman came over the mountains from a specific direction and into the glen. The man was large and powerful, but his wife was twice as big. The woman was pregnant. The people who lived in the glen at this time built and thatched a house for the strangers. The woman gave birth to a daughter, and the family lived in the

The little house and anthropomorphic goddess and god stones in Glen Lyon, Scotland. *(David Clarke)*

glen thereafter. They blessed the glen and its people, and ordered that a particular ritual be carried out each year.

Ross conducted fieldwork, making the tortuous journey to the top of the remote glen. The site itself is a tiny earth house; in winter it has stones laid on the top, and in summer, up until World War I at least, it was thatched. The three strangers – deities or semi-divine beings – are represented by three anthropomorphic-looking but natural, water-worn stones from the stream in the glen. Ross found that the shepherd tending his flocks in the upper glen is charged with bringing the stones, the ancient visitors, out of the house at Beltane, and putting them back at Samhain (1 November). They stay inside all winter. A large quartz stone was placed on the house as a marker, so it could be easily distinguished at a distance. Ross learned that the house has a Gaelic name meaning the Hag's House. She also was told that the Gaelic name for the stream is the Hag's Stream, and that the hill behind the house is called in Gaelic the Hag's Mountain.

Ross arrived on 1 May and saw that the stones had indeed been put out. The people in the lower glen who charge the shepherd with his ritual task believe that if it were not performed their crops and livestock would suffer. The stones are extraordinary, and the largest, **goddess** stone actually has an archaic, somewhat baleful face carved on its top. The streams in the area tend to wear stones into fanstastic shapes, and the waters are venerated and accredited with magical powers.

Ross is herself a Scottish Highlander and Gaelic speaker, and got to know the shepherd. Over numerous visits, she learned much of the lore of the locality from him. She found it to be very much a ritual landscape and discovered some examples of ancient ritual still being observed. She was shown stones further down the glen that were seen by locals as creatures belonging to Celtic myth and other stones with particular shapes that were thought to have healing power. Ross remarked that the veracity of the ancient nature of the Hag site and ritual she had confirmed was provided by the testimony of the associated place-names and the oral tradition in the glen. She argues that Celtic religion and superstitions are written into the landscape in the form of place-names 'which persist and are archaic'. The lesson of this would seem to be that instead of always seeking paper documentation, academics should more often attempt to read the ancient landscape.

As far as the lore of ancient monuments is concerned, a number of recurring themes can be identified in Britain as relating to prehistoric sites, especially megalithic ones. This lore variously states that stones at a site had healing properties – if the stones of **Stonehenge** were splashed with water, for example, the liquid would acquire curative properties; the

old sites were likely to bring down thunder and lightning if interfered with; stones in a circle could not be counted, were capable of movement (usually at night) or were people turned to stone for trangressing some taboo. This theme of petrifaction is very widespread. For example, a set of standing stones south of Morlaix in Brittany is called An Eured Ven (the Wedding Party), a group of people turned to stone because they blocked the way of a priest; the Stanton Drew circles in Somerset are likewise said to be a wedding party turned to stone for allowing revelries to continue into the Sabbath. Exactly the same legend attaches to a stone circle near Kaur, in the Gambia, Africa.

Another theme often associated with prehistoric sites is that of a tunnel, said to link to other monuments (or an old church) in the district. Certain sites are said to be the haunt of **fairies**. Yet another key ancient sites folklore motif is the idea that the old stones can promote fertility. In Brittany, for instance, the dolmen of Cruz-Moquen, also known as La Pierre Chaude (see **Carnac**), which has been Christianized by a cross affixed to the capstone, was where women used to raise their skirts at full moon in the hope of becoming pregnant. Some standing stones around the world have been shaped into phalli, such as in the Soddo area of Ethiopia, and others fashioned into the forms of an Earth Goddess, as in the Channel Islands. All these associations relate to fertility and fecundity. Further ancient monument lore includes themes involving giants and the Devil (often interchangeable), buried treasure, **dragons** and **divination**.

Such folklore motifs are so widespread that earth mysteries students feel that they may hold information, no matter

The King's Men circle, Rollright, in Oxfordshire. This site has one of the richest collections of attached lore of any in Britain. The stones are a king's army turned to stone by a witch — one day the spell will be broken and the stones will become flesh and blood once more. The stones can't be counted — a baker once tried by numbering loaves and placing one on each stone, but the devil removed each loaf behind the baker's back. The stones go down to a brook to drink at midnight. The tallest stone in the circle was taken to form a footbridge, but it took tremendous effort and bad luck followed, so the farmer brought it back, and it came with ease. Associated monuments nearby, the King Stone and the Whispering Knights, have additional lore attached to them.

how garbled, reaching back into prehistory. Do dancing stones, countless stones and divination and petrifaction themes contain vague hints of what went on at the sites originally? Do healing themes relate to rituals conducted at the sites? And so on. It is all too speculative to be certain. That folkore and legends *can* transmit information is probable, however. In *Hamlet's Mill* (1969) Giorgio de Santillana and Hertha von Dechend argued that signals can be transmitted through early data, lore, fables and sacred texts, and they specifically posited that some myths could perpetuate complex astronomical data.

See also **Archaeoastronomy; Celts; Cognitive Archaeology; Druids; Feng Shui; Maypole; St Michael Line**

FOUR DIRECTIONS

See **World Navel**

Rock carvings swirl around curious holes in this stone in the chamber at Gavrinis.

other segments of this huge former standing stone built into their fabric too, deducible by matching the fragments of the representational carvings. (The stone from which these segments originated must have stood around 40ft (12m) tall.) What is of significance is that the style of the carvings on this re-used monolith is completely different to the now-visible abstract patterns carved into the interior walls of Gavrinis. It seems that something rocked the cultural boat around 4000 BC – some archaeologists have suggested that it may have been the arrival of a 'psychedelic' cult from the Mediterranean region, for unusual ceramic objects dating to about that time were unearthed at Er-Lannic and other Breton sites, which are thought to have been used as braziers, perhaps for opium or even cannabis (*see* **Hallucinogens**).

In the wall about halfway down the entrance passage at Gavrinis is a distinctive quartz rock that is not covered with the rock art. It has been noted by prehistorian Aubrey Burl that the passage accommodates two astronomical orientations, one to the midwinter sunrise, the other to the most southerly moonrise during the major lunar standstill. It has been calculated that these two alignments intersect in the passage level with the quartz stone. So it is possible that this distinctive rock actually marks this astronomical conjunction within the site and, indeed, may have shone out with a ghostly glow during these solar–lunar events.

Archaeological investigation suggests that Gavrinis was ceremonially sealed between 3340 and 2910 BC. There is evidence that the closure was preceded by a series of rituals, as excavations of the ground beneath a pile of rubble closing off the front of the cairn revealed an extensive area of burning, evidence of postholes and concentrations of flint, three polished ceremonial axes and other stone tools, pottery and an animal bone. It was clear to the excavating archaeologists that the pile of rubble had been placed almost immediately after the timber structure indicated by the postholes had been burned.

Gavrinis, like other passage 'graves', is unlikely to have been simply a tomb. The living probably mixed ritually at times with the bones of the ancestors within it. As there appears to be a chronological overlap between the passage graves, the stone circles and the great stone rows of the region, it may be that these were all part of a single religious system.

See also **Archaeoastronomy**; **Atlantis**; **Carnac**; **Trance**

GEOMANCY

The proper use of the term geomancy means 'earth **divination**'. This was a fortune-telling procedure, probably originating in Africa and involving the casting of loose, dry soil (or seeds, pebbles or similar small particulate objects) on to the ground and reading the configurations produced, somewhat like tea-leaf reading. The method could range from being as simple as this to more sophisticated versions using pen and paper or even cards. In some more complex, non-folk versions of geomancy, certain dot patterns were categorized for formal divinatory schemes.

The meaning of the word was given a topographical dimension by the European missionaries who visited China during the Victorian era and encountered the **feng shui** system of landscape divination there. Some of these Western observers referred to this system as 'geomancy', and it was through this channel that the term was picked up by the pioneer earth mysteries buffs of the 1960s. They used it in an increasingly generalized way in the context of **leys**, ancient sites and ceremonial landscapes – in short, as a loose reference to all aspects of ancient sacred geography. The term is less often used in this context nowadays, and when it is it tends to be employed in even more multifarious and ill-defined ways.

GEOMETRY (Sacred)

Sacred or canonical geometry is not some arbitrary invention of the human mind, but an extrapolation by it of the implied patterns found in nature, ranging from the logarithms of growth in plants and organisms, to the geometry inherent in the vibration of atoms and molecules and the spin and

When one looks at a forest, a garden or even a single flower or cactus, one sees an eruption of geometry from the earth clothed in organic form. (*John Glover*)

motion of planets, stars and galaxies. One can dissect a plant or planet and not find the Maker's blueprint anywhere in sight, of course: it is inherent. The axis of a spinning sphere, for instance, is so real that we can measure its properties and location, yet it does not exist as an objective thing. A figure of sacred geometry can be seen as a frozen moment in the endless process of becoming.

Because sacred geometry derives from Nature's blueprint, it was obviously of great importance to temple builders, who wished to encode into their structures the ratios of creation, to mirror the universe, to create a microcosm of the macrocosm – 'as above, so below'. In such a way, the temple, the cathedral or whatever the sacred structure was, could become a point of integration between the outer world of matter and the inner world of consciousness.

The nature of sacred geometry is such that only straightedge and compass are required, for it is to do with ratio and proportion, not quantitative measure by number. Probably the best known element of sacred geometry today is the socalled Golden Proportion. In the figure shown here, the rectangle ABGH is a golden rectangle because the ratio of its length to its width is 1.618, a ratio referred to by the Greek letter ø (*phi*). The famed 'Golden Section' occurs on the line AH at D (AD:DH). Proportionally, the ratio works out at about 13 parts to 8. It has been claimed that in tests where large numbers of people have been asked to divide a line at a

point they find to be aesthetically pleasing, most do so intituitively at or around the golden cut. Now, a golden rectangle has the property that a square taken from it leaves a smaller golden rectangle, and this process can be repeated, theoretically, *ad infinitum*. Alternatively, a square can be added to the longer side to create an ever-enlarging proportional progression. A spiral can be generated from these proportional developments that is known as a logarithmic or growth spiral inherent in numerous examples of growth in nature. Other growth spirals can also be generated by golden triangles and proportional or 'root' rectangles.

Pentagonal geometry can be derived from Golden Section geometry, and this can be found in nature in the proportions of the human figure, in snowflakes and even in humble wayside flowers. A numerical analogue of the Golden Proportion exists in the Fibonacci series of numbers, where each number is the sum of the two preceding ones: 1, 2, 3, 5, 8, 13, 21, 34, 55 and so on. A classic natural example of this progression can be seen in the distribution of seeds on the head of a sunflower.

Another classic figure of sacred geometry is the *vesica piscis* (vessel of the fish), which is produced by two equal, overlapping circles, the circumference of one passing through the centre of the other. Architect Keith Critchlow feels that he detected this figure in the groundplan of the **Neolithic** stone circle at Castlerigg in the English Lake District, when he related the existing groundplan of the monument to the solar and lunar alignments incorporated into its structure. It also has esoteric associations with the womb and vulva, and was associated with the Blessed Virgin in arcane Christian tradition. (Some feel that the Virgin is a Christianized version of the pagan Earth Mother **Goddess**.) The fish-shaped vesica is particularly suitable for Christian esotericism, because the fish was the symbol of Christ – it is

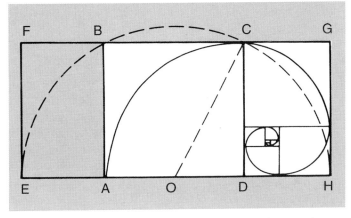

The Golden Proportion expressed as a rectangle and a growth spiral.

A ground marking 600ft (185m) long overlooking the Bay of Paracas in Peru, known variously as the Trident of Paracas and the Candelabra of the Andes and dated to 200 BC. Its meaning is unknown, but researcher Frank Joseph has suggested that it is a stylized depiction of Jimson weed (*Datura stramonium*). He has found a small version of the same design on a rock in California's Cleveland National Park, and proposes that the ancient people of Paracas voyaged up the Pacific coast to California to collect this particular species of the hallucinogen. (*Peruvian Embassy, London*)

illness, in puberty initiation rites, and for the production of visionary states. It characteristically generates the classic shamanic experiences of spirit flight and transformation into animals. In eastern North America, the Algonkian Indians issued a ritual drink, *wysoccan*, to youths undergoing rites of passage. The drink contained *Datura stramonium* or Jimson weed. The Chumash of coastal south California used the same hallucinogen for puberty rites and shamanic purposes, and its visionary effects are linked with the 'psychedelic' imagery in their **rock art**. The **Hopi** and Navajo of Arizona are other notable peoples in the American southwest who used *Datura*. The **Zuni** Indians of present-day New Mexico called it *a-neg-la-kya* and used it both ritually and medicinally. The Mexican Indians call the hallucinogen *toloache*, from the Aztec *toaloatzin*.

Remarkable hallucinogenic infusions (and occasionally snuffs) based on the vine or liana, *Banisteriopsis caapi* and other species of *Banisteriopsis*, are used by hundreds of Indians to this day in the western Amazon, the Orinoco, and on the slopes of the Pacific coast of Colombia and Ecuador. It is known by a variety of names in different places, including *caapi*, *ayahuasca* and *yagé* (*yajé*). It typically promotes a sensation of the spirit separating from the body, and although this is a common effect of many native hallucinogens,

Banisteriopsis concoctions seem particularly suited to producing this sensation. It is used in initiation ceremonies, for returning to the beginning of time to see the gods and for prophetic and divinatory purposes, including travelling in spirit (usually in the form of a bird or animal, such as a jaguar) to distant places.

Peyote must take pride of place as one of *the* hallucinogens of ancient Native America. Its usage in ancient Indian societies is demonstrated by such evidence as a ceramic snuffing pipe from Monte Albán, Oaxaca, in the form of a deer with a peyote cactus in its mouth, dating to c.500 BC, and a symbol employed in the Tarahumara Indian peyote ceremony has been found depicted in prehistoric rock carvings. The Huichol Indians of the Sierra Madre Occidental of northern Mexico still make an annual 300-mile (480km) pilgrimage to Wirikúta, a high desert area of ancestral significance to them, which is rich in the peyote cactus. The pilgrimage is, in fact, a ritual 'hunt' for peyote and contains some archaic themes that are thought to date back to palaeo-Siberian times. The peyote cactus appears as a rounded crown peeping above the ground, and it is this that becomes a 'peyote button' when cut off and dried. The most active 'visionary' alkaloid in the cactus is trimethoxyphenylethylamine, called mescalin. It can be eaten raw, or in dried form or taken as a tea or mash. The peyote experience is characterized by vividly coloured hallucinations, which often follow a sequence, starting with geometric patterns (*see* **Entoptic Patterns**) and progressing to more complex representational scenes. These visual effects can be accompanied by auditory hallucinations, which are known to have been the source of Indian songs and chants developed in fairly recent times – 'Heyowiniho', for instance, came to the 1890s Ghost Dance leader John Wilson (Nishkúntu) from a peyote perception in which he heard the

Huichol Indians collecting peyote during their annual pilgrimage to the sacred plateau of Wirikúta, Mexico. (*Dr Peter Furst*)

sound of the sun's rising. This inevitably raises the question of how much Indian traditional ceremonial song, dance and costume had its source in hallucinatory states.

One of the hallucinogens to have had the longest use in the Americas is undoubtedly the San Pedro cactus (*Trichocereus pachanoi*), found in the general Andes region of South America. It is used today for curing sickness, divination and sorcery in coastal and Andean Peru and Bolivia. There is a moon-oriented ritual, which has a Christian veneer, but its extreme antiquity in Native American shamanism is shown by its appearance on an engraved stone panel in the wall of the circular sunken plaza of the Old Temple at **Chavín de Huantar**, which belongs to the first millennium BC.

While the above represent the most important of Native American hallucinogens, there are many more known in the New World, not to mention those described by the Spanish conquerors that have yet to be identified.

In the Old World of Europe and Asia, the use of fly agaric as a shamanic sacrament among reindeer-herder tribes from the Baltic Sea to the Siberian wastes is the classic example of a sacred hallucinogen. A legendary Old World mind-altering substance, however, was soma, referred to in the Indian *Rig Veda* of the first millennium BC. What soma was remains a mystery. Suggestions have included fly agaric, Syrian rue (*Peganum harmala*) and psilocybin mushrooms. But now Andrew Sherratt of Oxford's Ashmolean Museum suggests that soma was a generic term covering a range of plant hallucinogens, for fairly new archaeological evidence is revealing that in the second millennium BC the desert plateau of Iran and its borderlands was a kind of 'contact zone' that between the old traditions of the central Asian steppes in which intoxicants were smoked and the Bronze Age development around the eastern Mediterranean of taking intoxicants in liquid form. A series of mud-brick, citadel-like sites has been excavated, revealing temple complexes containing ash deposits from sacred fires and preparation rooms with vats and strainers for liquid. Furthermore, traces of opium, cannabis and the intoxicating ephedra plant were found. Sherratt suggests that ritual plants traditionally inhaled as smoke from braziers were being prepared as mind-altering drinks and that soma was a drink involving the infusion of ancient hallucinogenic plants.

Hemp or cannabis is certainly an ancient Old World psychotropic plant, and its early use in Asia has been established. The oldest archaeological evidence has been found in a 10,000-year-old village in Taiwan in the form of ceramics that had been decorated by hemp cords impressed into the soft clay. Hemp fibre was also of great importance in China.

Copper censers for burning hemp, from Barrow 2 at Pazyryk, on the Outer Mongolia/Siberia border. (*After S.I. Rudenko*)

While it had use for making clothing and ropes, it is unlikely that its mind-altering properties would have gone unnoticed – in fact, some authorities argue that they would have been known about first, with the more pragmatic use of the plant developing later. At any rate, it was being referred to in a ritualistic context in the China of the fifteenth century BC. The Indians knew cannabis as 'the heavenly guide', and it was closely related to religious life. Knowledge of cannabis spread to Saudi Arabia and to Africa.

The Greek writer Herodotus (born c.485 BC) wrote in his *Histories* that the Scythians used hemp for making clothes and also ritually, by throwing hemp seeds on to hot stones inside a tent held up by a framework of sticks. 'At once it begins to smoke,' he wrote, 'giving off a vapour unsurpassed by any vapour-bath one could find in Greece. The Scythians enjoy it so much that they howl with pleasure.' (The name 'Scythians' was given by the Greeks to nomadic tribes originating in central Asia who inhabited the steppes to the north and east of the Black and Caspian seas from around the eighth century BC.) Many modern scholars frankly doubted the veracity of Herodotus' account, until 1924 when Russian archaeologist S.I. Rudenko discovered a set of five burial mounds or barrows in the valley of Pazyryk on the border between Siberia and Outer Mongolia. In a series of excavations Rudenko examined all five barrows, which were pit graves or *kurgans* constructed between 500 and 300 BC. They had been flooded by water, which had become frozen, so their contents were superbly preserved. In one of the mounds copper vessels were found containing the charred remains of hemp seeds and the stones used to heat them. Furthermore, a tent frame consisting of metal rods was also found. Herodotus' account was therefore shown to have been extremely accurate.

Another mind-altering staple of the Old World was opium, made from the milky liquid that exudes from the seed capsule of the opium poppy (*Papaver somniferum*). Relics from **Bronze Age** Greece and Crete, such as terracotta figurines from Knossos with incised capsules as coronas, a Cretan Poppy Goddess effigy with poppy pods sticking out of her headband, found buried near a pottery opium pipe by volcanic ash and earthquake debris, curiously long, poppy-headed needles found at Mycenae, which were eventually recognized as being for handling small pieces of opium, as well as various decorative depictions of poppies, all testify to the importance of opium in Mycenaean and Minoan societies. Opium was known also to the Egyptians. For example, the Ebers Papyrus of c.1500 BC contains medical notes, including copied references to opium, from a source at least a thousand years earlier, and Pharaonic tomb paintings dating to between 1600 and 600 BC show opium poppies and other psychoactive plants. (Cocaine has also been detected in an Egyptian mummy – a bizarre anomaly.) Cuneiform tablets from Sumer (a region between the Euphrates and Tigris rivers, now southern Iraq) also mention the use of opium.

It now seems that opium also had a presence in northern and western Europe as least as old as that recorded in Sumer. Prehistoric burials in a Spanish cave were found to be accompanied by large numbers of opium poppy capsules, which radiocarbon dated to c.4200 BC – the early **Neolithic** period. Poppy seeds have been uncovered at Neolithic lake villages and at some 17 other Neolithic sites, in Switzerland. Seedheads found in Neolithic contexts in Switzerland and Spain show them to have been from domesticated poppies. Seeds have also been found at ten sites of the later Bronze Age in Switzerland, with similar finds made in Italy and Germany.

Quite recently, archaeological attention has begun to be focused on the possibility of hallucinogen usage in the megalithic world of western Europe. What may be cannabis pollen has been found inside a stone chamber on the Channel Island of Jersey, and numerous richly decorated ceramic objects showing traces of burning have been found at megalithic

sites in Brittany and on the Channel Islands. The suspicion is that these were braziers for burning cannabis or opium. They first appeared in Brittany in the early fourth millennium BC, coincident with the sudden change in the types of ceremonial monument being built in the region and the appearance of a distinctly different style of **rock art** (see **Gavrinis**). In Britain Neolithic pottery vessels called 'grooved ware' have been found at ceremonial sites such as **henge** monuments throughout the country, and archaeologists have wondered if they were special vessels for sacred, and therefore potentially hallucinogenic, drinks. This speculation received support when the seeds and pollen of the psychoactive herb henbane (*Hyoscyamus niger*) were found in an encrusted deposit on shards of grooved ware at a megalithic ceremonial complex at Balfarg in Fife, Scotland. As henbane is not found naturally at this latitude, it must have been deliberately imported.

There is doubtless much more yet to learn about the role of hallucinogens in the ancient world, and much to be understood about how hallucinogenically altered states of consciousness in ancient times might affect how we should interpret some archaeological sites and artefacts.

See also **Delphi**; **Eleusis**; **Shaman**; **Shamanic Landscapes**; **Trance**; **Xochipilli**

HENGE

This is a type of **Neolithic** ceremonial earthwork found only in Britain, consisting of a circular area defined by a ditch with a bank *outside* it, thus not conforming to the arrangement of a defensive structure. Henges can be anything from a few hundred to almost 2000ft (600m) in diameter and have one or two causeway-style entrances. The term 'henge' apparently derives from **Stonehenge**, meaning, basically, 'hanging stones', a reference to the lintels on the upright stones within the ditch of the earthen henge at that site. It is rather ironic that the site-type name for an earthwork monument should derive from a term associated with a unique stone monument.

Henges can contain standing stones, postholes denoting former timber circles, pits and burials. In 1997 magnetometer studies of the ground beneath the Stanton Drew stone circles in Somerset revealed that there had formerly been a henge monument there encompassing a mighty timber structure some 300ft (100m) across, with over 400 massive wooden columns. The stone circles had been erected on the site a few hundred years after the demise of the timber temple.

HILL FIGURES

This term is applied to images cut primarily in the chalk hills of southern England. The figures stand out white against the green grass and when well kept can often be seen from many miles away. Most have been cut in the last few hundred years or even more recently, but a few do date back to ancient times. Controversy surrounds the actual dates and nature of these older figures.

A classic example is the White Horse of Uffington, Oxfordshire. It is 360ft (110m) in length, cut out of the chalk on the shoulder of the hill containing the **Iron Age** earthworks of Uffington Castle and is best seen from an aerial perspective. It is a highly stylized image of a galloping horse, using slender, flowing lines that merge somewhat with the contours of the hill, and some people have insisted that it is actually a depiction of a **dragon**. (As it happens, the effigy overlooks the small Dragon Hill. This has a seemingly artificially flattened summit on which there is a bare patch where grass never grows. **Folklore** has it that this is where St George killed the dragon and marks where the dragon's blood was spilled.) The single eye in the curiously beaked face is 4ft (1.2m) across. Drawings of the figure over the centuries show it in slightly differing forms, but this is to be expected: for any ancient ground image to remain visible in British conditions, it has to be recut and cleaned periodically. At Uffington, there was a traditional 'scouring' of the horse

The Cerne Giant chalk hill figure, Cerne Abbas, Dorset. (*Mick Sharp*)

every seven years, at Whitsun or Michaelmas, and it was a great event accompanied by fairground-like festivities, according to *The Scouring of the White Horse*, written in 1857 by Thomas Hughes (author of *Tom Brown's Schooldays*). Over the centuries, the outlines of the horse have varied, and even its position may have 'crept' uphill.

There have been conflicting views as to the age of the figure. Until recently scholars' opinions centred on it being either a Celtic image or a Saxon one. The **Celts** revered the horse, and ancient British coins and other artefacts show stylized depictions of horses vaguely similar to the Uffington figure. On the other hand, there were Saxon land charters for the area, Norse myths were preserved in the region, and suggestions have included that the horse relates to Odin or celebrates a battle in which King Alfred defeated the Danes. In fact, it now seems that all these guesses were too conservative. In 1996 scientists using a new, sophisticated technique that, in simplistic terms, can measure when soil was last exposed to sunlight, arrived at a late **Bronze Age** dating for the hill figure, making its orginal creation possibly as early as 1400 BC.

Two other noteworthy chalk hill figures of some antiquity are the Cerne Abbas Giant in Dorset and the Long Man of Wilmington in Sussex. Again, guesses abound concerning actual chronology. For the Cerne Giant – a naked male figure with an erect phallus 30ft (10m) long and wielding a club – suggestions have ranged from its being an **Iron Age** Celtic fertility symbol to a Romano-British depiction of Hercules to a seventeenth-century folly! The Long Man is the featureless outline of a human figure over 230ft (70m) in length, holding staves in both hands. It was overgrown and known as the Green Man until the nineteenth century, when it was recut and the outline filled with white bricks by a local antiquarian. It is now marked out by white concrete blocks. It is known that the Long Man once had facial features, and resitivity tests in the soil hint that it once had a helmet and plume and held a scythe or spears – but these are possibilities only. A belt buckle unearthed in an Anglo-Saxon cemetery in 1964 was decorated with the image of a helmeted warrior holding two spears, and this resemblance to the Long Man has led to speculation that the hill figure is indeed of Anglo-Saxon origin and may depict one of Odin's special, fierce warriors, the Berserkers. Then again, other suggestions for the Long Man have included that it represents, variously, Beowulf, Thor, Apollo and Mercury. Alfred Watkins, the man who brought us the **ley** theory, was convinced that the figure represented the prehistoric surveyor who laid out alignments with the ranging rods in his hands.
See also **Acoustics**; **Nazca Lines**; **Shamanic Landscapes**

HOLLOW EARTH

A nineteenth-century pioneer of this belief was the American John Cleves, who unsuccessfully petitioned Congress for funding to conduct an expedition to the poles to gain entry to what he claimed were five concentric spheres within the Earth that could sustain life. The obsession was continued by Cyrus Reed Teed (called by his followers Koresh), who developed a cult in America. This was introduced to Germany by World War I pilot Peter Bender, and it eventually came to Hitler's attention. According to some neo-Nazi beliefs, Hitler escaped at the end of World War II through a hole at the South Pole into a world inside the Earth. Other rumours say that he sent elite troops on an expedition aimed at locating the polar entrances to the underworld before the war even began.

The idea of a Hollow Earth obtained a new lease of life by becoming enmeshed in the rising tide of flying saucer **folklore** in the 1940s and 1950s. This process was encouraged by Ray Palmer, editor of *Amazing Stories* and *Fate* magazines. One of the stories he floated was that Admiral Richard Evelyn Byrd, the American polar explorer, had found the entrance to the interior of the Earth during his expeditions. Elements of the Hollow Earth theme have surfaced periodically on the fringes of modern ufology ever since – especially in South America. The basic notion is that flying saucers enter our world from and disappear back through holes at the poles. In this scenario, the ufonauts are not extraterrestrials but representatives of the peoples from within the Earth, who are sometimes cast as the survivors of lost **Atlantis** or **Lemuria**. British ufological writer Brinsley le Poer Trench (who became Lord Clancarty) even deluded himself into thinking he had discovered a space-satellite photograph of a polar hole. In reality, the picture was made up of a montage of satellite images, which built up the picture of the polar region over a period of time. The evolving polar night occupied a rotating part of each photograph, creating the impression of a dark circle or 'hole' at the centre of the montage. *See also* **UFOs**

HOPEWELL INDIANS

The Hopewell culture was at its height between 150 BC and AD 500, and its influence can be found far afield from its Middle Ohio Valley heartland. Rather than being a distinct tribe, the Hopewell culture was a religious phenomenon, a sphere of influence. We know that the Hopewell religion was shamanically based, as is evidenced by finds in the Mound

City necropolis at Chillicothe, Ohio, which include deer-antler headgear, bird-claw and other shapes cut from mica designed to hang on ceremonial robes, and a copper-sheathed wooden effigy of a hallucinogenic mushroom. The Hopewell, following on from the Adena people, who were also probably shamanic, built burial mounds and huge geometrical earthworks covering many acres, effigy mounds, earthen pyramid-like platforms and linear features, which seem to have been ceremonial roadways.

Many Hopewell earthworks were destroyed during the Colonial period, but fortunately some survived. The inhabitants of Marietta, Ohio, took pride in the ancient earthworks they found, and their library can be found even to this day perched on a Hopewell mound! They also preserved the course of a Hopewell graded, ceremonial way leading from the Muskingum River to a 50-acre (20ha) enclosure containing truncated earthen pyramids. Its straight course can be traced by the pink-surfaced road called Sacra Via.

In 1995 Bradley T. Lepper, curator of archaeology at the Ohio Historical Society, announced the finding of a lost Hopewell ceremonial road 60 miles (96km) long connecting modern Newark and Chillicothe in a straight line. At

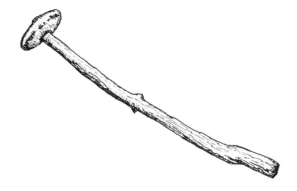

A drawing of the copper and wood 'magic mushroom' effigy found in a Hopewell shaman's grave at Chillicothe, Ohio.

Newark, is Octagon State Memorial Park, which contains a circular earthwork over 1000ft (300m) across connected to an octagonal earthwork covering some 50 acres (20ha). Parallel earthen walls, extending 2½ miles (4km) southwards from the octagon, mark the beginning of the road. By combining information from nineteenth-century accounts of

The Hopewell mound known as Conus, in the cemetery at Marietta, Ohio.

This modern road in Marietta, known as Sacra Via, traces the straight course of a 2000-year-old Hopewell ceremonial way.

explorers' findings, the observations of pilots flying over the Ohio countryside, data produced by specialist infrared surveys and his own field observations, Lepper was able to plot the course of the lost Hopewell road on a map. It terminated at another circle-and-octagon earthwork complex, very similar in size to that at Newark, on the banks of the Scioto River opposite Mound City in Chillicothe. Although there are no surviving records or traditions about these long-distance Hopewell features, it is probable that others await discovery.

See also **Effigy Mounds; Hallucinogens; Leys/Leylines; Shaman; Shamanic Landscapes**

HOPI

The people of this Pueblo Indian tribe consider themselves to have been the first inhabitants of America, and it is probably at least true that they have descended wholly or in part from the lost **Anasazi** and Sinagua peoples (as possibly did some other Pueblo Indian groups, such as the **Zuni**). The Sinagua ruins of **Wupatki** are considered an ancestral site by the Hopi, and as recently as the 1930s Hopi pilgrims on their way to the sacred San Francisco Peaks stopped to pray at Elden Pueblo, another Sinagua ruined site near Flagstaff, Arizona. In the 1990s Hopis have been noticed quietly visiting little-known Anasazi sites in Utah – perhaps as part of a spiritual process of ancestral reclamation.

Today's Hopi reservation covers some 4000 sq miles (10,000 sq km) deep within the much larger (25,000 sq miles/64,000 sq km) Navajo reservation in Arizona. Hopi villages cluster on three dramatic mesas or escarpments , 600ft (185m) high. On Third Mesa is Old Oraibi, the oldest continuously inhabited settlement in the United States. Radiocarbon dating indicates that the village goes back to at least AD c.1100. These mesa villages look so ancient as to seem completely out of place in modern-day America. The dark, deeply lined faces of the Hopi appear almost Tibetan in appearance, and this, along with the antiquity of their culture, makes it is easy to understand how New Age speculation has it that they did indeed have archaic connections with the Tibetans. Whatever the truth of such notions, the Hopi undoubtedly have a living body of lore, tradition and ritual that goes back to ancient times, perhaps providing a window on to the worlds of lost peoples like the Anasazi. The Hopi have also been a time capsule for ancient practices such as the use of 'horizon calendars'. In the 1930s anthropologist Alexander Stephen found that such a 'sunwatcher' role was still being observed: from a given location, a designated functionary would observe the position of the sun over specific horizon features such as peaks and notches to tell the time of day, and the setting or rising of the sun over such identified skyline features would tell the times of year for planting or harvesting.

There are approximately 9000 surviving Hopi, and their language belongs to the Uto-Aztecan family.

See also **Archaeoastronomy; Hovenweep**

HOVENWEEP

Situated in eastern Utah, 40 miles (64km) west of Cortez in Colorado, Hovenweep National Monument consists of six groups of **Anasazi** buildings approximately 800 years old. These are situated in and around the edges of small box canyons (Hovenweep is the Ute Indian term for 'deserted valley'). The sites were not documented until 1874, and very little archaeological work has gone on there.

The buildings are today much as the Anasazi left them, except for the depredations of time. Those known as the Square Tower group, at the head of Little Ruin Canyon, display the Anasazi skill in stone-coursed masonry, and it is remarkable how they managed to build in such a perilous, rocky place. The group of D-shaped towers and walls called Hovenweep Castle still rise up to 20ft (6m) in height, even if some of them are now leaning a little, and it is here that archaeoastronomer Ray Williamson suggests a possible set of solar alignments (see **Archaeoastronomy**). Among other astronomical possibilities at Hovenweep, he has also noted that a panel of ancient **rock art** beneath an overhang close to another building group, Holly House, seems to interact with a 'serpent' of sunlight cast on it during the summer solstice. This serpent-shaped lightplay, and the form of the rock art (which includes two circles, each with a central dot, probably symbolizing the sun) seems to provide a kind of re-enactment of certain myths and rituals held by the **Hopi**, another Pueblo Indian tribe.

The nature of most of the structures at Hovenweep is not fully understood: there are, for example, towers on the canyon floors at the head of the canyons, next to vital water sources, and clusters of other buildings perch precariously on the edges of the canyons or even on top of rock outcrops. Some doorways open out on to open space and were presumably reached by rope ladders, while at least one building has no doorway at all, access to it probably being through the roof. The buildings have tiny apertures or peepholes for windows. Theories abound, but there are no firm answers. Without doubt, there is much still to be learned at the remote Hovenweep sites.

See also **Simulacra**

Hovenweep Castle in Utah.

A precariously perched Anasazi building at Hovenweep.

J K

JERUSALEM

Sacred to Judaism, Islam and Christianity alike, Jerusalem has special status as a sacred centre. The most ancient, sacred core is Temple Mount, the area of the Rock, a natural outcrop beneath which was said to be the primeval waters, the *tehom*. Here was built the legendary Temple of Solomon. Before the Jews, the Canaanites worshipped Baal there, and after King David's conquest of Jerusalam it became a *kibleh* or point of worship. A series of temples was reconstructed on the spot after various sackings of Jerusalem, but the Romans destroyed the last temple structure in AD 70. A temple to Jupiter was erected on the site, and this lasted until the Christianization of the Roman empire, when a church was built there. From AD 325 Jerusalem experienced 300 years of Christian domination. The Christians saw the hill of Golgotha as the place where the skull of Adam was buried. In AD 638 the Muslims took over the city, destroying most of the Christian features that had developed in those three centuries, and a mosque, the Dome of the Rock (Qubbat al Sakrah) was built, enclosing a bare surface of the Rock, supposedly the spot from where Muhammed ascended to heaven. Nearby, a small cupola, the Dome of the Spirits, covers another area of exposed rock where the Tablets of the Covenant were said to have rested and which is, some researchers now claim, the true foundation stone of Solomon's temple.

To Islam, Jerusalem is the most sacred city after Mecca and Medina, so for around 4000 years Jerusalem has been a sacred centre, a **World Navel**, to some great religions. The medieval Christians expressed this explicitly in their *mappae mundi* (maps of the world), which were schematic religious diagrams showing Jerusalem in the centre. The Ebstorf map of 1235 is one of these schematic maps, with Christ's head in the north, the hands at the east and west sides of the circular border, and the feet at the south. Jerusalem is specifically placed as Christ's navel. In *Talmudic Miscellany* we can read the equally explicit Jewish conception: 'The land of Israel is

Jerusalem is shown as a round form at the centre of the *mappa mundi* in Hereford Cathedral. (*Dean and Chapter of Hereford Cathedral/ The Hereford Mappa Mundi Trust*)

situated in the centre of the world, and Jerusalem in the centre of the land of Israel, and the Temple in the centre of Jerusalem, and the Holy of Holies in the centre of the Temple, and the foundation stone on which the world was founded is situated in front of the **ark**.'
See also **Pilgrimage**

KEYHOLE TOMBS

These are a type of Japanese tomb constructed in the *zempokoen* style, which has a distinctly keyhole-shaped groundplan. A classic example is the mound at Hashihaka, dating to the Kofun period (AD 300–700). Located close to the holy mountain of Miwayama, it is over 800ft (245m) long, and its highest point is in the round part of the 'keyhole' at 89ft (27m). It was built with stones, but is now covered in trees, forming a keyhole-shaped copse in the surrounding flat countryside. A moat orginally encircled much of its perimeter, but only two large ponds now remain. The axis of the mound aligns on the summit of a hill 2 miles (3km) distant, over which the summer solstice sun rises when viewed from Hashihaka.
See also **Archaeoastronomy**

KIVAS

These are semi-subterranean ceremonial structures associated with the Pueblo Indians of the American southwest. They first appeared in the **Anasazi** culture a thousand or more years ago, originating in the Anasazi pit houses, which gradually changed from providing secular and domestic functions to ritual ones. Kivas took various forms: although typically a circular roofed structure set into the ground, they could also be included in pueblos standing above ground, be in two tiers or even be linear in shape. There were small kivas, perhaps for group or clan use, and the larger, more impressive Great Kivas, which served wider communities. The distinction between these types is readily visible in the ruins of Pueblo Bonitio in **Chaco Canyon**. The largest Anasazi kiva to have survived is Casa Rinconada, also in Chaco Canyon, although the nearby Chetro Ketl kiva is some 50ft (15m) across. At Aztec, another Anasazi centre, the Great Kiva has been carefully restored.

Kivas were the darkened places where the mysteries of the tribe were divulged and the magical maintenance of material tribal life was conducted. Activities would have included chanting, ritual, praying, smoking, storytelling (mnemonic

The great kiva of Chetro Ketl in Chaco Canyon, New Mexico. This would have been capped by a roof supported by massive timbers. The timbers were themselves placed on great sandstone discs brought from a source some 40 miles (64km) distant – some of them can still be seen scattered on the kiva floor. Similar discs can be found at Aztec kiva and elsewhere.

methods of preserving the tribal myths), dramatic theatrical events (there was an underground entrance to Casa Rinconada, for example, for the sudden, magic-like appearances of costumed participants representing – or embodying – mythic personae), and quite possibly the sacramental use of mind-altering plants, usually Jimson weed (*Datura*) (see **Hallucinogens**). Kivas were entered through the smoke-hole in the roof and had specific features, such as niches in the wall, an encircling bench, a central raised firebox structure by the fire hearth and a *sipapu* – a hole in the ground symbolically representing the point of entry from a previous world used by the mythic first members of the tribe. The *sipapu* is the classic Pueblo Indian version of the **World Navel**, representing the Centre.

LABYRINTHS

Unlike the maze, there is only one path to follow in a labyrinth, but it takes a profoundly circuitous route to the centre. Some large-scale labyrinths laid out in boulders, or smaller versions carved on rocks, have considerable antiquity. Examples of prehistoric rock-carved labyrinths are to be found in Val Camonica, Italy, and at Pontevedra, Spain, while several hundred labyrinths formed from rocks laid out on the ground have been recorded in Scandinavia, Iceland, Russia and the Baltic countries. One survives also in Britain, in the Scilly Isles off the Cornish peninsula. (This had its ancient shape modified a little in recent years by New Age dowsers, who felt driven to move the stones so as to mark 'energy patterns' in the ground that they believed they could detect with their **dowsing** rods.) Some of these labyrinths are probably prehistoric – a group in the Solovecke Archipelago are thought to date to 4000 BC, for example, and meander patterns, from which the labyrinth configuration can be developed, have been found on mammoth ivory figurines from Siberia dating back around 20,000 years.

One use for the prehistoric labyrinth seems to have been as a **spirit trap**. The Saami of Lapland would walk around labyrinths in order to ensnare trolls and other evil spirits that might be following them. The spirits would be unable to escape from the labyrinth when the person stepped out of it. This implies that curved lines could hinder spirit movement, and thus by implication suggests that straight lines could assist it (see **Spirit Ways**). The same concept is indicated by the last known use of labyrinths on the Baltic coast: fishermen would traditionally do a circuit of a stone labyrinth before boarding their boats so as to attract good luck in their fishing and to neutralize dangerous winds, which may also have equated with the 'laying' of any bad spirits that might be following them. A **Bronze Age** stone labyrinth known as the Rösaring located amid the stone cairns (mounds) of a mixed Bronze Age and Viking burial ground at Laassa in Uppland, Sweden, may have been intended to ensure that the spirits of the dead did not wander out of the necropolis. A similar idea might be encoded in a meander carving on a

The pattern of a stone labyrinth at Visby in Gotland, Sweden.

stone found at the **Neolithic** stone chamber of Bryn Celli Ddu on the island of Anglesey, Wales.

The most famous prehistoric labyrinth, of course, is the Cretan labyrinth, the lair of the mythic Minotaur, a fearsome half-man, half-bull creature. The labyrinth was at Knossos, one of a number of Minoan palace-temples on Bronze Age Crete and the centre of a bull cult. Although the original form of the Cretan Labyrinth is not now known, as Knossos was destroyed and rebuilt a number of times over the centuries before its final abandonment c.1400 BC, late prehistoric Cretan coins show a classic labyrinth design. This design became popular with the Romans, who employed it for mosaic floor patterns.

The labyrinth experienced something of a revival in medieval Europe, primarily in the forms of open-air turf labyrinths, and in the nave pavements of Gothic cathedrals such as **Chartres**. The turf sites are formed by grassed earthen ridges, creating a gully between them that serves as the path. They measured up to 60ft (18m) across and were usually circular, though square and other rectilinear shapes also existed. Several hundred such sites have been documented, but only about a dozen still survive, in England and Germany. **Folklore** indicates that turf labyrinths (often, if incorrectly, referred to as 'turf mazes') were typically incorporated into spring fairs. They were situated on village greens, near churches and sometimes at remote sites such as hilltops. Taken together, these factors can be seen as possibly offering circumstantial evidence for a distant pagan context. One documented account describes a game in which young men would race one another through a labyrinth to be first to reach a girl standing in the centre. Another records a festival at a huge former labyrinth site in Poland, in which a man would hop lapwing-fashion around the winding path while attempting to drink a long glass of beer! (Labyrinth scholars have also uncovered curious links between the crane and the labyrinth, a link that seems to relate to the intricate courtship dance of the bird.) The patron of the Polish labyrinth festival was the local shoemaker's guild, and, interestingly, shoemakers were also associated with a former turf labyrinth in Shrewsbury, Shropshire.

The centres of turf labyrinths were typically occupied by a mound or a tree. The tree seems to be an expression of the World Tree – one of the many images of the **World Navel**. But there were exceptions – for instance, available documentation indicates that the centre of the Shrewsbury labyrinth had an archaic ground drawing of a face.

The cathedral labyrinths were used as penance paths, and the name sometimes given to them was the 'road to **Jerusalem**'. At least some of the turf mazes shared this function, and there is evidence that monks did penance on their

'The turf maze' at Wing in Rutland.

knees in the great Saffron Walden turf labyrinth in Essex.

Some researchers have suggested that a three-dimensional labyrinth is impressed on the slopes of Glastonbury Tor. There is no doubt that the terracing visible on the sides of the Tor today do approximate to a labyrinth pattern when viewed from above, and it is just conceivable that they are the remnants of a long-forgotten and possibly pagan initiatory pathway up the Tor. But it remains a controversial idea.

The labyrinth design also makes its appearance in the Americas. Proto-labyrinth spirals and meanders appear in **Anasazi** and **Hopi** rock art and are etched into the desert surface at **Nazca**. Meanders also appear in pre-Columbian decorative art. The labyrinth design appears in the basket decoration of southern Arizona Indians, but whether this is a genuine pre-Columbian survival or a result of European contact is hard to determine for certain.

The labyrinth pattern might possibly represent a deep, archetypal pattern of the human mind. If so, it would account for its cross-cultural occurrence. C.A. Meier, one-time head of the Jung Institute in Zurich, reported on the spontaneous production of the labyrinth pattern in the mind of a woman patient, and Geoffrey Russell, the man who first put forward the idea of the Glastonbury Tor labyrinth (above), has described an experience in 1944 when he was transported into a visionary state while listening to music. Having no knowledge of the labyrinth pattern at the time, Russell described what he saw in his vision as looking like 'a pair of kidneys stuck together'. He was later able to identify this as the classic labyrinth pattern.

At the end of the twentieth century, the labyrinth has become a popular image yet again. Specialist journals and

Anasazi rock carvings (above and below) of linked spirals and meanders in Arch Valley, Utah. Experts consider such types of marking to prefigure labyrinth designs.

books are devoted to it, and earth mysteries lecturers and workshop leaders throughout Europe and America delight in having their students make new labyrinth sites to the ancient pattern.

See also **Leys/Leylines**; **Mythic Geography**

LEMURIA

This is a lost land that was supposed to have existed once in the Indian Ocean. It was first suggested by a zoologist, P.L. Sclater, in the nineteenth century as a way of explaining how the lemur used to be found in Africa, Malaysia and Sri Lanka

(today the true lemur is found only in Madagascar and nearby islands). Lemuria would have been the lost homeland, forming a land bridge that allowed dispersal of the primate around the Indian Ocean region and beyond. The famous scientist T.H. Huxley also backed the basic idea of a lost continent in the Indian Ocean, as did Alfred Wallace (who developed a theory of evolution contemporaneously with Darwin). Ernst Haeckel in Germany suggested that Lemuria may have been 'the cradle of the human race'.

In reality, Lemuria is a symbol of the relatively limited scientific understanding of the day, when factors such as continental drift were not yet known. But the attraction of Lemuria extended beyond scientists trying to explain the geological, fossil and botanical similarities and anomalies they were uncovering on separated land masses: it became a convenient place for religious literalists to locate the Garden of Eden, and occultists attached themselves to it as they did to the ideas of **Atlantis** and **Mu**. For example, Madam Blavatsky, one of the key founders of **Theosophy**, identified Lemuria as the place where the third 'root race' had lived, though she believed that the lost continent had extended into the Pacific Ocean.

LEYS/LEYLINES

The term 'ley' is used in earth mysteries circles to denote an alignment of ancient places – a straight line of sites across country. It seems an innocuous idea, yet it has caused fierce controversy down the decades, not only between ancient mysteries followers and archaeologists (who have always viewed it as a heretical notion), but also within earth mysteries circles themselves. The subject of leys may generally be viewed as one of the minor themes of the earth mysteries canon, yet it lies at the heart of the whole movement in a subtle, deep-rooted way. Because of this inherent importance, a reasonably comprehensive 'mini-history' is required here in order to untangle the misunderstandings that surround the topic.

The story of leys effectively begins in 1921, when the English businessman, pioneer photographer, inventor and amateur archaeologist Alfred Watkins had what he felt was an insight while looking at a map of the Herefordshire and Welsh Borders countryside. He saw that various prehistoric places, such as standing stones, earthen burial mounds, earthworked hills and other such features, fell into straight lines for miles across country. Watkins went on to spend many years studying such alignments on the ground and on maps. He used his pioneering photography skills to take photographs of his alignments, wrote books and gave lectures. In response to his work, especially to his most important book on the ley subject, *The Old Straight Track* (1925), the Straight Track Club was formed, in which members all over Britain conducted field research and exchanged postal portfolios on their findings.

Watkins initially referred to his alignments as 'leys', an Anglo-Saxon word meaning 'cleared strips of ground' or 'meadows'. Watkins' theory was that leys were old, straight traders' tracks laid down by **Neolithic** surveyors using sighting rods, and it was this line-of-sight method that led to the straightness of the old tracks. The tracks ran from hilltop to hilltop 'like a fairy chain', as Watkins put it. They cut through wild country, and through the valleys where there was dense forest. Over time, this was cleared along the course of the straight tracks, Watkins surmised, and this was the reason he used the word 'ley'. However, by 1929 he referred to his alignments only as 'old straight tracks' or 'archaic tracks'.

Watkins felt that many of the key sighting points along these old straight tracks evolved into sacred sites, such as standing stones and burial mounds. He felt that eventually the old straight tracks fell into disuse, and so we only have the aligned sites today to indicate their former courses. He also theorized that in the historic, Christian era, some of the prehistoric, pagan sites became Christianized and this explained why he found so many ancient churches standing on his alignments (it is certainly a fact that some such sites did become Christianized).

Watkins had not been the first to suggest that ancient sites fell into straight alignments: a number of British, American, French and German researchers had been making similar suggestions from at least the eighteenth century. The German researchers tended to emphasize astronomical aspects, but Watkins's German contemporary, Wilhelm Teudt, was putting forward a quite similar idea with his *heilige Linien* ('holy lines'). Much of the German linear research became associated with Nazi philosophy and was suppressed after World War II. It was Watkins's work that survived the best and was the most complete and free from political agendas.

Watkins died in 1935. The following year, the British occultist Dion Fortune wrote a novel, *The Goat-Foot God*, in which she introduced the notion of 'lines of force' connecting megalithic sites. In 1938 Arthur Lawton, a member of the Straight Track Club, wrote a paper in which he claimed that leys were lines of cosmic force that could be dowsed. He was a dowser himself and was impressed with the German geopathological **dowsing** that was then taking place and French dowsing work involving standing stones. In 1948 the

Alfred Watkins photographing one of his leys. (*Major F.C. Tyler/NEM*)

Straight Track Club closed down as there were only a few surviving members and no new work was being done. The idea of Watkins's leys was kept alive by a few fringe writers and researchers in Britain during the 1950s.

From 1960 the ley idea took on a new lease of life. An ex-RAF pilot, Tony Wedd, was very interested in flying saucers or **UFOs**. He had read Watkins's *The Old Straight Track* and also a French book, *Flying Saucers and the Straight Line Mystery* (1958) by Aimé Michel, in which it was (falsely) suggested that sightings during a 1954 French flying saucer outbreak fell into straight lines or 'orthotenies'. Wedd made the excited conclusion that Watkins's leys and Michel's orthotenies were one and the same phenomenon. He had also read an American book by Buck Nelson called *My Trip to Mars, the Moon and Venus* (1956) in which Nelson claimed to have flown in UFOs and to have witnessed them picking up energy from 'magnetic currents' flowing through the Earth. In addition, Wedd would also doubtless have read the best-selling *Flying Saucers Have Landed* (1953) by UFO 'contactee' George Adamski, with Desmond Leslie, in which Leslie waxes on about UFOs following 'magnetic paths' across the planet. In 1961 Wedd published a pamphlet called *Skyways and Landmarks* in which he theorized that UFO occupants flew along magnetic lines of force that linked ancient sites, and that the ancient sites acted as landmarks for UFO pilots. It all relied very much on the notions and experiences of an old-fashioned terrestrial air pilot rather than on extraterrestrial technology!

Wedd formed the Star Fellowship, which aimed to contact the 'Space Brothers'. It enlisted the aid of a psychic called Mary Long, who referred to 'lines of force' and

Part of the 'Saintbury ley' on the northern edge of the Cotswolds – a Watkins-style ley that aligns with a section of ancient track, passing through an old crossroads and preaching cross, a very old church and two prehistoric burial mounds beyond. The section between the cross and the church later turned out to be part of a funeral or corpse way. (See Death Roads for more on these features.)

'magnetic nodes' in the landscape. (She also channelled communications from a 'space being' called Attalita.) In 1962 a Ley Hunter's Club was set up by Jimmy Goddard and Philip Heselton, with Wedd's encouragement, and by 1965 it had produced the first few copies of *The Ley Hunter* journal under Heselton's editorship. Interest in leys started to widen from this time onwards, as it very much fitted in with the new surge of fascination in occultism, UFOs and ancient mysteries that was emerging during the psychedelic decade – the period that also saw the birth of what have become known as the Human Potential and New Age movements. In addition to Heselton and Goddard, a small group of 'ley hunters' emerged and was the foundation of what came to be called earth mysteries. This embryonic ley movement was soon embraced by the maverick scholar John Michell, who brought a new depth of erudition to it along with esoteric ideas originating in – among other sources – the **Theosophy** movement of several decades earlier. Also, at the same time,

archaeology was undergoing profound changes caused by new dating techniques, serious archaeoastronomical propositions and the collapse of certain long-held theories. In 1967 Michell wrote his first book, *The Flying Saucer Vision*, in which he talked about UFOs, ancient sites, Alfred Watkins and leys. In 1969 he produced his seminal work, *The View Over Atlantis*, in which he fused the ley theory with ancient, sacred geometrical and number systems, the Chinese system of landscape divination called **feng shui** and dowsing. This book had a great effect on the new generation of ley hunters. In that same year *The Ley Hunter* journal came under the editorship of Paul Screeton. Under the later editorship of myself and then architect Danny Sullivan, it remained in continuous publication until 1999. It was the nearest thing the ley-hunting field has had to a journal of record and was the first dedicated English-language earth mysteries periodical.

In 1972 Janet and Colin Bord published their widely read *Mysterious Britain*, which summarized the new wave of ideas about leys and mixed it in with themes from **folklore**. In 1974 Paul Screeton wrote *Quicksilver Heritage*, in which he further dveloped ideas about leys, earth energies and mystic, occult themes. John Michell also published a book at this time, *The Old Stones of Land's End*, which somewhat bucked the then current trends, in that it described alignments of standing stones in Cornwall: this was classic Alfred Watkins ley hunting. In this same year of 1974 the first article on leys was published in the United States by the then president of the American Society of Dowsers, Terry Ross. He had read the Bords' *Mysterious Britain*, and he talked only about leys as being lines of energy. This was gradually picked up by various elements in American dowsing circles and the New Age movement. In the States there was little knowledge of Alfred Watkins or the original theory. In 1976 British dowser Tom Graves published a new book on dowsing in which he reinforced the idea of leys as being energy lines and described how to dowse them. This was a popular work and greatly strengthened ideas about dowsing what were becoming known as 'leylines'.

Towards the end of the 1970s ley hunting had begun to divide into two halves. One side treated leys as lines of energy, while the other, lesser known group was more research oriented, studying possible actual alignments in the landscape in the old ley-hunting tradition. Ian Thomson and myself published *The Ley Hunter's Companion* (1979), encouraging this kind of approach, but the idea of energy lines grew at a greater pace, and became a part of the New Age stock in trade. These energy line and dowsing-based notions have subsequently become the most publicly known version of the subject, taken as standard by those whose knowledge has come only from the same New Age sources and who perpetuate them.

By the early 1980s those actually engaged in ley research had not only dismissed the 'energy line' idea but were coming to realize that Alfred Watkins's idea of leys was also untenable. This was because the British Isles has been very extensively photographed from the air since Watkins's time. Air photos can show where ground was disturbed even thousands of years ago, and there was no evidence of any 'ley system' with old straight tracks criss-crossing everywhere. Also, protracted debate with statisticians had made some of the research-based ley hunters more aware of the role chance could play in the aligning of sites, especially with regard to lines drawn on maps. But by now, the ley researchers were becoming increasingly intrigued with actual, physical straight linear features, such as the **Nazca lines** in Peru and similar features in Bolivia, which had been brought to their attention by British film-maker Tony Morrison. They were to learn that there were numerous others such features in the Americas (*see* other entries, including those on the **Anasazi**, **Chaco Canyon**, **Cuzco**, the **Maya** and **Shamanic Landscapes**).

These were not leys, but they offered similar challenges regarding interpretation. There were linear archaeological features in Europe, too, such as the Neolithic **cursus** type of monument in Britain. And more physical mystery lines began to be learned of in ancient sacred landscapes world-wide.

If not energy lines, if not traders' tracks, then what were such linear features all about? In *Lines on the Landscape* (1989; with Nigel Pennick), I suggested that they may have been 'spirit lines' of various kinds and provided some evidence for this. After the book came out, a stream of further evidence supporting this approach began to fall into place. Information began to be accumulated about medieval **death roads** in Holland and elsewhere, about mysterious, non-physical **spirit ways** that existed in folklore in parts of Europe and other, similar traditions in several areas of the world. Further, spirit-and-line ideas were found associated in folklore with threads and string. Australian Aborigine healers use a filament thread secreted by an insect to act as a 'road' for a sick person's spirit to return to their body, and Siberian Buryat shamans used taut threads as spirit roads in both healing and shamanic initiation. There are many other examples.

It seemed that to the ancient mind in various parts of the world, straight lines of all kinds – whether marks on the ground, folk concepts or threads – were associated with the movement of spirits. Curved, twisted or jumbled lines, on the other hand, were thought by our forebears to bind spirits. This idea was a founding concept in feng shui in China, and stone and turf **labyrinths** in old Europe were also used to trap spirits, while tangled threads in bottles put over entrance doors, or webs woven across hoops and placed on old paths, were thought able to ensnare spirits (*see* **Spirit Traps**).

The core group of objective ley researchers wanted to know what lay behind this ancient, deep-rooted and cross-cultural 'spirit-and-line' concept. The obvious place to look in connection with cross-cultural concepts is shamanism, itself a universal expression of the human mind. The **shaman** entered the spirit worlds by means of an ecstatic (out-of-body) 'journey' during **trance**. This trance was induced by a variety of techniques, including the ingestion of plant **hallucinogens** that specifically promote the dissociative, out-of-body sensation. This still goes on among some surviving tribal peoples, while in Europe there were hallucinogenic 'flying ointments' used by medieval (and earlier) so-called witches. The idea began to dawn on some of the 'new ley hunters' that this shamanic 'aerial journey' may have been translated on to ancient landscapes in the Americas as straight lines – an archaic variant, perhaps, of the 'tunnel' image reported in today's near-death and out-of-body experiences.

As research continued, the work of American anthropologist Marlene Dobkin de Rios was encountered. In a 1977 paper she had already openly stated that this is what the Native American lines were all about. The new ley hunters later learned that the Kogi Indians in Colombia, a people who still hold pre-Columbian beliefs, claim that some of the ancient pathways in their territory are physical traces of spirit paths their shamans follow during their entranced journeys in the spirit world. It appeared to some of the ley researchers,

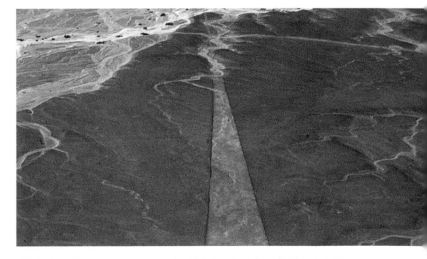

Mysterious lines engraved on ancient Native American landscapes now attract the attention of the new ley hunters. (*Peruvian Embassy, London*)

side of the church was a liminal zone, the Devil's area, for that was where the building's shadow fell. Suicides, transgressors and unbaptized children would be buried in that part of the churchyard. Shadows were seen as liminal in many cultures, and the great German researcher of the **Nazca lines** in Peru, Maria Reiche, noted that the Indians would not walk where the shadow of a rock touched one of the mysterious desert lines because it was hallowed or, conversely, full of evil spirits. (A vestige of such kinds of avoidance probably survives in the childhood game of not walking on the cracks in sidewalk paving.)

Physical boundaries were by definition liminal zones. From at least the sixth century the Christian church encouraged the Beating of the Bounds, in which young boys were taken around the parish limits and were beaten or dragged along at various points *en route*. It was felt that by this means the position of the boundaries would be ingrained into the memories of the upcoming generation. In Ireland at liminal Beltane the father of the house would light a candle and bless the threshold, the hearth and the four corners of the house, while the boundaries of the farmstead might be marked by the mother carrying a pail of well water around them or by putting sprigs of rowan in the four corners of each field. Land boundaries also functioned in a psychological sense to separate the human, lived-in land from the wilderness beyond, where spirits and witches roamed. A witch was herself a liminal personality, as was the **shaman**, who could cross the boundaries between the human and spirit worlds. Turner also felt that jesters, clowns and poets inhabited the border realm where outlaws and initiates sojourned temporarily.

Many kinds of sacred sites are themselves essentially liminal, being where contact with the world of spirits could be made, where the veils between this world and the otherworld are at their thinnest.

Time has its liminal aspects. In the Celtic year, the festivals of Imbolc, Beltane, Lughnassadh and Samhain (Hallowe'en) were times when the threshold between the human and supernatural worlds was open, an idea that survives in our own Hallowe'en festivities today. Samhain was the Celtic New Year, and the time of New Year is a threshold period in all cultures. As with the year, so with the day. Midnight is an obvious liminal time, being the 'witching hour'; noon is another moment of 'time outside time', when shadows are at their shortest but have not commenced lengthening; and twilight is a particularly potent example of a 'crack between the worlds'. In the human lifetime, the greatest threshold is death.

In funeral traditions in the Celtic countries of Europe's western fringe, we can see a wide scope of liminality being involved, ranging from the social to the physical. In the first instance, the period between death and burial was profoundly liminal: the dead person had left the world of the living but had not yet physically left the community. The corpse would have its own boundaries defined: its eyes and mouth would be closed and its other orifices plugged, before it was wrapped in a winding sheet and placed in the coffin. From the moment of death, the thresholds of the house took on special importance, and windows would be closed and drapes drawn. It was important that the corpse be carried out across the threshold of the house feet first and never by the back door. Ideally, the corpse's feet had to be kept pointing away from the house all the way to the grave so as to reduce the chances of haunting.

Most country funerals in former times in Europe were walking funerals, with a procession of mourners carrying the coffin along specially designated pathways or **death roads**. The procession would stop at certain points along the corpse way, and these would typically be liminal locations, such as bridges over streams, ancient stiles, crossroads and the boundary of the churchyard itself – a factor that a church's 'lych gate', or corpse gate, recalls. Such corpse ways were liminal space extended in linear fashion. Not only were they associated with the carriage of the dead from home to burial, but they were also seen as ways of the spirit through the land. *See also* **Omphalos**; **Pilgrimage**; **Sacred Place**; **Shamanic Landscapes**; **Sitting Out**; **Spirit Traps**; **Spirit Ways**; **Sweeping**; **Trance**; **Vision Quest**; **World Navel**

LOUGHCREW

This complex of **Neolithic** chambered cairns (stone mounds) lies 50 miles (80km) northwest of Dublin near Oldcastle in County Meath, Ireland. The cairns, in varying conditions, from ruinous to fairly intact, are scattered along the spine of the Loughcrew hills, clustering on and around the four main peaks of the ridge, especially the two highest ones, known as Carnbane East and Carnbane West. The range of hills is also known as Slieve na Calliagh, the Hill of the Witch or Hag.

One of these is Cairn T, standing like a giant nipple atop Carnbane East. It is 120ft (37m) in diameter and has a 369ft (113m) circumference. A short entrance passage leads to a main chamber, which has three side-chambers. Both passage and chamber have several richly carved stones, in particular the backstone of the main chamber. Among the prehistoric designs carved on this stone are rayed motifs like sun symbols. That this *is* their meaning has become clear as a result of pioneering research by American researcher Martin Brennan in 1980. He and

A ruined cairn on Carnbane West at Loughcrew in County Meath, Ireland, aligns to the giant mound of Cairn T in the distance.

colleagues discovered that the rising sun shines into the chamber in the days around the equinoxes, in March and September each year. Because of the configuration of the stones in the passage, the sunbeam is sculpted into a fairly regular rectangular form. As the sun rises, this rectangle of golden sunlight drops slowly across the rock carvings, ultimately framing the most complete of the stone's sun symbol carvings, located at the furthest point from the entrance.

Another researcher, Tim O'Brien, conducted further observations on the equinoctial sunbeams at Cairn T between 1986 and 1990. He arranged the removal of an entrance stone that had been incorrectly replaced during reconstruction and had the existing security door replaced. These had interfered with what would have been the original course by which the sunbeams would have entered the cairn. He was able to see and photograph the true form of the light as it passed across Stone 14 and to make useful additional observations. He noted carvings consisting of vertical spines with regularly spaced horizontal lines across them that looked like grading or scale marks – it turned out that these marked the edges of the rectangular patch of sunlight, registering its shifting angular position day to day on the backstone. O'Brien was able to show that the cairn builders could have measured solar motion by these grading marks with sufficient accuracy to identify the leap-year cycle of four years.

The other site at Loughcrew with solar significance is Cairn L on Carnbane West. At 435ft (134m), this has a larger circumference than Cairn T. A passage leads into a chamber whose most arresting feature is a freestanding white monolith, over 6ft (2m) high. Brennan and his cohorts found the cairn was oriented towards sunrise during the November cross-quarter day period. They saw the rising sun at that time shoot a sunbeam into the chamber with such precision that it initially struck just the white standing stone. The sunlight lengthened its rectangular glare down the stone over a 16-minute period, before slipping off and shining into a side stall in the chamber containing a stone basin and rock carvings. A dazzling Neolithic lightshow.

As well as light, research indicates that sound might also have played a part in the ceremonial significance of the cairns. Acoustical tests inside Cairn T indicate that the chamber resonates at the same frequency as the male baritone voice. Interestingly, another local tradition is said to be attached to the Loughcrew complex claiming that oracular pronouncements issued from the cairns.

It is the varied aspects of sites like Loughcrew that particularly appeal to the cross-disciplinary preferences of earth mysteries enthusiasts.

See also **Acoustics**; **Archaeoastronomy**; **Oracles**; **Rock Art**; **Trance**

The rock art on the backstone in the chamber at Cairn T at Loughcrew. Note the rayed 'sun symbols' and the ruler-like calibration markings.

breakdowns. Maya culture continued in the Yucatán, and remnants of this survived until the Spanish Conquest in the sixteenth century. Even today, there are several million Indians who still speak the Mayan language, a member of the Totonac-Mayan (Penutian) family, along with Spanish. They are now ostensibly Roman Catholic, but in their book *Maya Cosmos* (1993) Freidel, Schiele and Parker have demonstrated that Mayan shamanism has continued from ancient times right up to the present day.

The Maya built stepped pyramids, temples, ball courts, platforms and many other buildings with remarkable masonry skills. They used ceremonial astronomy, a sophisticated form of arithmetic (it incorporated the concept of zero, which eluded the ancient Greeks and Romans, and used a vigesimal – 20-based – counting system) and kept records, using a heiroglyphic form of writing on stone and in plaster-coated bark paper or animal skin books now referred to as Codices. They also had a complex and accurate dating system using integrated calendars based on different schemes. One involved a 365-day year consisting of 18 periods or 'months' of 20 days plus an unlucky period of five days, another was a 260-day sequence, and then there was a 'long count' denoting an era that commenced at a base date of 3113 BC in our calendar, long before any Mayan monuments were erected. There has been much speculation about this early date, and there is an opinion among some scholars that in the Mayan cosmology it may have represented the last creation of the world (the Maya belief was that we are now in the fifth world and that there had been four previous creations). The full cycle of integration between the 260-day period and the 365-day system took 18,980 days (52 of our years) and is called the Calendar Round. Certain day names were associated with various other factors such as colours and directions. It is thought possible the system was invented by the **Olmec** rather than the Maya, but this remains uncertain.

Venus was a major player in Mayan cosmology, being one of the twins (Hunahpu) in the Mayas' epic poem *Popol Vuh* (the other twin being the sun). It was associated with warfare and death. Blue was the symbolic colour for Venus, and sacrificial victims were sometimes painted in that colour prior to death. Maya priests had almanacs recording the cycles of Venus, and these were keyed with their overall calendar, so that they could identify propitious times for ritual combat and sacrifice. This was a complicated business. Five 584-day Venus cycles fortuitously equal eight 365-day solar cycles or years, so an eight-year Venus almanac was devised. But that in turn had to mesh with the 260-day system, which involved a cycle combining a sequence of 13 sacred numbers with another of 20 named days. This resulted in a 104-year Great Venus Almanac, which incorporated 65 Venus cycles.

Two aspects of the ancient Mayan culture hold particular fascination within some earth mysteries circles. One is the *sacbes* or *sacbeob*, Mayan for White Ways. These were straight causeways that interconnected plazas and temples within some of the Mayan ceremonial cities and also linked cities themselves. They now exist only in fragmentary sections, the longest known surviving sacbe being the 62-mile (99km) section running between Coba and Yaxuna in the northern part of the Yucatán peninsula. This was discovered by explorer Thomas Gann in the 1920s. He described it as 'a great elevated road, or causeway thirty-two-feet wide ... This was one of the most remarkable roads ever constructed, as the sides were built of great blocks of cut stone, many weighing hundreds of pounds ... It was convex, being higher in the centre than either side, and ran, as far as we followed it, straight as an arrow, and almost flat as a rule.' Altars, arches and curious ramps are associated with the sacbeob, and according to local Mayan tradition, the physical network is augmented at various places by non-material routes: there are said to be undergound sacbeob and others than run through the air known as Kusam Sum. One of these 'air lines' is said to link Izamal with Dzibilchaltun. The sacbeob are interesting to some ancient mysteries scholars because they may contribute towards an understanding of **shamanic landscapes**, a more ethnology-centred approach to the old **ley** belief within earth mysteries. Other scholars have speculated that astronomical alignments found at Mayan centres such as Uxmal were, in effect, transcribed on to the ground on a huge, territorial scale by means of these ceremonial causeways.

The other specially interesting Mayan mystery is the possibility that these remarkable people incorporated an acoustic element into some of their key ceremonial structures, including their ball courts, which seem to have had more of a ritual function than one of mere entertainment. (*see* **Acoustics**).

As 'millennium fever' develops in our own times, belief in so-called Mayan prophecies is exercising the imaginations of many New Agers, but it is the past of this great culture that may hold the more important secrets.

See also **Archaeoastronomy; Atlantis; Chichén Itzá; Shaman**

MAYPOLE

May Day was superimposed on the Beltane festival of the pagan **Celts** and in the Celtic parts of the British Isles is known to have been marked by bonfires symbolizing the sun.

Maypole at Padstow, Cornwall.

centre in the middle of a wood in southern Denmark. It was bedecked with coloured rags and was clearly a tree shrine still locally acknowledged.

The maypole obviously has phallic associations, at the deepest level symbolizing the bringing of the revivifying powers of the gods in the heaven worlds down through the conduit of the Cosmic Axis and, at the more popular level, linked to the theme of May greenery and foliage, symbolizing fertility and fecundity.

From the descriptions in the documentation and **folklore** available, the May Day practice involved cutting a tree from the woodland and stripping off its branches – except sometimes for the very top ones, which were left to symbolize new life – and bringing it into the village, usually by youths, where it would be erected on the green and decked out with flowers and ribbons and perhaps painted with coloured stripes. Preferred trees were hazel, ash, oak and yew. Foliage

The point at which the maypole was added to the festivities is obscure, as first clear documentation of them anywhere in Europe goes back only to the fourteenth century. Folk historian Ronald Hutton offers as one possibility in *The Rise and Fall of Merry England* (1994) that the maypole was introduced by the Anglo-Saxons into England, where it replaced the fire-ritual aspect of May Day, but this continued for many centuries longer in the Celtic fringes of the islands.

Many folklore scholars, especially within earth mysteries circles, see the maypole as a survivor of pagan tree worship and ultimately of the World Tree, a representative of the Cosmic Axis that held together the underworld, the 'middle Earth' of the physical world and the upper worlds of the gods. In Norse tradition the World Tree was the great ash tree, **Yggdrasil**, the German Irminsul. In turn, these are, in essence, manifestations of the **omphalos** or **World Navel**. In pagan Ireland, sacred trees were known as *bile*, and in England there are named trees like the former Copt Oak in Leicestershire, and a range of 'Gospel' and other oaks that possibly represent the survival of pagan ideas. In 1968 the editor of the British archaeological journal *Antiquity* described encountering a tall tree with a hole through its

A sapling is co-opted as a *Maibaum in situ* at Burtscheid, Germany.

NAZCA LINES

Etched on a 30-mile (48km) stretch of desert plains between Nazca and Palpa, Peru, is a seemingly chaotic cross-hatching of ruler-straight lines of varying widths, and lengths up to 6 miles (10km). Sprinkled among them are over 100 spiral designs plus a few dozen figures depicting birds, whales, lizards, monkeys, spiders, flowers, seaweed and abstract forms. These ground drawings are nowadays called 'geoglyphs', and they range from about 50ft (15m) to over 1000ft (300m) in length. They are typically unicursal, which means that a single line delineates them without crossing back over itself. Because this means that the line can be followed on foot without hindrance all around the image, some investigators have suggested the geoglyphs were dancing grounds, allowing processional dancing.

Because these desert drawings can be seen best from the air and because they are remarkably symmetrical, some researchers wondered if the ancient Nazcans had perhaps been able to fly by means of hot-air balloons. In order to test this idea, American explorer Jim Woodman tried out a hot-air balloon (made from fabric that matched samples found on mummies in Nazca graves) over the pampa in 1975. After some minor hitches, the balloon, which was 90ft (28m) tall, rose slowly and majestically into the air. But this dramatic display did not convince everyone, because of one key factor: a substantial fire pit had been necessary to generate the smoky, hot air for the balloon, and there were scant signs of such features on the desert. Although there are stone heaps at the end of some lines and within some of the trapezoid clearings that show signs of blackening, these are almost certainly due simply to ancient campfires.

The age of the 'Nazca lines' has mainly been inferred from pottery fragments found among the markings. The bulk of these ceramic pieces belong to the Nazca culture, which developed out of the earlier Paracas culture around the second century BC. There has been much uninformed speculation about how difficult it would have been for such an ancient culture to have made the markings. In fact, they

Lines overlay geoglyphs in a complex of ground markings at Nazca, Peru. (*Peruvian Embassy, London*)

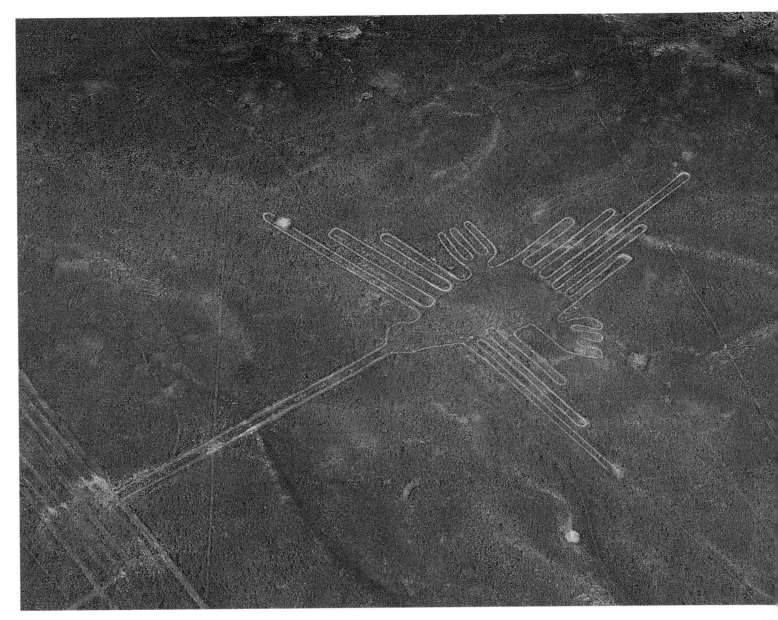

The ground drawing (geoglyph) of a humming bird, over 200ft (60m) in length, on the Nazca pampa in Peru. (*Peruvian Embassy, London*)

were all made quite simply by the removal of the darkened, oxidized desert pavement or crust revealing a lighter subsoil beneath. Modern tests have shown that they could have been laid out relatively speedily, though the lines would have required accurate ranging to make them so straight, and the geoglyphs would have demanded planning and exceptional artistic skill to have been etched into the desert in so proportioned and symmetrical a manner. Although the markings are most numerous near Nazca, south of the Ingenio valley, other examples can be found quite widespread on various desert areas of the western Andes.

As commercial air traffic started overflying such remote reaches of the Andes in the 1930s, reports describing strange desert markings began to come from pilots and passengers. But the lines had first been discovered in 1926 by archaeologists Alfred Kroeber and Toribio Mejia Xesspe, who had been searching for archaeological remains on the Nazca pampa.

Climbing a low hill, they were surprised to see curious furrows in the stony surface of the level desert beneath them. They initially took these to be ancient attempts at irrigation channels, but years later Xesspe was able to appreciate their greater mystery. The rumours about the desert markings eventually reached Paul Kosok of Long Island University. Visiting the pampa in 1941, he saw the markings as making up 'the largest astronomy book in the world'. He passed on this opinion to Maria Reiche, a German mathematician. She studied the lines, walked them, measured them, mapped them, protected them and lived with them from the 1940s until a few years before her death in 1998. In 1968, Gerald Hawkins of the Smithsonian Institution carried out ground, aerial and computer surveys of the desert lines. Hawkins was

Researchers walk a Nazca line. (*Gary Urton*)

Nazca lines of varying widths radiate from (or converge on) a line centre. (*Gary Urton*)

already famous for 'decoding' **Stonehenge** as a prehistoric astronomical computer, but his studies at Nazca showed no astronomical orientations that breached the level of random chance.

The most comprehensive work on the Nazca markings was conducted over several seasons in the 1980s by a diverse body of investigators co-ordinated by astronomer Anthony Aveni of Colgate University, New York. These researchers compiled extensive new information on the features. Maria Reiche had noted what she called 'star-like centres', which were raised hillocks or promontories that lines seemed to radiate from or converge on. These centres were also interconnected. Aveni's multi-disciplinary team uncovered more such 'ray centres' or 'line centres', as they came to be called. It was also found that numerous lines contained deeply worn footpaths, suggesting that they had been used for sacred walking or pilgrimages, although it was not clear what the exact nature of such activity had been. Detailed study of the lines indicated that some appeared to be associated with ancient cemeteries out on the pampa and also with ancient aqueducts and arroyos (the dried beds of occasional streams). Some lines seemed oriented to mountains where the Indians traditionally believed water or rain gods dwelt. There were stone piles and curious clearings among the markings, and broken pottery – probably left as votive offerings – was found associated with some markings. Finally, the new survey confirmed Hawkins's earlier findings that there was little evidence to indicate that the lines had astronomical significance.

Of all the many attempts to unravel the secret of the markings, the one that has most caught the public's imagination was the assertion by Erich von Daniken in *Chariots of the Gods?* (1968) that the markings looked like an airfield. He felt that the Nazca lines were a signal to the 'gods', ancient spacemen. He further suggested that they could have been landing strips for ancient spacecraft – a kind of prehistoric space centre. But the pampa surface is so delicate that the markings made by landing spacecraft on the Nazca 'runways', and the blast effects of their propulsion systems would have left marks. There aren't any. Von Daniken tried to make out that the lines were *themselves* the tracks of spacecraft, but they are, in fact, constructed features. In any case, as the late astronomer and writer Carl Sagan observed, why would a spaceship capable of crossing intergalactic space need a landing strip like one of our relatively primitive aircraft?

The main reason why von Daniken's late-twentieth-century notions are wrong, however, is simply because the Nazca lines are merely the most famous of many other straight-line features to be found throughout the Americas (*see* **Shamanic Landscapes** and other entries in this book). The place to start looking for the answer to the straight-line mystery of the Americas seems to lie in the religious life of pre-Columbian Indians rather than the technology of extraterrestrials.

See also **Chaco Canyon; Cuzco; Death Roads; Effigy Mounds; Hill Figures; Leys/Leylines; Rock Art; Shaman; Spirit Ways; Trance**

NEOLITHIC

This term means 'New Stone Age', and the Stone Age is the first broad technological period of the 'Three Age' chronological system put forward by Christian Thomsen and J.J. Worsaae (see **Bronze Age**). The Neolithic era can be seen as dawning at varying times in the Old World from about the eighth millennium BC and was generally characterized by the emergence of farming and husbandry – as distinct from an earlier hunting and gathering pattern of life – and the building of monuments and dwellings. But no hard-edged definition is possible – 'Neolithic' must be a seen as a very generalized term.

See also **Iron Age; Palaeolithic**

NEWGRANGE

This Irish **Neolithic** chambered mound, some 36ft (11m) high and 300ft (100m) in diameter, occupies a large bend in the River Boyne in County Meath, north of Dublin, along with two companion chambered mounds – Dowth and Knowth – and a variety of other smaller, earthen and megalithic monuments. Around the base of Newgrange is a kerbing of 97 stones lying on edge, acting as a retaining wall. Three of these stones are decorated by carvings. Lying horizontally in front of the mound's entrance is a stone (Kerbstone 1) incised with a rich variety of spiral and lozenge designs. The entrance gives access to a passage 62ft (18.9m) long which ends in a corbelled stone chamber 20ft (6m) high. The passage averages about 4ft (1.2m) in height and its floor rises steadily from the entrance to the chamber, which has three side-chambers or recesses, one at its end or back (opposite to where the passage enters the chamber) and one at either side. Large stone basins were found in these recesses. There are stones decorated with **rock art** in both the passage and the chamber recesses, including a famous triple spiral carving in the end recess.

The entrance stone at Newgrange in County Meath, Ireland. Note the roof-box above the passage entrance, and the vertical line in the top middle of the entrance stone's spiral carvings. (See text.)

Ringed by an incomplete circle of massive standing stones, Newgrange has been dated to at least 3200 BC, making it considerably older than Egypt's Great Pyramid and one of the oldest roofed structures in the world. It was known in Irish myth as Bru na Boinne, the palace by the Boyne, and was where the ancient Lords of Light were said to dwell. This is a particularly appropriate legend because the monument aligns to the rising winter solstice sun, providing one of the most dramatic and best confirmed examples of ancient astronomy. For centuries local **folklore** rumoured that on a special day sunlight entered what was then the tumbleddown mound of Newgrange. In 1909 Sir Norman Lockyer, the founder of **archaeoastronomy**, mentioned that Newgrange was oriented to the midwinter sunrise, and in 1912 folklorist W.Y. Evans Wentz similarly remarked that Newgrange was astronomically aligned. For decades archaeologists tended to dismiss such lore and observations as wishful thinking, but attitudes began to change as a consequence of excavations carried out at the site between 1962 and 1975 under the directorship of Michael J. O'Kelly. His work uncovered a curious rectangular opening above the passage entrance. The top lintel of this structure, an engraved slab, had been visible prior to the excavations, but O'Kelly revealed the full nature of what he called the 'roof-box'. The archaeologist suspected that this was for the admission of the rumoured midwinter sunbeams into the chamber, and he noted that a line drawn from the backstone of the end recess

in the central chamber through the roof-box would go to the point on the horizon where the midwinter sun would have risen 5000 years ago.

On 21 December 1969 O'Kelly became the first modern observer of the Newgrange sunbeam phenomenon. A pencil beam of direct sunlight shot through the roof-box, along the passage and across the chamber floor as far as the basin stone in the end recess. Because of precession, the Earth's slow polar axial 'wobble', the sun's rising position at midwinter has moved slightly, so the roof-box sunbeam cannot now reach to the very the back of the end recess as it would have done originally. 'As the thin line of light widened to a [8in] 17cm band and swung across the chamber floor, the tomb was dramatically illuminated and various details of the side- and end-chambers as well as the corbelled roof could be clearly seen in the light reflected from the floor,' O'Kelly observed. 'At 10.04am (British Standard Time) the [8in] 17cm band of light began to narrow again and at exactly 10.15am the direct beam was cut off from the tomb.' Direct sunlight through the passage doorway cannot reach as far as the chamber itself because of the upward slope of the passage floor and the arrangement of the upright stones or orthostats that form the passage walls.

Over a two-year period in the 1980s, Irish researcher Tim O'Brien made special studies of the midwinter lightbeam in Newgrange. He recorded the maximum length of the light-beam on the chamber floor at just greater than 3m (10ft). His vertical sequence photographs show it like the glowing hand of a clock sweeping across the chamber floor like a clock dial. He showed that two of the passage orthostats, known as L20 and R21, lean into one another to form a triangle that controls and sculpts the sunbeam from the roof-box. In 1989 Tom Ray, an astronomer at the Dublin Institute for Advanced Studies, provided statistical proof that the midwinter sunbeam event at Newgrange occurs by design and not by chance. So the phenomenon of Newgrange finally made the long journey from legend to scientific fact.

We can be certain that Newgrange holds further secrets to be uncovered. For example, American artist Martin Brennan and colleagues like Jack Roberts noted that the rock art on the entrance stone, Kerbstone 1, is divided by a straight vertical line. On the diametrically opposite side of the mound is Kerbstone 52, also richly carved, and it too has a broad, vertical line dividing it half. Both these stones stand on the line of the midwinter sunbeam at Newgrange, so it is as certain as can be that the vertical markings represent this

The winter-solstice rising sun shining into the entrance passage at Newgrange. (*Duchas, The Heritage Service*)

solar alignment (John Michell first noted this possibility several years earlier). In addition, Brennan suspects that shadows cast by certain stones in the megalithic circle surrounding Newgrange may have been designed deliberately to point out carvings on the kerbstones.

Further research by Brennan and company at nearby Knowth has revealed other vertical markings on stones that were placed on the line of the sunbeams that enter that site at the equinoxes. This Boyne Valley work, together with their research at other sites such as the cairns of **Loughcrew**, indicate that at least some of the Irish rock carvings may be decipherable as being symbology interactive with sunlight and shadow. Although they got some of their calculations wrong, Brennan and helpers have been shamefully ignored or dismissed by the mainstream for the general thrust of their efforts in opening up this intriguing area of enquiry.

See also **Acoustics**; **Atlantis**; **Entoptic Patterns**; **Trance**

Rock carvings above one of the mysterious stone basins inside Newgrange (right). (*Brenda Dunne*)

Kerbstone 52 (below) at the rear of the Newgrange mound. Note the vertical line, thought to indicate the solar alignment through the mound. (See text.)

OGHAM

This is a form of notation, probably invented in Ireland in the fifth century AD and associated with the Celtic god Oghma. It is the last-known form of writing used by the ancient **Celts** and has been found only in the western parts of the British Isles where Roman influence was least strong. The script consists of 20 alphabetical units formed from between one and five lines or strokes or staves, cut into wood or stone in a slanting or horizontal fashion either side of a vertical line or corner. It was initially a secret writing, probably used for magical purposes by the **druids**. Irish Celtic texts actually refer to druidic yew wands engraved with ogham characters. Ogham was suitable only for short inscriptions and came to be used mostly on stone pillars and slabs marking graves. Interestingly, one such slab, found on the Isle of Man, had an inscription that has been interpreted as reading *Dovaidona Maqi Droata* ('Dovaidona son of the Druid').

See also **Runes**

OLMEC

These people first appear in the archaeological record *c*.1200 BC on Mexico's Gulf Coast in an area covered by parts of today's states of Veracruz and Tabasco, from where they spread their influence over a much wider area. Their culture peaked in the first millennium BC and had declined by *c*.300 BC. They were among the first Mesoamericans to transform from a village-type society to a complex, stratified culture. Key Olmec sites include San Lorenzo Tenochtitlan (*c*.1200–900 BC), Laguna de los Cerros and La Venta (*c*.1000–600 BC), and the later Tres Zapotes.

The Olmec left behind many tantalizing artefacts, including cave paintings, iconographic imagery carved with supreme skill in serpentine, jade, wood and basalt, stone sculptures depicting snarling 'were-children' displaying the fangs and claws of jaguars and being held by regal-looking adults, dwarfs and foetuses and large, natural rubber balls,

Ogham along the edge of a stone that originally stood outside but has long since been incorporated into a windowsill in the ancient church at Nevern, Wales.

A gigantic Olmec stone head at La Venta park, Villahermosa, Mexico. (*Klaus Aarsleff/ Fortean Picture Library*).

which may indicate the presence at this early time of the mysterious and apparently ritualistic ball game that required the ball courts found at numerous Central American and Mexican archaeological sites and even at ancient Indian sites in Arizona (*see* **Wupatki**). It is possible that the Olmec used the magnetic compass, because a lodestone magnet carved into the shape of a grooved oblong bar was unearthed at San Lorenzo and was found to orient quite accurately to magnetic north. They also worked in iron, and concave, mirror-like iron objects have been found, which were worn as pendants. Carved reliefs on basalt altars or thrones and stelae show kings or priest-chieftains in elaborate costumes accompanied by supernatural creatures.

In addition to all these remarkable artefacts, the Olmec constructed ceremonial centres incorporating large-scale earthen and clay monumental works such as pyramids and platforms for buildings. They used coloured clays and sands in building these ceremonial centres, which must have given them a rich appearance – 'psychedelic' as one archaeologist put it – although with the depredations of time this is no longer evident. Complex stone drainage systems built by the Olmec were also found.

The Olmec had a profound influence on the **Maya** culture that followed them and on later Mesoamerican cultures generally. For instance, Olmec sculptures and paintings frequently display the jaguar image – some show half-human, half-jaguar creatures, which are quite probably an expression of shamanistic experience – which appeared later in varying religious and iconographic contexts throughout pre-Columbian Mesoamerica, and even in some South American cultures, notably that associated with **Chavín de Huantar**.

The mystery most popularly associated with the Olmec is that of the colossal basalt heads up to 10ft (3m) tall and weighing as much as 20 tons that were unearthed at Olmec ceremonial centres. The nearest source of the stone lies well over 50 miles (80km) to the west. The heads are carved to show tight-fitting helmets and thick-lipped, flat-nosed facial features. This has caused some scholars to argue for trans-atlantic contact with African peoples, or even with marooned Polynesians. But most archaeologists point out that such physical features are within the range found among the Mesoamerican peoples. In a more extreme vein, the depiction of helmets automatically gives licence to believers in ancient **astronauts** to speculate about extraterrestrial contact, but most scholars feel confident that the stone heads are actually portraits of specific Olmec rulers.

See also **Hallucinogens**; **Shaman**; **Shamanic Landscapes**

OMPHALOS

This is a conical 'navel stone' found in ancient Greece and other ancient eastern Mediterranean cultures symbolizing the centre of the world, or **World Navel**. Notable among these were the carved and plain ones found at **Delphi**, a plain one found at Claros, and omphaloi with carved serpents coiling round them at Delos, Greece, and Pergamum, Turkey.

The navel or belly button in human beings is located halfway down the body, so is physically central, but it is also the point from which the embryo grows in the womb, and so can be seen symbolically as the centre of life. But as the navel is usually a depression in the stomach, it is initially difficult to understand why the ancients used a dome of stone to symbolize it. The answer may have been found by scholar Marie Delacourt, who has pointed out that not only does the navel of a pregnant woman at the end of her term protrude, but so does that of a newborn baby. This might arguably indicate the vestigial hints of Earth Mother **Goddess** associations in the classical omphalos stone.

There is a holed slab at Delphi, which may be a different kind of omphalos stone. There is evidence that smoke issued through it.
See also **Yggdrasil**

A Roman copy of one of the omphaloi stones found at Delphi in Greece. It has a curious lattice motif known as an *agrenon* or net carved on it. No one knows what it symbolizes, though it has been suggested that it represents strands of wool, while others have argued that it refers to an archaic system of latitude and longitude. There has also been speculation that it symbolizes alignments of ancient Greek temples.

ORACLES

An oracle is first and foremost a place where prophecy or advice was sought, ostensibly from the gods or spirits. Often, this process involved an intermediary such as a priest, priestess or other form of seer, and these may also be referred to as oracles. Oracles are usually associated with the proto-historical world of the eastern Mediterranean – the classic example being the oracle of **Delphi** – but in point of fact many cultures around the world had various forms of oracles. An Azende of the Congo region of Africa, for example, would consult a termite mound by sticking two leafy branches into the mound, then address questions to the termites and leave the branches in place overnight. The 'yes' or 'no' answer to the question would be revealed the next day, depending on whether or not the leaves on the branches had been eaten by the termites. Trees were resorted to as oracles by many cultures in Arabia, Persia and Armenia, among other places, such as Rome where there was an oracular ilex grove on the Aventine hill.

Oracle sites often made use of sound – waterfalls or burbling springs, for instance, were typical oracle locations for peoples as diverse as the ancient **Celts** and pre-Columbian Indians. A good example of an acoustic-based oracle site in ancient Greece was Dodona, where the primary method was the interpretation of the sound of the wind in the foliage of a great, sacred oak tree. The other oracular function there involved a 'sounding brass', descriptions of which vary but essentially involved a brass bowl or cauldron of some sort that was made to reverberate. Again, at the Greek oracle site of Lebadea, about 20 miles (32km) from Delphi, there is a rock-hewn cell in a ravine, situated over a murmuring underground stream. This was a 'direct' oracle, where the voice of the gods could be heard without a human intermediary. Princeton psychologist Julian Jaynes thinks such sites helped trigger auditory hallucinations that were interpreted as divine speech by people of the 'age of oracles' due to the way their minds functioned (see **Bicameral Mind**). Whether or not his theory is correct, there is no doubt that the 'pink-noise' effect of wind in foliage or roaring water can readily be interpreted as voices by anyone, even today.

See also **Acoustics**; **Divination**; **Sibyls**

The Colossi of Memnon, 60ft (18m) tall, in the Valley of the Kings, Luxor, Egypt. These giant statues are actually representations of Amenhotep III, which originally flanked the entrance to his now-vanished mortuary temple. In Graeco-Roman times the northernmost statue (on the right in this view) was famous as an oracle. After an earthquake in 27 BC had caused cracks in it, the statue would issue a sound at sunrise – presumably due to expansion in the fissures. It was variously described as sounding like a trumpet blast, a cord snapping or a musical note. The Greeks flocked to it. Questions would be asked of the statue, and the sound it made interpreted. When the Romans repaired the cracks early in the third century AD, the Colossus fell silent.

PAGANISM

The term 'pagan' derives from the Latin *paganus*, which can be interpreted in a range of related ways: a villager, a person from a rural area or a heathen – a person 'from the heath', that is, from the wild countryside beyond the pale of the town. The word 'peasant' derives from the same source. 'Paganism' tends to be used today in a religious context to refer variously to nature-based religions of ancient or indigenous peoples or to spiritual inclinations outside the main religious denominations of the world, especially Christianity, which are sometimes equated with irreligiosity by members of those religions.

There is a quite widespread modern Romantic movement in which certain individuals and groups lay claim to a pagan spirituality. In reality, these people can only be *neo*pagan, because it is virtually impossible for anyone living in a First World country today to have the sort of life experience, spiritual sensibilities or worldview of the pagans to whom the Romans referred or of any pre-industrial peoples. Even the most ardent neopagans are ineluctably tainted by the modern industrialized world and rely on it in one way or another for their very existence. Indeed, most neopagans derive their nature-based religious outlooks primarily from beliefs concocted by Romantics of earlier generations and disseminated through a slew of New Age books offering information of usually dubious provenance. In addition, neopaganism is often inextricably mixed in with equally Romantically invented notions of witchcraft or 'wicca', with modern magical movements and with ecological concerns. It also usually blurs into the ancient earth mysteries constituency, which itself is not a religious movement. In Western countries neopaganism in general tends to represent the more impecunious end of the spectrum, which has relatively well-heeled New Age and Human Potential movements and groups at the other end.

While neopaganism cannot replicate authentic paganism or indigenous nature religions with anything more than a superficial veneer (if that), it can nevertheless become a vehicle for an individual's love of nature, an openness to nature

The Roman relief of Sulis-Minerva at Bath, England, representing the spirit of the sacred waters. This is a hybrid of a pagan Celtic god and a Roman goddess.

mysticism (a non-denominational spiritual condition that does not, of course, need any 'ism', pagan or otherwise, to validate its existence) and eco-activism. It can also provide many people with the context for exploring inner, psycho-spiritual states that they might otherwise not work to cultivate.
See also **Gaia Theory**; **Goddess**

PALAEOLITHIC

This word means Old Stone Age. It refers to an extremely long period of time, which begins with the appearance of early humans and the first stone and bone tools and continues through the last Ice Age. It is usually subdivided into Lower (oldest), Middle and Upper, the latter period stretching from about 40,000 to 10,000 years ago. The Upper Palaeolithic is marked by new stone technology in tool-making and the appearance of highly developed cave art discovered at a number of sites but most famously at Lascaux in France and Altimira in Spain. There is also noteworthy evidence of calendrical notation on bones during this era.
See also **Archaeoastronomy**; **Bronze Age**; **Iron Age**; **Neolithic**; **Rock Art**

PILGRIMAGE

Pilgrimage is seen by most of the great religions as one of the classic personal acts of spiritual devotion and cleansing. The essential aim of a pilgrimage was, and is, to visit a specific shrine or sacred complex important to the religious life of the pilgrim in order to 'witness things that are of benefit' (as the *Koran* puts it). In addition to being simply an act of devotion, a pilgrimage might also be undertaken to gain spiritual credit, to expiate sins or to seek healing or be offered for the repose of dead relatives. More simplistic – and perhaps slightly baser – motives can include pleading for greater prosperity and good luck, not to mention taking the opportunity to 'get away from it all'.

The structure of the traditional pilgrimage was more complex than just going to a shrine. There would be sacred sites *en route*, and there would be the arduous act of travelling, often to remote and strange locations. In addition the act of pilgrimage was one of liminality, in that the pilgrim left the routine of normal life and while on the pilgrimage was neither here nor there, 'betwixt and between' a normal state of being. Because they were outside the normal social structure, pilgrims could strike up friendships with one another across social class, and a sense of comradeship –

what anthropologist Victor Turner called *communitas* – was a marked feature of pilgrimage.

Pilgrimages could take days, weeks, months, even years, and would in many cases be the peak experience of a person's life, dreamed about, waited for, saved up for – a great 'holiday of the soul', to use the phrase of the editor of the journal *Resurgence*, Satish Kumar. The thrust of perception and expectation was different from that in mundane life; the marvellous, the magical and the spiritual were in the forefront of the traveller's mind. The 'set and setting' was distinctly different for the lay person when on a pilgrimage compared with their everyday life. Pilgrimage was a physical act that moved the person out of the normal cultural domain and into nature, out of the mundane routine to conditions that exposed the mind to the possibility of new sensibilities, perhaps even to the extent that visionary experience might be provoked. In his *Placeways* (1988), Victor Walter remarks that the sacred places that formed the destinations of pilgrimage journeys had to be able 'to absorb varieties of interpretation ... capable of accommodating diverse meanings and practices'.

Pilgrimage has occurred within many diverse cultures. In Ireland, the tradition of the *turus*, the journey or pilgrimage, is of considerable antiquity. For example, archaeologists have uncovered physical evidence of a very early Christian pilgrimage centred on Brandon Mountain near the end of the Dingle peninsula, which extends into the Atlantic from southwest Ireland – a typically liminal place, at the edge of the ancient world. This pilgrimage was almost certainly based on earlier pagan practice, for Brandon Mountain seems to have been sacred to Lug, the god of light to the pagan **Celts**, and was a site used for Lughnassadh harvest festivities. Parts of a path known as the Saint's Road lead up towards the peak from the south coast of the peninsula and form one of two pilgrimage routes ascending the mountain. On the way are features that give an insight into aspects of the pilgrimage. These include occasional stone pillars and natural rocks carved with leaf-like crosses and archaic **ogham** script. One of these scripts says simply 'Colman the pilgrim'. Next to the marked boulders are small hollowed-out stones known as *bullauns*. The water that collected in them would have been considered holy, and passing pilgrims would have collected it for healing purposes.

Also on the Saint's Road is the now-ruined twelfth-century church at Kilmalkedar, in the grounds of which is a stone carved with markings that have been interpreted as a sundial for telling pilgrims the hours of the day for their prayers. At this site there is also a drystone oratory, a most ancient design of cell or religious refuge in the shape of an

Imhotep's stepped pyramid at Saqqara in Egypt.

astronomical skills on the part of its builders, but also the role of heavenly bodies in ancient Egyptian cosmology and temple-building practice is well known. The internal passages and shafts of the Great Pyramid have come under particular scrutiny in an astronomical context. The nineteenth-century astronomer-antiquarian Richard Proctor pointed out that the Grand Gallery leading up to the King's Chamber was aligned with the local celestial meridian and its opening (which points southwards) could have been used to time the transit of the stars, had the pyramid ever been open (there is some speculation that it may have been open for some time before the structure was fully closed in).

More interestingly, it was noted in 1964 by the Egyptologist-astronomer team of Professor Alexander Badawy and Dr Virginia Trimble that the so-called 'ventilation shafts' connected to the King's Chamber may have considerable astronomical and cosmological significance. There are two of these shafts, opening respectively in the north and south walls of the King's Chamber, and leading all the way through the surrounding mass of the pyramid to the outside. They have a section 9in (23cm) square and Badawy pointed out that these could hardly have functioned as air tubes for the chamber, and in any case no other Egyptian tombs were known to be ventilated. (Few archaeologists now put much credence on an air-shaft explanation for these features.) What Badawy and Trimble did find, though, was that the north shaft aligned to the star Thuban in its uppermost arc in the sky, while the southern shaft aligned well for transiting the sky where the three prominent stars forming the 'belt' of the constellation of Orion would have passed in 2700–2600 BC. According to the Pyramid Texts (engraved prayers found inside Fifth and Sixth Dynasty pyramids

Egyptians had excellent, tempered copper tools to shape and finish stone and, along with chisels and wedges, to quarry it. Hodges went back to the account of the ancient Greek historian Herodotus, who was told by the Egyptians over 2000 years ago that the blocks making up the Great Pyramid had been lifted by unspecified mechanical means from one tier to another and that the structure had been completed in 20 years. Hodges knew the ancient Eyptians did not have pulleys but realized that until the final casing stones were put in place the Great Pyramid was, in effect, a stepped pyramid consisting of hundreds of tiers. He was able to show that these could themselves have been used rather than ramps and scaffolding as the building progressed upwards. He demonstrated in both theory and practice that small teams could quite easily have raised the coarse blocks by means of long levers (apparently also depicted in the Djehutihotep illustration) and packing from one level to another, and could also have manipulated the stones horizontally with precision. Keable confirmed this and refined Hodges's theory. He found working a lever 'to be a pleasure' and that 100 sets of timber levers would have been sufficient for the job. Careful calculations showed that a few thousand skilled workers could have done the job in 17 years, working year-round. The remaining years would have been used for fitting and smoothing the casing blocks (chippings from this process have been found around the Great Pyramid).

It is only to be expected that the Great Pyramid has been studied for possible astronomical alignments, for not only is it accurately aligned to the compass points, thereby indicating

The Great Pyramid at Giza. Appearing so perfect at a distance, it can be seen at close range to be made up of tiers of coarse blocks of stone. For scale, note the car at lower left.

15 miles (24km) from the Great Pyramid), Thuban was the equivalent of our pole star for the Egyptians of the time (Polaris did not mark the pole for them as it does now for us due to precession, the Earth's slow axial 'wobble'), and was one of the circumpolar stars that never set. It was to these Imperishable Stars that the pharaoh's spirit journeyed after death, there to 'regulate the night' and 'send the hours on the way'. The pharaoh's spirit also made a celestial trip to Orion, which to the ancient Egyptians symbolized Osiris and the great cycle of birth, life, death and resurrection. Here the pharaoh, in the company of Osiris, was to maintain the round of the seasons. Badawy and Trimble therefore seriously raised the possibility that the shafts leading from the King's Chamber were made to allow the pharaoh's soul to travel to the heavens to perform its post-mortem duties.

A new twist has been given to this idea by writer Robert Bauval, who used an astronomical computer program to be able to claim that five of the seven Fourth Dynasty pyramids on the Giza plateau – the Great Pyramid, Abu Roash, the Pyramid of Chephren, the Pyramid of Menkare and Zawiyet El-Aryan – were laid out on the ground relative to one another in replication of the pattern of the stars forming the Orion constellation. Their configuration symbolically hid Osiris in the land, thereby bringing the god to Earth. Bauval calculated that the south shaft was specifically targeted on Zita Orionis in the belt of Orion and that the Great Pyramid represented that star in the 'constellation map' formed by the

The pyramids of Chephren (Khafre) and Menkare, companions of the Great Pyramid at Giza, Egypt.

pyramids on the ground. Bauval found that the positions of the other two Fourth Dynasty pyramids on the plateau, the Red Pyramid and the Bent Pyramid, related to the stars Epsilon Tauri and Aldebaran representing Set, the murderous brother of Osiris, in Egyptian skylore. In this overall scheme, according to Bauval, the Nile represented the course of the Milky Way in the heavens. Furthermore, he worked out that a shaft leading from the Queen's Chamber in the Great Pyramid pointed to Sirius, identified in the ancient Egyptian mind with Isis, wife of Osiris. Critics have argued, however, that Bauval's ideas work only because he has ignored pyramids that do not support his scheme. (In later work, where Bauval has teamed up with the journalist Graham Hancock to speculate about supposed associations between the Egyptian pyramids and the Sphinx with topics like a lost super-civilization, prophecies and supposed pyramidical features on Mars, criticism has become more audible.)

In the end, there can be only two things certain about the Giza features – more of archaeological value is waiting to be learned about them and they will continue to exercise the imaginations of those who become awestruck by them. The challenge is to be able to sort the one from the other.
See also **Archaeoastronomy; Aztecs; Cahokia; Chichén Itzá; Geometry (Sacred); Olmec; Ziggurat**

A classic 'cup and ring' type of rock art marking. Tentatively dated to the Bronze Age, such markings are found on rock faces and boulders in various parts of the British Isles and elsewhere in western Europe. Some archaeologists are mapping the locations of these petroglyphs in an attempt to gain some understanding of their meaning or function.

This trance-shamanism revolution in the interpretation of rock art has now reached into studies of western European Neolithic rock markings. A classic case seems to be that of **Gavrinis** in Brittany. The strange fingerprint-like whorls and clustered lines on the interior of this so-called passage grave are now seen by some archaeologists as being effectively the psychedelic signatures of Neolithic people in altered mind states.

Further evidence for a trance basis to the rock art of Neolithic chambers in Europe has been provided by

Cambridge archaeologist Jeremy Dronfield. He has conducted computer-aided analyses of pattern shapes in the rock art of 12 Irish passage tombs and compared these with similar patterns drawn by modern Westerners and traditional people experiencing entoptic imagery resulting from the administration of hallucinogens. Dronfield was able to distinguish results from different hallucinogens. He went further than this, however, and included entoptic patterns drawn by modern Western subjects as a result of controlled electrical stimulation of the eyes. While this method would not have been available to the megalith builders, it happens to mimic closely the effect of facing a powerful light source such as the sun with eyes closed while creating a strobing effect by clapping hands, waving fingers or other actions between the eyelids and the light source. In addition, Dronfield took account of distinctive types of entoptic imagery produced in pathological conditions, such as migraine and forms of epilepsy. All these were compared with a randomly generated control sample of patterns. This scientific analysis showed no significant matching between Neolithic tomb art and the random control set, as expected, and cannabis imagery did not match either. Interestingly, there was matching in some sites with entoptic imagery produced by migraine and epilepsy. As these conditions tend to occur in genetically related groups, especially in the maternal line, Dronfield implies that such conditions, seen as disabilities by our culture, might have been a prized ability in a shamanic society. Hallucinogens such as psilocybin (in 'magic mushrooms') showed correlations with the megalithic art in about half the sites in the test sample. But the most prevailing correlation was between the rock art and light-flicker entoptics. This, of course, has great significance, as most of the chambered mounds were astronomically oriented and so had searchlight-like beams of sunlight directed down their passages at key calendrical points in the year.

It could also be the case that trance experiences were source elements in the cave art of the Upper Palaeolithic era. At painted Palaeolithic caves such as Les Trois Frères, Niaux, La Mouthe, Lascaux and Altamira, among others, dots, zigzags and grids are ubiquitous, and it is not difficult to pick out possible entoptic form constants. Further, Palaeolithic rock art contains clear examples of both shamanic imagery and shamans themselves. A famous example is the so-called antlered sorcerer in the cave of Les Trois Frères in France, which is a classic therianthrope with a mixture of animal and human parts. At Lascaux there is the depiction of a man in a supine position wearing a bird mask, alongside a bird-headed stick, a type of artefact noted as being symbolic of shamanism in Eurasia even up to recent centuries. It may also be significant that the location of Palaeolithic rock art is in deeply subterranean, natural rock chambers where utmost darkness and silence prevails or, conversely, where reverberating drumming and chanting along with flickering flames would have provided unsurpassed conditions for producing trance states. In 1994 a remarkable Palaeolithic painted cave, Chauvet, was discovered in the Ardèche region of France. This contained a block of stone on which a bear skull had been deliberately placed perhaps 25,000-30,000 years ago. It looked like an altar of some kind, and bear cults are known indicators of archaic shamanism.

See also **Acoustics; Atlantis; Entoptic Patterns; Shamanic Landscapes**

Ancient rock art in Boca Negro Canyon, New Mexico. Those researchers who feel that some rock art is based on ritual hallucinations would interpret this snake-like zigzag marking as a 'construal-iconic' image, referring to flickering mental patterns seen in trance states that are halfway between simple abstract, geometrical shapes and representational forms.

RUNES

These are letters of the earliest Germanic alphabet, used by north Europeans and Scandinavians from about the third century AD. The term 'rune' comes from a root meaning 'secret' and still echoes in the modern German verb *raunen*, 'to whisper'. Runes were designed to be carved rather than written, and are found engraved into wooden articles like the Norse magic wand or rune-staff, on metals (especially swords and other weaponry), on tombstones, and on jewellery.

Runes were magical symbols as well as an alphabet, used for spells, charms and **divination**. Myth has it that the god Odin hung on the World Tree, **Yggdrasil**, for nine days and nights in order to gain the knowledge of the runes. Although the occult use of the runes could be practised by a person of any religious background or none, rune magic was suppressed by the Church as it was strongly associated in the Christian mind with pagan practices.

The use of the runes fed the occult leanings of German nationalists and Nazis in twentieth-century Germany, and they have become a popular form of divinatory device for today's neopagans, New Agers and others.

See also **Ogham; Paganism; Simulacra**

has been widely and repeatedly described in the New Age literature and beyond for decades. At that level it certainly does exist, and there is no harm in that; the danger arises in there being a crucial intellectual failure or sheer lack of will to distinguish a pet fantasy, however charming and attractive, from an actuality concerning the past. Anyone who is not a committed believer is hard pressed to consider the St Michael Line as anything other than an idea, for if that were not the case, how could it shift its physical position? For example, the change from the old to the new model of the line occasioned a northward shift of 3 miles (5km) or more in western Cornwall. Stripped of the romantic claims surrounding it, even the most benevolent sceptic is obliged to see the St Michael Line as an artefact of the modern mind rather than the product of ancient intent. Wilfully to blur this distinction is a kind of modern intellectual imperialism that, in the end, can advance no genuine understanding about the thinking, beliefs and practices of pre-industrial and prehistoric societies that inhabited the landscapes of southern England long before our culture was able to develop maps and rulers.

SEIDHR

This was a form of **trance divination** practised by women in Scandinavia. The *seidhonka* (or *volva* or *spakona*) would travel around farmsteads and hamlets predicting the future. The seidhonka's ritual costume consisted of a blue cloak, jewels and a headpiece of black lamb with white catskins. She carried a staff and conducted her divination from a high platform while seated on a cushion of chicken feathers. The woman would go into an ecstatic trance, so the practice was shamanic.

The goddess Freya was said to be the mistress and first teacher of seidhr. Freya was closely associated with Frigg, wife of Odin, in Norse myth, and the two are generally considered to be the same mythological element, with Frigg emphasizing the maternal principle, and Freya fertility. Freya's carriage was pulled by cats, and she has been depicted in the cloak of a seidhonka flying on the back of a large striped cat. This is just one example

Drawing of the mural in Schleswig Cathedral showing Frigg on a broomstick, recently declared a forgery.

of 'flight' imagery associated with Freya and Frigg, which is a reference to the ecstatic, soul-flight experience at the heart of all shamanic practice. Freya also owned a magic feather garment, which enabled her to fly, and she taught Odin to fly, which he was able to do after donning a garment made of falcon feathers.

See also **Shaman**; **Shamanic Landscapes**; **World Navel**; **Yggdrasil**

SHAMAN

Shamanism was (and is) a religious phenomenon of primarily tribal societies, and the shaman was the person who acted as an intermediary between the tribe and the otherworlds of spirits. A shaman would heal sick tribal members by locating their lost souls, perhaps entering the otherworld to reclaim them, or by deflecting bad spirits and invisible influences. There was also a variety of other reasons for entering the spirit realms, such as accompanying the souls of dying people or seeking information from the spirits or ancestors. Another role for the shaman is to protect the tribe from the malevolent actions of rival shamans in other tribes, so the shaman must be proficient in using sorcery as both a defensive and an offensive tool: shamanic 'wars' were more or less regular facts of life for shamanic peoples.

A Siberian shaman wearing antlers and drumming himself into a trance state. (*Nicolas Witsen, 1705*)

A rare photograph of a Hmong shaman in northern Thailand, entering trance. He had been asked to heal a sick man. The shaman set up a visual device on a wall of the patient's home to represent a portal through which the shaman's spirit could fly. He then arranged a small altar beneath the portal device, placed a mask over his face and sat on a stool facing towards the altar. This picture shows his outlines somewhat blurred because he is rocking rapidly back and forth to induce a trance in which he can fly through the magic portal to the spirit world in order to rescue the sick man's soul. (*Chris Ashton*)

The shaman employed a wide range of methods to produce the **trance** states necessary for the ecstatic or soul-flight condition that is at the core of shamanism – what we nowadays call the out-of-body experience. These 'techniques of ecstasy' (to use Mircea Eliade's term) can include drumming, dancing, chanting, fasting, sensory deprivation, hyperventilation and the ingestion of hallucinogenic substances. Quite often, there is a mix of such methods. In addition, the shaman usually tends to be a person who by nature can shift easily into other mental realities (who is particularly prone to dissociative states, to use modern terminology). This

tendency, aided and abetted by trance-inducing techniques, was often a consequence of what we would consider to be a prevailing medical or psychological condition, or of some trauma in childhood or in initiation. The shaman's social position could vary dramatically in different societies: in some tribes he could be a key figure, even a leader, while in others he was a shadowy, feared liminal figure, almost an outcast, living on the edges of the main group.

Strictly speaking, the term shamanism applies only to its occurrence among Siberian and Central Asian tribes, for it derives from the Tungus word *saman* (though there are some suggestions that the word is foreign even to that language), but it is used widely nowadays in both popular and academic literature to describe healers and spiritual practitioners world-wide who employ ecstatic trance as part of their proceedings (it does not follow, therefore, that all witch doctors, medicine men or sorcerers are necessarily shamans). Shamanism arose out of animism and is, therefore, one of the oldest and most universal expressions of human spiritual sensibility. Although it was absorbed into larger and more organized religions in many parts of the world, it still survives today in some tribal societies.

See also **Druids**; **Hallucinogens**; **Liminality**; **Nazca Lines**; **Rock Art**; **Shamanic Landscapes**; **World Navel**

SHAMANIC LANDSCAPES

This term was first coined by myself to designate unusual and poorly understood ancient ritual landscapes and ceremonial features in the Americas that seem to have developed out of pre-Columbian shamanic traditions. Such landscapes contain distinctive ground markings or figures, which fall into three basic categories: terrestrial effigies or 'geoglyphs' abstract geometric and meander linear patterns, and straight-line markings and tracks. Locations such as the **Nazca lines** contain examples of all three categories, but they can also occur separately and in isolation. The features are constructed in various ways depending on terrain and local conditions: petroforms (outlines in small rocks and boulders); intaglios (etchings or engravings into desert surfaces) and earthwork structures. In complex and hierarchical prehistoric Native American cultures, like that of the **Maya**, the straight-line markings sometimes developed into more formalized and ceremonial engineered structures, such as roads and causeways.

The terrestrial effigies are found on prehistoric landscapes in various locations in the Americas, a classic example being the **effigy mounds** of Iowa and other north midwestern

Serpent Mound, Adams County, Ohio. The earthen effigy is ¼ mile (0.5km) long and is between 1500 and 2000 years old. It may relate as much to the Adena Indians as to those of Hopewell. (Ohio Historical Society)

American states – the complex and sophisticated geometric earthworks of the **Hopewell** culture in Ohio, for instance. These ancient geoglyphs take many forms, depicting animals, human beings, and strange creatures that are half-human, half-animal, as well as geometric-shaped features. An example of a giant human effigy can be found in the Gila River area of southwest Arizona. Known as Ha-ak Va-ak ('Ha-ak Lying'), the figure is an 'intaglio' creation, essentially formed by a scraped line 18in (0.5m) wide and dozens of yards (metres) long. The ancient image relates to a creation myth and is still a shrine to the Pima Indians. Other earth figures along the Colorado River valley, which divides the southern parts of California and Arizona, include giant depictions of humans, rattlesnakes, lizards and mountain lions. Some of the figures are thought to be up to 3000 years old and may have lain on a **pilgrimage** route of the Yuman Indians.

But these southern extremities of Arizona and California are by no means the only places in the Americas where geoglyphs occur. In more northerly reaches of the Americas similar ground figures are to be found, though in these cases small rocks have been carefully placed to mark out figures. One of the most important of these northern sites is in Whiteshell Park, Manitoba, Canada. In the last Ice Age glaciers here scraped bare expanses of granite bedrock, which form the surfaces on which these petroforms have been laid. Saskatchewan, Alberta and British Columbia also

boast examples of animal and human petroforms, and south of the Canadian border, in Montana, petroform effigies of three-legged anthropomorphs occur on the Blackfoot Indian reservation. Humanoid and animal figures outlined in a similar way are found in various locations in South Dakota. Even as far south as Kansas, there is the Stone Man of Penokee, a giant figure with pronounced ears and phallus, outlined with small stones. In South America, there are numerous geoglyph locations in the Andes, notably the Nazca lines, as already mentioned. Here, dozens of animal, insect and other images are scattered among the straight lines and may possibly be older than them. One of the most dramatic of South American geoglyphs, however, is to be found at the **Olmec** site of San Lorenzo; this complex is located on a plateau that the Olmecs physically modified with artificial ridges and appendages to form a gigantic terrestrial image of a flying bird.

In addition to creating giant terrestrial effigies, the prehistoric American Indians marked out strange geometric patterns, enclosures, meanders and other curvilinear markings. Such ancient patterns can be found in various parts of southern California, on the shimmering-hot floor of Death Valley and nearby arid valleys, where serpentine lines of stones extend for hundreds of feet, connecting cell-like enclosures. Although these look like casual arrangements of stone, they have been found to contain features suggesting that they were planned constructions. The Manitoba petroforms also contain abstract, geometric patterns.

A giant human form etched on the desert near Blythe, California, in pre-Columbian times. (Imperial Valley College Museum)

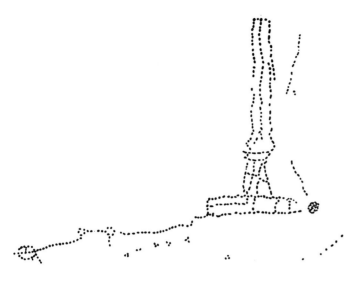

A plan of one of many curious designs on the floor of Death Valley (north at top). It extends over 200ft (62m) east to west and is constructed from fairly small rocks and cobbles placed on or embedded into the desert surface. The feature seems to have been developed over a long period of time, with the east–west line being one of the older elements. Shaman's hearths have been identified amid some of the designs in this region. (*From* Spirits of the Earth, *Jay von Werlhof/Imperial Valley College Museum*)

A huge humanoid figure marked on pampa slopes near Nazca, Peru. (*Peruvian Embassy, London*)

The third category of shamanic landscape characteristics are straight-line markings and other direct linear features, and these are of special interest to those **ley** researchers seeking genuine, archaeological features to study. Though they should not be taken out of context with the other two categories of ground markings already described, there is no doubt that the straight lines present a particularly challenging enigma. The Nazca lines are, again, the classic example of such features, but there are many others throughout the Americas, such as those mentioned in the entries on **Anasazi, Chaco Canyon, Chichén Itzá, Cuzco, Hopewell Indians** and the **Maya**. And there are many more examples than these of prehistoric straight, linear features in the Americas.

In the California Sierras, the Miwok Indians left behind the remains of tracks that ran straight over ridge and valley without detours. In Mexico 100 miles (160km) of ancient roads extend around the archaeological site of La Quemada in Zacatecas. Dated to AD 700–800, these are masonry structures built on the surface of the ground, forming causeways: two parallel rows of stone were laid out in a straight line, and the area between was filled with rubble and capped with flagstones. The first detailed written descriptions of the roads were made by an English mining engineer, G.F. Lyon, in 1828. He described perfectly straight roads, including one that had one end at the foot of a cliff beneath a cave and the other at an artificial mound. Similar straight causeway features occur in at least five other areas of Mexico, in addition to the Mayan *sacbeob* to be found in many parts of the Yucatán and Central America. Other straight roads, built by other cultures for carrying the dead, have been detected by NASA high-tech aerial photography running through the mountainous rainforest of Costa Rica. The Sierra Nevada de Santa Marta on the northern coast of Colombia is the territory of the Kogi Indians, and archaeologists have so far found about 200 miles (320km) of ancient paved roads or paths there. The Kogi consider the roads to have been built by the ancestors and therefore to be sacred; their traditions place them under a spiritual obligation to maintain and walk the roads.

In the Andes region of South America we encounter a number of different 'roads', desert lines and alignments in addition to the Nazca lines. Lines also criss-cross the altiplano of western Bolivia. These can reach lengths of 20 miles (32km), considerably longer than any found at Nazca. French anthropologist Alfred Métraux came across them in the 1930s, when he investigated earthen shrines set out in a straight row from a small village and found them to be standing on a pathway that was 'absolutely straight, regardless of

A colour infrared aerial image of the course of a Maya causeway or *sacbe* entering the archaeological site of El Mirador in the northern Peten, Guatemala. (*NASA*)

the irregularities of the ground'. The lines are, in the main, simply ways cut through the bushes, and cleared of any debris. Consequently they can easily grow back into the landscape. The shrines along them were of various kinds – Christianized adobe structures, piles of rocks, places where lightning had struck and similar sanctified spots. There were also churches standing on some of the lines, as at the community of Sajama, for instance.

Prehistoric straight roads are now also known to exist in the lowland, rainforest parts of South America, east of the Andes. Researchers know of over 900 miles (1440km) of ancient causeways in the Llanos de Mojos, a savanna in the upper Amazon region of northeastern Bolivia. Archaeologists have remarked that many are 'unusually straight', despite the difficulties of building them that way in the forest and savanna environment. It has further been observed that the causeways occur in dry, drained ground and not just in wetlands, and thus they take on other significance than can be explained merely by providing dry transport across swamp country.

Elsewhere, archaeological knowledge of prehistoric roads is still sketchy. Some have been seen leading out from the eastern Andes to the edge of the tropical lowlands, but little is known about them and they have not even been properly mapped. There are rumours of straight roads and causeways in the Mato Grosso of western Brazil, and causeways connected with artifical mounds have been given cursory study in the Orinoco Llanos of Venezuela.

The meaning of these shamanic landscapes is yet to be understood fully, but the pieces are slowly coming together. First, are they shamanic at all? The presence of stone vision questing rings and the ancient traditions of the local Indians suggest that the intaglios of Arizona and California, for instance, are associated with shamanism. This is further supported by the fact than many of the ground figures occur near prehistoric **rock art** sites containing similar, if smaller, imagery. These locations were where shamans interacted with the spirit world. The figures of animals and anthropo-morphs may in some cases have represented mythic person-alities and served general tribal ceremonial purposes, but many may have depicted spirits and shamanic 'familiars' or power animals.

Along with the meanders and complex enclosures, there are circular stone settings, thought to have been used by shamans as 'rings of power' for their seances or **vision quests**, suggesting the shamanic associations of these curious ground figures. Some markings may have been dance grounds. Ethnological evidence indicates that at least some of the meandering lines in the American southwest were part of a magical geography and represented symbolic 'mountain ranges' laid out by tribal shamans to block the influence of neighbouring hostile sorcerers and shamans.

Virtually all the known straight-line features occur in the territories of peoples known to have practised shamanism – usually based on sacred **hallucinogens** – and were built contemporaneously with the height of those cultures, so they must presumably, therefore, be inherently shamanic. The more engineered, causeway-type straight ways have been considered as military and trade routes by those favouring conservative archaeological opinion, but this view is increas-ingly finding less favour with informed investigators. Although everyone agrees that some of these features served multi-functional roles, it is their ceremonial and ritual aspects that require the greatest attention. Also, the simpler desert lines, like those at Nazca, were clearly religious in some way, not trade routes or military roads.

It is the unusual, almost obsessive *straightness* of all the pre-Columbian 'roads' and 'lines' that begs most questions. The late John Hyslop of the Museum of Natural History in New York, a veteran of Inca roads research, commented that roads constructed in extraordinary ways may reflect ritual or symbolic concerns. He warned Western interpreters not to project their own cultural prejudices and to be prepared to accept that prehistoric Native American roads had meanings and conceptual uses not found in our present-day idea of roads. He was convinced that attempts to interpret all aspects of prehistoric roads in purely materialistic terms were

A Kogi Indian *mama* or shaman, Colombia. These people may hold key information regarding the meaning of the mystery roads and lines of the ancient Americas. (*The Hutchison Library*)

form from **entoptic patterns** experienced in shamanic trance (as is now argued for some Native American rock art imagery), and the fact that they seem to have been conceptualized to be seen from above related to the aerial journey or out-of-body spirit flight of the **shaman**. (We do not need to believe that literally happened, but if the makers of the lines did so, then that is all that matters.) The geoglyphs could have been signs of power to intimidate the flying spirits of enemy shamans, while the lines, like the 'tunnel' entoptic pattern often reported today in near-death experiences, might have represented spirit trajectories or routes – literally a spirit geography. This would only have been the esoteric and original association with the form, of course, and it would have been presented in exoteric religious ways to ordinary tribal members. The lines or paths would become pilgrimage ways, ceremonial routes and, in later hierarchical Native American cultures, such as that of the Maya, roads for elite royal, military and trade purposes while still embodying their aura of sanctity.

This is not mere supposition. In 1990 Alan Ereira filmed the remote Kogi Indians for BBC television. The Kogi are among the least acculturated of surviving Native American tribes with strongly surviving pre-Columbian traits. They are ruled by a shamanic theocracy. These shamans or *mamas* ('enlightened ones') explained to Ereira that their roads held spiritual importance for them, and that the Earth Mother had instructed them that the roads must be often walked (some similar idea to this would explain the tracks formed by ancient feet inside some of the Nazca lines). Ereira was shown a stone road that was straight and that the *mamas* said was the trace of a spirit path in the otherworld, what they call *aluna*. They claim that such spirit routes could be 'seen' by them even where they were not marked by physical roads. The Kogi have a standing stone criss-crossed with straight lines, said to be a map of the spirit paths in the Kogi territory. Only some of these had physical 'traces' on the ground.

This ethnological revelation came at a time when some earth mysteries researchers were increasingly turning their attention to the Native American lines and roads. I myself had independently come to similar conclusions to Dobkin de Rios, albeit more than a decade after her, and a 'school' of earth mysteries enthusiasts began to emerge that started exploring a 'spirit line' approach to ancient straight landscape markings. These people have dismissed both the Alfred Watkins idea of leys as old traders' routes and New Age beliefs about 'leylines' being channels of **energy**; instead, they are asking if the all-pervading element of straightness in the pre-Columbian ground markings came in shamanic baggage brought over the Beringia land bridge many

bound to fail. Perhaps Hosteen Beyal, a Navajo elder, put it most succinctly – if enigmatically – when he told archaeologist Neil Judd in the 1920s that the Chaco roads may look like roads but were not roads.

While there are enough fragments of ethnology to give us a faint understanding of what the geoglyphs and patterns might have meant to their makers, the straight lines and roads remain a deep mystery. If they were shamanic, as seems certain, why the obsession with straightness? This is their fundamental characteristic, found in those belonging to Native American societies widely separated in both time and space. It is unlikely that their cultural context remained constant, but their essential *form* clearly did; it suggests some physiological or neurophysiological factor common to all peoples of ancient America.

Anthropologist Marlene Dobkin de Rios of the University of California suggested in 1977 that the lines, however they were later developed and formalized, derived their original thousands of years ago by the palaeo-Indians. If this were true, could there be similar landscape traces in the Old World? This highly contentious part of the current earth mysteries story is described in greater depth in the **Leys/Leylines** entry.

See also **Chavín de Huantar**; **Death Roads**; **Mythic Geography**; **Spirit Traps**; **Spirit Ways**; **Trance**

SIBYLS

These were the divinely inspired prophetesses of Classical antiquity who travelled and uttered in ancient Asia Minor, Egypt and parts of Europe, especially Greece. They were the mouthpieces of the gods – the word 'sibyl' is a composite Greek noun apparently deriving from the words for 'god' and 'advice'. Some sibyls boasted of being related or married to certain gods, and claimed incredible longevity. One of the more famous sibyls is probably the Sibyl of Cumae in southern Italy, who uttered in a hewn-out cave and guided Aeneas through the underworld. A sibyl would claim that a god (identified by the Hellenic Greeks as Apollo) spoke through her, but was not possessed: as the scholar of sibylline prophecy H.W. Parke put it, a sibyl was a clairvoyant rather than a medium.

The Rock of the Sibyl at Delphi, Greece. It is said that the sibyl Herophile, who claimed she was half-mortal, half-divine, stood on this rock and chanted her prophetic verses. The Delphic sibyl is not to be confused with the prophetesses of the Temple of Apollo at this site.

Sibyls used elliptical or ambiguous terminology in hexameter verses, rather than uttering direct prophetic statements, as this was considered to be a suitable way for the gods to address mortals (and, the cynic might add, gave the sibyl more latitude in which to 'score' with her predictions). Sibyls did not act as **oracles**, in that they did not respond to specific questions or tell the future for individuals but dealt more generally with major events, such as wars and disasters. These utterances were circulated by the *chresmologoi*, the 'tellers of oracles' who recycled sibylline and other oracular pronouncements for the general populace – and probably tampered with some of them. The developed form of sibylline prophecy, containing earlier material, was assembled in the *Oracular Sibyllina* by a Byzantine scholar in the sixth century AD, but there is evidence that pagan scholars were not familiar with the prophecies in this form.

Although they were usually peripatetic, sibyls tended nevertheless to be associated with places, although it seems that certain localities would claim the utterences of different prophetesses under one name. A sibyl designated as of a specific place, therefore, may have been a gloss for several prophetesses who visited the locality. The fourth-century writer Lactantius felt able to ascribe only the work of the Erythraean Sibyl to an individual prophetess, the other works being 'mixed up', the result of multiple authorship. Some sibyls were literary devices invented by later writers.

It is uncertain how far back in time the sibylline tradition reached, but there is evidence of sibyl-like oracles in the Syria of *c*.700 BC.

See also **Bicameral Mind**; **Delphi**; **Divination**

SIMULACRA

A simulacrum is something that coincidentally looks like something else, such as the design on the wings of a butterfly looking like eyes or the texture of bark on a tree trunk conjuring the appearance of a person's face. Castles in the clouds. This somewhat dreamy way of perception was the subject of a fascinating book, *Simulacra* (1979), by John Michell. It has relevance to earth mysteries concerns because it was a way of looking that seems to have been fostered by ancient and traditional peoples.

Just how relevant to ancient studies simulacra can be became apparent in a dramatic way to Egyptologist Anthony Donohue in 1991, while he was studying the New Kingdom temple of Queen Hatshepsut at Deir el-Bahri near the Valley of the Kings. This has long been admired as one of the great achievements of ancient Egyptian temple architecture and is

The highly eroded natural statue group in the cliff-face behind the temple of Hatshepsut in Egypt. The head of the pharaoh, with head-dress and ceremonial beard, can be made out, as can the cobra rearing above. (*N. Griffiths, courtesy of V.A. Donohue*)

angles looks strikingly like a man with his arms raised, as if tied to the rock. This phenomenon has long been noted, and there has been debate that it represents Odin hanging on the World Tree or Christ on the Cross. Recent technical examination has in this case apparently indicated that this natural simulacrum was worked with tools to enhance its anthropomorphic appearance.

Traditional peoples often saw gods, goddesses and heroes in the lie of the land. The shapes of mountains, already associated in ancient times with spirits and the abode, or seat, of the Earth Mother **Goddess**, the Mountain Woman, were particularly important elements in this mythic, 'dreamscape' perception of the topography. One example, which has roots at least 4000 thousand years old, is to be found at Callanish, a group of remarkable stone circles on the Isle of Lewis off

focused on a column of rock that obtrudes from the cliff-face and reaches to the full height of the cliffs behind the temple. It appears as a human form wearing the headdress and beard of kingship. Behind this figure rises a cobra, symbol of kingship in ancient Egypt, which has a distended hood. This colossal figure group, hundreds of feet high, is heavily eroded but still discernible for those who have the eyes to see. It awaits further technical investigation to determine whether or not this is a case of untouched simulacra or of suggestive natural features being enhanced by human art. The implications are intriguing. In either case there had to be human recognition of the forms in the column, which means that people must have looked at the natural topography for symbolic meaning. Either they projected into the natural forms an expression of their own religious ideas, or, more startlingly, the western mountain with its pyramidical peak and goddess column may have promoted royal and religious iconography in the minds of the Egyptians. Donohue has identified other temple locations along the Nile that also incorporate such rock-face simulacra.

Another simulacrum exists in a quite different context at the **Externsteine** rocks in Germany. On one of the rock columns there is an overhanging segment that from certain

The giant figure in the rock at the Externsteine, Germany. Odin or Christ? Note the hole in the figure's side – was this a way of Christianizing the natural effigy, the simulacrum, so as to represent Christ's spear wound during the crucifixion?

Scotland's west coast. The Callanish stones seem to have been associated with the observation of the moon. At their latitude during the major standstill period every 18.61 years in the long and complex lunar cycle, the moon appears to rise out of the Pairc Hills, which from the area of the Callanish stones resemble the form of a woman reclining on her back. Sometimes called the Sleeping Beauty, her Gaelic name is Cailleach na Mointeach, the Old Woman of the Moors, a pseudonym for the Hag or Earth Mother. She is well known to the present inhabitants of the Callanish area and was doubtless so to their distant ancestors.

Something similar happens at **Ballochroy** lower down the Scottish coast, when the sun appears to set into the Paps ('Breasts') of Jura. The symbolic importance of these breast-like mountains in prehistory has been further confirmed by an archaeological discovery in 1994 on the island of Islay, close to Jura. Geophysical investigation on the shores of Loch Finlaggan revealed the remains of an alignment of stones that oriented on a gap in the skyline that perfectly frames the two main, breast-like peaks of the Paps of Jura. Near Killarney in Ireland are two peaks that similarly stand out distinctly from the hill country around them and are profoundly breast-like in their symmetry and roundness, an impression enhanced by teat-like cairns on their summits. They are known as the Paps of Anu. Anu was the mythical mother of the last generation of gods who ruled the Earth, the Tuatha De Danaan. Celtic scholar Anne Ross has written that the hills personify the powers of the goddess embedded in the land.

Seeing mythic beings in mountains was a cross-cultural phenomenon in the ancient world. In ancient Greece, for instance, twin-summit or cleft-peak mountains visible from temples like **Eleusis**, the Parthenon or the Cretan palace-

Mount Kerata rises above the cement works surrounding the Mystery temple of Eleusis, Greece. The mountain's name means horns, a reference to its split peak.

temple of Knossos were seen as representing the Earth Mother Goddess. Again, the evolved temple site of **Borobudur** in Java is so positioned that part of the Menoreh mountain range visible on the southern horizon as viewed from the top of the temple looks like the profile of a man on his back, with the nose, chin and lips clearly delineated. It has been local **folklore** since records began that this figure is Gunadharma, the original architect of the temple. In the Americas similar ancient **Dreamtime** visions are to be found within the topography. An example is the **Anasazi** site complex of **Hovenweep**, which looks out towards an isolated mountain ridge now known as the Sleeping Ute. It looks very much like a sleeping chieftain beneath his blanket, and the legend has it that he will awake at the time of greatest need. If this mountain has insinuated itself into Ute mythology, we need have no doubt that the Anasazi saw something very similar. The Australian Aborigines, too, saw Dreamtime beings in the topographical configurations of their landscapes.

To the ancient Dreamtime peoples of the world the physical environment could take on the texture and ambiguity of a dream; myth was reinforced by forms in the landscape. *See also* **Cognitive Archaeology**; **Mythic Geography**; **Songlines**

SITTING OUT

This was a practice of unknown antiquity that was conducted in Iceland, Scandinavia and northern Europe in the historical era. It involved the seer (a **shaman**-like practitioner of European tradition) entering a **trance** in order to summon

The Paps of Anu, Ireland.

spirits for **divination** or go on 'seers' journeys' – a clairvoyant exercise or perhaps a version of the ecstatic soul flight associated with shamanism. In Norway this tradition is recorded in the context of men sitting out on burial mounds in order to receive occult wisdom. In Iceland (and probably elsewhere in Britain and Europe) seers repaired to specific, isolated crossroads at certain dates such as New Year's Eve or the eve of St John's Day (24 June) in order to become entranced and to summon spirits from church cemeteries either lying on the roads meeting at the crossroads or else visible from there.

See also **Death Roads; Liminality; Shamanic Landscapes; Spirit Paths**

SONGLINES

During the timeless time of the *tjukuba* or **Dreamtime,** the tribal lore of the Australian Aborigines says that giant totemic beings travelled over the country, which in that mythic era was flat and featureless. In the course of their journeys they created the features of the landscape that now exists. They left their tracks across the surface of the world, and when the Dreaming came to an end they turned into rocks or entered the ground. Aborigines, for unknown generations, have re-traced the journeys of these Dreamtime ancestors. These routes are called *djalkiri* by the Yolngu of Arnhemland, a term often translated as 'footprints of the ancestors'. They are variously known by non-Aborigines as 'dream journey routes', 'dreaming tracks' and, probably most of all, as 'songlines', due to the success of Bruce Chatwin's *The Songlines* (1987), rather than for any special ethnological reason.

It was really the anthropologist and explorer C.P. Mountford who started to bring the phenomenon of dream journey routes into focus for non-Aborigines. In repeated travelling across the central regions of Australia, he noted that he kept encountering similar myths which he came to realize had a linear geographical distribution over large distances. Then, in 1960, he was led by elders of the Ngalia and Walbiri tribes along the 200-mile (320km) route of the dreaming track of Jarapiri, the Snake Man (a version of the Rainbow Serpent) and his companions. As Mountford recounts in *Winbaraku and the Myth of Jarapiri* (1968), his guides, the tribal elders, felt that the course of the dreaming track would be best preserved with him, as the normal succession of knowledge to the young men of the tribe was being disrupted by the influence of non-Aboriginal culture.

The birthplace or emergence point of Jarapiri was Winbaraku (Blanche Tower), a twin-peaked hill in the western Macdonnell Ranges. From there, the route stretched north through a string of sacred places such as a pile of stones where the spider Mamuboijunda appeared, caves that were the vulvas of the Nabanunga women, and a line of rocks that represented the track of Jarapiri and his party. At the rocky outcrop of Ngama, a rock shelter contains a huge painting of the snake Jarapiri. Mountford mapped the course of the dreaming track, and noted that a precise route was followed, apparently known to the Aborigines since time immemorial. At a certain point on the route, Mountford's Ngalia guides became uncertain as to the position of the next sacred site and the words of its associated chants. When he asked why this was so, he was told that the Ngalia 'line of songs' finished at Walutjara and that those dotted along the remainder of the totemic route belonged to the Walbiri tribe to the north. A boundary marked by myth and song.

Some of these dreaming tracks were followed by whole tribes, often as part of their seasonal, nomadic circuits over the outback, but they can also be followed individually by tribal members, giving rise to the 'walkabout', so misunderstood by non-Aborigines. Sometimes information on dreaming tracks previously unknown by a tribal group can be transmitted to a tribal member through the medium of a dream, and new rituals and songs are produced. The country an Aborigine traverses on a dream journey route is charged with meaning, so that ridges, water soaks, rocks, caves and other features are transformed from mere topography into a spiritual, **mythic geography**. Each significant place along a dreaming track would have its song, its dance, its ritual. There would also probably be secreted *churingas*, ritual objects of flattened stone, wood or bark. These would be covered in motifs, which would, in effect, be a map of their part of the Dreamtime route. A *churinga* also told the stories of the Dreamtime beings associated with the site and informed the initiated elder what songs and dances were associated with that spot.

The vast wilderness regions of Australia may look desolate to non-Aborigines, but in a mythic and therefore cognitive sense they are criss-crossed with these dreaming tracks. These gave much spatial information to the Aborigine, always linking one area with another, and they were integrated with the overall tribal lifeway. Anthropologist Helen Watson calls this collective system a 'knowledge network', with each tribal member being responsible for their part of it, and constantly requiring activity, singing, dancing and painting for its maintenance.

See also **Sacred Place; Shamanic Landscapes**

SPHINX

Sphinx is a Greek word said to derive from the Egyptian expression *shesep ankh*, 'living image'. A sphinx is a statue that represents a mythological creature having a lion's body with a human head. The effigy type is found among the ancient Syrians, Phoenicians and Greeks, but it originated in Egypt, where a crouching lion's body is often shown with a ram's head and was a solar symbol and mark of royal power. In Egyptian belief, the sphinx was the guardian of the gates of the underworld on the eastern and western horizons, while the lion was considered the guardian of sacred places from unrecorded antiquity in Egypt.

The largest and best known sphinx is that accompanying the **pyramids** at Giza. It is 240ft (74m) long and 66ft (20m) high, and was sculpted from a natural rock outcrop and had masonry additions. Dated by orthodox Egyptologists to *c*.2500 BC, the Sphinx's head is thought to depict the pharaoh Chephren, but this is by no means certain. The nose and beard were apparently shot off by a Mamaluke sultan who used the Sphinx as target practice for his artillery. The Sphinx was probably covered for much of its existence by shifting desert sands, and this doubtless explains why that great historian and traveller of antiquity, Herodotus, made no mention of it.

The Giza, Great or Giant Sphinx, as it is variously called, is virtually synonymous with enigma, for the strange effigy in the desert with the distant, inscrutable eastward gaze has tantalized human curiosity and imagination down the ages.

The Sphinx and Great Pyramid of Giza, Egypt.
(*Michael Howell/Images Colour Library*)

Even a mere thousand or so years after its construction, it was being identified with the god Harmachis, and it had its own cult. The Arabs regarded the Great Sphinx in some awe, referring to it as Abu Hol, 'Father of Terror' (although Egyptologist Selim Hassan argued that the term actually meant 'The Place of the God Hwl'). Jumping ahead to the early decades of the twentieth century, Edgar Cayce, the so-called 'sleeping prophet', foretold in his trances that the 'Hall of Records', detailing the history of **Atlantis**, would be found in a chamber beneath the Sphinx around the end of the millennium. At roughly the same period as Cayce's prophecies were becoming known, the ghost of Atlantis was also invoked by the French mathematician and symbolist (and maverick scholar), R.A. Schwaller de Lubicz, who was studying the remains of ancient Egypt and came to comment on the eroded appearance of the body of the Sphinx. It was generally assumed that this was due to the action of wind-blown sand, but Schwaller de Lubicz argued that it was due to water erosion. Geologically, Egypt is believed to have been subject to severe flooding due to the melting of the ice at the end of the last Ice Age, about 10,000–15,000 years ago. If the erosion on the body of the Sphinx were due to these waters, the implication is that the Sphinx had been produced 10,000 or more years ago by some lost high civilization.

Popular Egyptologist John Anthony West has long championed the idea that the Sphinx is older than the dates offered by orthodox scholarship, and he brought the work of Schwaller de Lubicz to wider attention. This helped to re-ignite the debate about the age of the Sphinx. A problem with the wind-driven sand explanation for the erosion on the Sphinx is that the effigy was covered by the desert for much of its existence, so protected. Another explanation for water erosion suggests that it was caused by groundwater rising through capillary action into the body of the Sphinx and reacting with the salts in the limestone. There have been arguments against this possibility, too, one of them being that the level of the water table may have been too low in Chephren's time for it to happen.

In 1989 American geologist Robert M. Schock joined forces with West to start exploring the matter further. Schock's subsequent on-site examinations have convinced him that the weathering on the Sphinx is indeed due to the action of water, specifically rainfall, which he infers was due to the moist climate of pre-dynastic Egypt. From studying a complex of other data, ranging from **folklore** to seismic surveys, Schock and West have concluded that the initial carving of the body of the Sphinx was begun in pre-dynastic times, though the head was probably re-carved in its present form much later — the original image might have been quite different.

They have naturally met with opposition and the presentation of alternative explanations. James Harrell of the University of Toledo has suggested that the erosion was caused by wet sand in historic time, for the lower layers of the Sphinx lie only a few yards above modern Nile flood levels, and floodwater with occasional rainfall could have soaked the sand for long enough to cause erosion damage. Harrell also offers alternative interpretations of seismic survey results presented by Schock. Zahi Hawass, curator of the Giza monuments, and Mark Lehner, director of the American Research Center in Cairo (and originally chosen by the Edgar Cayce Foundation as its scholar), have detailed further archaeological evidence that links the Sphinx with Chephren's mortuary complex. Hawass and Lehner also dispute some of Schock's geological interpretations. K. Lal Gauri and colleagues from the University of Louisville, Kentucky, have argued that differential weathering characteristics of the limestone from which the Sphinx is formed could result in wind-created weathering effects that look like water erosion. They also point out that observed rapid deterioration in the Sphinx during the twentieth century indicates that erosion effects could have occurred in historic times. And much other evidence against the Schock–West view has been presented. Schock has replied to his critics, however, and at the time of writing the debate continues.

There is, however, a possible third line of approach to the riddle of the age of the Sphinx that lies between the orthodox, conservative linkage of the Sphinx to the mortuary complex of Chephren (Khafre) and speculations about a super-civilization older than the Ice Age. It has been suggested to me by Egyptologist Anthony Donohue, who has discovered slightly modified likenesses of pre-dynastic deities and proto-sphinxes in natural outcrops of rock and cliff-faces along the Nile (see **Simulacra**). He suspects that the rock outcrop that was worked into the present image of the Sphinx may have been a natural simulacrum that was considered sacred from pre-dynastic times and may even have been artificially modified from time to time to enhance the imagery those people saw in its natural lineaments. Donohue, too, feels that it is possible that the 'Chephren' head dates to dynastic times and that the orthodox dating of that may well be correct, but the outcrop that provides the body of the Sphinx may have been noted and even modified in pre-dynastic times. This would allow for the water erosion now being claimed, without invoking some lost high civilization.

Such 'home-grown' approaches do not sit well, however, with those who are anxious to find the fingerprints of Atlanteans, ancient **astronauts** or other types of unknown

Ram-headed sphinxes line the entrance to Karnak.

super-races in the remains of the remarkable civilization of ancient, dynastic Egypt. The latest round of this kind of work has come through the best-selling books – under sole and joint authorships – of Robert Bauval and Graham Hancock. Bauval has argued that the Giza pyramids relate to the Orion constellation (see **Pyramids**). He says that the region of the sky containing Orion was known to the Egyptians as Duat, which also encompassed the constellations of Canis Major and Leo. This part of the night sky is where Osiris lived, according to Egyptian myth. Using computer programs to recreate the ancient Egyptian sky, Bauval claims that the gaze of the Sphinx is fixed on the horizon point of the equinoctial sunrise, and the monument was oriented on the heliacal rising position of Leo in 10,500 BC. A lion-bodied creature is, of course, the ideal earthly representative of that constellation. The authors find the Orion alignments in the Giza pyramids to work best at that remote date, too. The implications are obvious to them and their many devoted readers. But though Bauval and Hancock are vastly superior writers and researchers to many before them convinced of lost super-civilizations based on Atlanteans or ancient astronauts (or both), sceptics sense a similar obsession – an obsession that can be seen as deriving more from modern sensibilities than those actually harboured by the ancient mind. Sceptics claim that one can pick stellar alignments from any age and find monuments around the world that can be claimed as aligning to them. To be fair, Bauval and Hancock provide a rich tapestry of evidence – although all of it could be said to be serving a pre determined model or belief – but doubts begin to creep into even the most benign sceptic's mind when Hancock can

This 1976 photograph by the Viking 1 spacecraft of an area of Mars has given rise to much speculation about a face and pyramids on the red planet. Most experts feel that the features result simply from the impressions given by the play of light and shadow on distant mesa-like geological forms. (See also Simulacra.) (*NASA*)

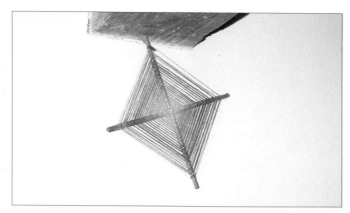

A Bavarian spirit trap of traditional design, just inside a doorway.

make associations between the Giza monuments and a mile-wide supposed Sphinx-like face and ruined pyramids in the Cydonia region of Mars.

But what of the Hall of Records beneath the Sphinx? To find this would undoubtedly and rightly be a sensation, perfectly timed for the millennium. Various attempts at checking around the Sphinx for underground anomalies have been made, including using boreholes and acoustic techniques. Nothing particularly unusual was found, except for a seismic survey in 1992, undertaken as part of Schock's work, which detected what seemed to be a rectangular cavity beneath the forepaws of the Sphinx. In addition, Dr Zahi Hawass has found a tunnel that leads beneath the Sphinx from the southeast, although he strenuously separates this from any talk of Edgar Cayce's prophecies about a Hall of Records. But there are claims and counterclaims surrounding this topic, and increasing bad blood between orthodox and unorthodox researchers, as the minutes tick away to the end of the millennium...

See also **Archaeoastronomy**

SPIRIT TRAPS

To the pre-industrial societies of Europe and elsewhere the physical environment contained spirits and demons as well as human beings. Precautions had to be taken. One of these was the idea of the spirit trap, which essentially consisted of a net or tangle of threads or similar convoluted artefact, as this could bind spirits and stop their movement – especially their entry into a house. (By a similar token, straight features were seen as being able to enhance the passage of spirits; *see* **Spirit Ways**.) One typical device consisted of a copper loop criss-crossed with threads – traditionally red in colour – fixed to the top of a wooden stave. This would be inserted into the ground at some haunted spot or on an old, rarely used track – especially one leading to or from a cemetery. 'Witch bottles' were bottles filled with tangles of coloured threads; placed over an entrance door, they were thought to prevent the entry of the spirits of witches flying out and about at night.

In Bavaria spirit traps could take the form of a complex pattern of pebbles on the ground in front of an entrance door or of a circuit of threads or wires on a small wooden frame inserted into the ceiling beams just inside the door. In Russia it was traditional to throw a fishing net over a bride dressed for her wedding to prevent her being reached by malevolent influences from sorcery. Nets and 'cat's cradles' of threads

A spirit trap protects the entrance to an Indonesian village. (*Chris Ashton*)

were placed on corpses in various parts of Europe to prevent the ghosts of the recently deceased from wandering. At least one use of the ancient stone **labyrinth** site was to trap or bind spirits. In Tibet 'devil traps' were placed on houses, described by one writer as looking like 'wireless aerials, but much more complicated'. In China **feng shui** practitioners would erect mirrors or place fearsome door-guardian sculptures to frighten off troublesome and evil spirits or erect other kinds of spirit baffles. The American Indian 'dream catcher' is reminiscent of some European spirit traps – a hoop holds a web of threads to snare bad dreams, but there is a hole in the centre to let pleasant dreams through.

Today's researchers and scholars often overlook the fundamental difference in former and modern worldviews: the old one teemed with spirits, ours is empty of them. It can make all the difference when trying to interpret certain kinds of obscure ancient site, landscape or tradition.

See also **Shamanic Landscapes**; **Sweeping**

SPIRIT WAYS

As noted in the previous entry, in former times the landscape was seen as being inhabited by spirits as well as people. There was an invisible dimension to the environment, and this dimension had its own geography, especially the notion of spirit ways through the land. This is indicated in Britain and elsewhere in Europe in the way some old roads and tracks were considered to be holy or haunted – an example can be found at Steeple Barton in Oxfordshire, where there was a path was known as Demnesweye (Demon's Way) in Anglo-Saxon times. This view was not universal, but it was nevertheless broadly cross-cultural, as can be seen from the following examples.

In old Germany there were the *Geisterwege*, ghost or spirit paths. German researcher Ulrich Magin found a reference to them in the *Handwortbuch de deutschen Aberglaubens*. It stated that these ghost paths were invisible but were located in specific places known to the local folk (who avoided them because they were where one was likely to encounter a ghost). The paths always ran in a straight line over mountains and valleys and through marshes. In the towns they passed the houses closely or went right through them. The paths ended or originated in a cemetery. Magin was subsequently able to confirm that references to *Geisterwege* go back to at least the nineteenth century, relating, of course, to older traditions. The places where these ghost path traditions were strongest – Saxony, the Voigtland, Silesia and parts of the Oberpfalz – were outside the great early medieval

A length of country road coincides with the course of a fairy pass in County Sligo, Ireland.

German empire and so were closer to pagan and Slav traditions, which might indicate great antiquity for the concept of *Geisterwege*. Although these paths are themselves invisible, they seem rather reminiscent of the features described in the **Death Roads** entry.

In Ireland, there were the famous 'fairy passes': invisible paths that ran from one *rath* (prehistoric earthwork) to another. In Irish folk tradition, it was considered unwise to build on the course of a fairy pass; to do so would be to invite bad luck. It is unclear whether these fairy routes were straight or not, but in *The Middle Kingdom* (1959) Dermot MacManus implies that they were straight, and cites the cases in County Mayo where certain houses had their corners cut off because they jutted out on to a fairy pass. He also mentions that if a bush grew on a fairy pass, the marching fairies would go round it and then continue onwards.

Irish fairy lore curiously recalls ideas forming the basis of the ancient Chinese landscape divination system called **feng shui**, in which straight features in the landscape – roads, ridges, river courses, avenues and such like – all attracted troublesome spirits, so if a tomb or building was on the course of such an 'arrow' in the land, then preventative measures had to be taken (*see also* **Spirit Traps**). In Indonesia, too, some temples have low walls inside their main entrances to deflect any straight-moving spirits from getting inside the sacred precinct.

A Bronze Age stone row at Merrivale on Dartmoor, Devon, one of about 60 surviving row complexes on the moor. Excavations have revealed no clues as to their purpose, but most lead to or pass through burial sites, so some researchers suggest that they may mark out spirit paths. Large terminus stones, as seen here in the foreground, are called blocking stones by archaeologists. Some earth mysteries researchers think they may be just that – erected to block spirit movement beyond the confines of the row, in accord with similar ideas about hindering the movement of spirits found in numerous traditional cultures.

In Laos the Hmong make sure that a new house in a village is not built directly in front of or behind another house. This is because they believe that spirits travel in straight lines and when corpses are moved from the house for burial they must go straight out of the house. Often the coffin will go through an opening specifically made in the wall and down to an open space at the other side of the village without passing around any other house. This is very similar to a belief system in the Gilbert Islands, an archipelago of about 50 islands in the western Pacific. Makin Meang, the northernmost island in this archipelago, is considered the halfway house betwen the living and the dead. On whatever island within the archipelago a person died, it was believed that the soul travelled northwards in a straight line – even sometimes taking a particular path – to a sandspit on Makin Meang known as the Place of Dread. From there, the soul departed across the ocean and over the western horizon *en route* to Matang, the land of the ancestors. Long ago, a supernatural being, Nakaa the Judge, gave the islanders a ritual called Te Kaetikawai, 'Straightening the Way of the Dead'. This ritual needed to be enacted around the body of the recently deceased, otherwise the departing spirit might travel in other than a straight line, in which case Nakaa would ensnare it. As with the Hmong, houses in villages were situated so as not to block the straight passage of any soul departing from any house.

In Europe, and particularly in Britain, the folk link between the physical corpse way or death road and invisible ghost path might have been provided by the tradition of holding vigils at the church door (or lych – corpse – gate) on New Year's Eve or St Mark's Eve (24 April), when the spirits of all the parishioners who are to die in the coming year are said to become visible, parading by in a line.

The church seems to have taken over the concept of spirit lines and Christianized it, according to research by Ulrich Magin. Between AD 900 and 1300 in Germany and Switzerland, at least, the church employed a specific type of sacred geography involving the creation of a cross formation marked out by alignments of churches radiating out in the cardinal directions from a central cathedral. Sometimes this giant cross formation would be enhanced by church roads running out along the alignments, too. At Worms, for instance, Magin counted seven churches on a 2-mile (3km) alignment, with a third of that distance being followed by a road. Such arrangements have been noted at Speyer and Zurich, among other cathedral cities. These features seem to have been a more purposeful and sophisticated version of church paths, and Magin has speculated that they were envisaged as conduits of the Holy Spirit.

or a run of a spirit or animal. Humphrey observes that in the 'purely shamanic' view, the world of the dead is not located in some separate underworld, but is sometimes nearby, across the mountains or round some bends in a river or inside a cliff. Ordinary people lack the abilities to see this, but the shaman can do so.

A similar idea is also found in Native America. In northern Colombia, for instance, the *mamas* of the remote Kogi Indians (*see* **Shamanic Landscapes**) have had strict training in childhood and are able to see the spirit world or *aluna* intermixed with the physical environment. When a *mama* sees a rock he also sees a spirit rock, and when he sees a river he also sees the spirit river. A network of stone pathways runs through Kogi territory, and these are sacred to the Indians. They have to be maintained (*see* **Sweeping**) and must be walked. Some of these are understood as being physical traces of spirit paths, although some spirit ways the *mamas* take in the spirit otherworld are not marked on the ground.

It is clear that many (though not all) ancient traditions associated spirit movement with *straightness*. This has not been lost on the new breed of **ley** hunter.

See also **Cursus; Liminality; Shamanic Landscapes; Stone Rows**

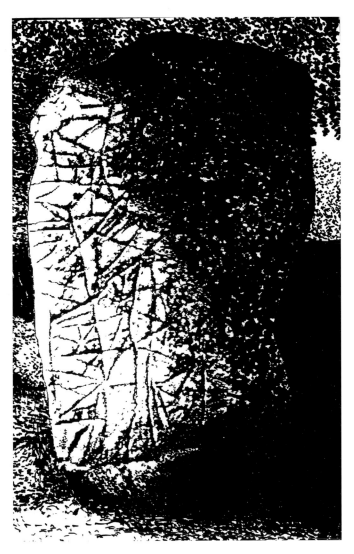

The Kogi Indian 'map stone', which shows the spirit paths taken by the Kogi shamans in the otherworld, and which are partially marked on the ground by physical pathways. (*Drawing after a photograph by Alan Ereira*)

There is no doubt, then, that a widespread belief in spirit ways crossing ancient landscapes in a variety of forms existed at various periods of time. There is a school of thought within earth mysteries research that considers that all these references to the passage of spirits through the land are echoes of an archaic Eurasian shamanism. Certainly, the idea of a spirit path was incorporated into Siberian shamanic beliefs, as noted by Cambridge anthropologist Caroline Humphrey. She found that the Buryat **shaman** is buried in a particular spot of which it is believed that the shaman's soul will become the spiritual guardian. From that place, the Buryat believe that the shaman's spirit can move out and about on 'journeys'. The Buryat word *güidel* means the track

STONEHENGE

This famous **Neolithic** site in Wiltshire is noted for its ancient astronomy and, moreover, for its role in the development of its modern study (see **Archaeoastronomy**). In 1961 the French architect G. Charrière noted that the key astronomical alignments of Stonehenge crossed virtually at right angles, thus allowing the four Station Stone positions in the groundplan to form a near-perfect rectangular setting. This is a function of the monument's latitude. If it were any great distance further north or south, the Station Stones would form an irregular groundplan. In fact, Gerald Hawkins, the former Smithsonian astronomer famed for his book *Stonehenge Decoded* (with John B. White; 1965), discovered that one has to go as far south as the 30th parallel to be able to place stones dealing with the astronomical alignments in a regular pattern. Interestingly, this is the line of latitude in which the Great Pyramid stands. Is this just a coincidence, or does this curious fact reveal that the builders of Stonehenge knew the dimensions of the Earth? One man who thinks so is John Michell. His studies of the measurements of Stonehenge have led him to feel that he has detected ancient metrological units in the proportions of Stonehenge and to note geodetic information such as that the lintel ring that once ran in a perfect circle supported by the outer sarsen uprights was a scale model of the Earth's meridian circumference.

The enigma of Stonehenge continues to fascinate. In *The Stonehenge Solution* (1992), for instance, meteorologist Terence Meaden observed that the shadow of the Heel Stone penetrates into the centre of the stone ring as the midsummer sun rises behind it. He suggests that this 'Midsummer Marriage' is symbolic of the Sky Father coupling with the Earth Mother, with Stonehenge representing her womb.

In considering astronomy at Stonehenge, however, one has to ask *which* Stonehenge one means, for the monument has evolved over a 2000-year period. In what archaeologists term Stonehenge I, dating to *c.*3300 BC, there was at first a timber structure 100ft (30m) in diameter, which had an entrance to the northeast and a narrower one to the south. This may have been a charnel house, perhaps also an observatory for astronomer-priests to make the first of a long series of observations of lunar movement from the site. About a

century after this, a circular ditch-and-bank enclosure was dug (the actual **henge**), a ring of pits now called the Aubrey Holes was dug and infilled around the inner rim of the ditch, and, probably, the Heel Stone (and a possible partner) erected outlying to the northeast. There was a causeway opening in the ditch-and-bank to the northeast, and two stones were placed there. Some timber structures also seem to have been erected at this time.

Stonehenge II was the first remodelling of the site, dated between 2200 and 2000 BC. The axis of the site was moved a little on to the orientation of the midsummer sunrise, and along this line an earthen avenue about 500yd (460m) long was built, approaching the entrance from the northeast. The two entrance stones were re-erected along the midline of the avenue. An incomplete circular setting of bluestones (the smaller stones now visible at the site today) was put up

Part of the outer sarsen circle at Stonehenge in Wiltshire, embracing the smaller, and earlier, bluestones.

within the henge. While the Heel Stone is of local sarsen stone, the bluestones are foreign to the area, brought there either by human transportation or by earlier glacial action. The stones were taken down again during this period (leaving what archaeologists call the Q and R holes). The four Station Stones (known as stones 91, 92, 93 and 94 on modern plans of Stonehenge) were erected on the edge of the Aubrey Hole circle either in this phase or at some unknown time after Stonehenge I.

The phase known as Stonehenge III is broken down into three or more divisions. The first is dated to around 2000 BC. The great lintelled sarsen structure most people think of as Stonehenge was erected. Ten huge sarsens were shaped to form the uprights of a central horseshoe arrangement, with massive lintels placed on top of each pair, forming five trilithons. An encircling set of 30 slightly smaller sarsen uprights supporting a continuous lintel ring 16ft (5m) off the ground was erected. Two other sarsen stones were also erected in the entrance to the henge (one of these survives today as the fallen Slaughter Stone). No one knows where the bluestones were during this phase, but they reappeared between 2000 and 1550 BC. About 20 were set up within the trilithon horseshoe. Holes (the Y and Z holes) were dug around the outer sarsen ring as if to accept more bluestones, but they seem never to have been used. The bluestones were rearranged yet again and from this time to around 1100 BC various alterations and tinkerings were made to the site, including a considerable extension to the length of the avenue and a turn in its direction.

The Stonehenge we see today is, therefore, not only complex, but it also represents what remains of a whole evolution of concepts, functions, symbolism and ground-plans. It may occupy a relatively small physical space, but it contains a deep well of time.

SWEEPING

Ritual sweeping was a cross-cultural procedure in societies that believed in the presence of spirits. In Europe old paths that had not been used for a long time were swept to rid them of any ghosts or unpleasant spirits that might be haunting them, and at liminal ('betwixt and between') times of year, such as New Year's Eve in Celtic countries, crossroads would be swept to clear them of spectres and demons – this was done in the Isle of Man, for example, well within living memory. Half the world away in Andean communities, Aymara Indians sweep the plaza in front of a church before a saint's statue is brought out in order to cleanse the ground of harmful influences accrued during the daily, secular use of the place and to transform it temporarily into a sacred space. This may have deep roots, for experts who have studied the **Nazca lines** in Peru think they see evidence that these ancient and mysterious lines were also ritually swept long ago, in the way that the Kogi Indians of Colombia clear their sacred pathways to this day.

See also **Death Roads**; **Leys/Leylines**; **Liminality**; **Shamanic Landscapes**; **Spirit Traps**; **Spirit Ways**

SYSTEM THEORY

General System Theory emphasizes wholes and interconnections – especially in terms of information and organization – rather than isolated elements or components. 'General System Theory' sounds very mechanistic, and used too literally it can, indeed, become over-rigid, but as a guiding principle it can prove to be extremely useful. While it has obvious value in organizing disparate teams or groups in, say, a large engineering project, it can also have applications in fields as diverse as physics and sociology, and even the 'most esoteric' subjects, too, as System pioneer Ludwig von Bertalanffy pointed out. He said that the method represented 'a change in basic categories of thought', and referred to it as a 'general science of wholeness'. Although System Theory can become very complex and technical depending on its applications, worn lightly it can be of great help to anyone faced with a problem with many aspects or variables. Sometimes emergent characteristics can be detected in this manner that are simply invisible when dealing only with the parts of a problem or a subject – as the phrase has it, 'the whole can be greater than the sum of the parts'. For example, most of us are now familiar with the term 'ecology', yet without System thinking the concept of ecology could not exist. (The related **Gaia Theory** is an exemplar of System thinking.)

The Systems approach has had a great impact on **archaeology** because of the wide range and types of data it has to consider together; in a similar manner, it is useful to take a System approach to the ancient earth mysteries area, as this is also multi-faceted and multi-mode. Even an ancient monument can be viewed in a General System way – in fact, a complex site cannot be fully understood without such an approach. (It might be noted that this encyclopedia can be a useful tool with which to explore a System approach to ancient earth mysteries: a classic case is the subject of **leys** – the new approach can be fully understood only by tracing several entries in this encyclopedia, as indicated in the Using the Encyclopedia section in the Introduction.)

TEOTIHUACÁN

This was a great religious and economic centre founded by an unknown people in the first century AD. Growing to dominate the Valley of Mexico between AD 350 and 650, its area of 10 sq miles (25 sq km) contained temples, shrines, plazas, dwellings and workshops. By the eighth century it was burned and abandoned, perhaps resulting from internal conflict rather than from invasion. The **Aztecs**, who encountered its awesome ruins centuries later, named it Teotihuacán – the Birthplace of the Gods. In their mythology it was where Nanahuatzin, a dying god, jumped into a ceremonial fire that the four creator gods (representing the four cardinal directions) were too fearful to enter. Thus turned to flame, Nanahuatzin became the Fifth Sun, the present world in Aztec mythic chronology. Nanahuatzin's companion, Tecciztecatl, joined him in the sacrificial fire and became the moon. The Aztecs thus decided that the two tiered **pyramids** that dominate Teotihuacán were dedicated respectively to the sun and moon.

The prime axis of Teotihuacán was actually set to the curious angle of 15.5 degrees east of north, and this initially puzzled archaeologists and astronomers. It was an orientation that had been strictly adhered to by the city's builders, for not only were streets and many of the buildings kept to it, even the course of the San Juan River, which runs through the site, was canalized to conform to it. This skewed north–south central axis is marked by the great ceremonial way the Aztecs called the Street of the Dead aligned to the Pyramid of the Moon, with the larger Pyramid of the Sun, 200ft (62m) tall, set just to its east. The answer to the riddle of the weird axial orientation lay with a cave discovered by accident beneath this pyramid. It is a four-lobed cave, with lava-tube extension, and clear evidence of ancient ritual and ceremony was found within it. The lava-tube passage, by remarkable coincidence, aligns to the setting point of the Pleiades, a constellation of great symbolic import for ancient Mesoamericans because its heliacal (first pre-sunrise) annual

The Street of the Dead, Teotihuacán, Mexico.
(*Patrick Horsbrugh/EFI*)

appearance heralded one of the two times each year at the latitude of Teotihuacán when the sun passes directly overhead. At noon on these days no shadows are cast, and it was said that the sun god visited the Earth briefly at these moments. The Pyramid of the Sun was built directly over this cave and given an orientation in line with the lava-tube passage, thus also aligning to the Pleiades setting point in AD 150. This founding axis of Teotihuacán actually crosses the Street of the Dead, and seems to have been marked out by 'benchmarks' consisting of pecked crosses.

See also **Archaeoastronomy**; **Hallucinogens**; **Quetzalcoatl**; **World Navel**

TERRESTRIAL ZODIACS

The notion of there being giant zodiacal figures laid out in the British landscape in ancient times has persisted for decades within twentieth-century earth mysteries circles. Pre-eminent among such supposed features is the so-called Glastonbury Zodiac, seen in a map of that area by Katherine Maltwood in 1925, and about which she wrote in *Glastonbury's Temple of the Stars* (1935) and other works. She studied airviews and maps of that area of Somerset, and identified topographical features she felt created a circle of terrestrial zodiacal effigies 10 miles (16km) wide, centred near the village of Butleigh. She became convinced that this was the reality of the Round Table in the legends of **Arthur**. Her ideas were championed and developed by others, notably Elizabeth Leader and Mary Caine (who has also declared the existence of a zodiac around Kingston-upon-Thames, Surrey), but doubters feel that the theory does not stand up to scrutiny. They point out that the figures are delineated by river courses, ancient roads, dykes, boundaries of woodland and other features that appeared at different times in the landscape and in some cases shifted over the years. A scatter of place-names and place-related legends have been found at appropriate places on the landscape figures of the Glastonbury Zodiac, and this has been presented as proof, but if several images can be seen in an inkblot, a map provides a much richer matrix out of which textual and visual patterns can be drawn.

It can be easier than might be thought to find 'zodiacs' on a number of Ordnance Survey maps of Britain, and several have been claimed over the years. They may have some psychological and poetical validity, but terrestrial zodiacs are not widely regarded as being actual physical features fashioned with human intent on the landscape.

See also **Grail**

THEOSOPHY

The Theosophical Society was founded in 1875 in New York by Helen Petrovna Blavatsky in association with Colonel H.S. Olcott and others. The society in general, and the person of Blavatsky in particular, represented the synthesis of the hungover anti-Christianity of the Enlightenment – when secular rationalism struggled to overcome fundamentalist Christianity – with the burgeoning occult interest of the period. This particularly included Spiritualism. Theosophy provided a royal road for oriental philosophy to reach broader Western attention, introducing concepts such as reincarnation, meditation and karma to many people.

Blavatsky was Ukrainian by birth, and only a few reliable details are known of her earlier life as she moved between her home country, Paris, Italy, Kiev, Egypt and New York. She mixed with various kinds of occultists and eventually set up a society for investigating mediums and occult phenomena in Cairo, but this soon collapsed. In 1877 she published her two-volume *Isis Unveiled*, a somewhat truculent and anecdotal mix of mysticism, **archaeology** and supposed lost wisdom. The great success of the Theosophical Society in its earlier period (it attracted many leading intellectuals of the day, such as W.B. Yeats) was doubtless due to the powerful presence of Blavatsky herself, but another reason was timing. There was a great need for some workable synthesis of rational 'modern thought' and the rise in occult interest – especially practical occultism. Indeed, the Theosophical Society embodied the *Zeitgeist* of its time to the extent of having a surprisingly strong Darwinian element, for one of its underlying beliefs was that humanity was evolving towards some new spiritual level. A third and important reason was that the aims of the Society were sufficiently vague for a wide range of general occult interest and spiritual yearning to be accommodated.

The Theosophical Society linked itself with a revived Hindu movement in India, founding a headquarters at Adyar, near Madras. Blavatsky blended Eastern spiritual philosophy with her own notions, and the theme began to emerge that the Society was under the guidance of hidden Masters – perfected beings living in Tibet – and its goal was to usher humanity safely along the path of evolution to a future psycho-spiritual dawn. Psychic phenomena were said to attend Blavatsky, and this also attracted much interest. However, a scandal broke out when an employee of the Society, Emma Coulomb, informed a Christian journal in Madras that she and her husband had been paid by Blavatsky to produce fake psychic phenomena in Cairo. As a consequence of this, the Society for Psychical Research in Britain investigated the Theosophical Society and produced a damning report. Blavatsky downplayed 'phenomena' thereafter, but otherwise the fortunes of the Society were not too badly affected. In Europe, Blavatsky settled to writing her main opus, *The Secret Doctrine* (1888), which contained the essence of what could be identified of Theosophical doctrine, including the idea of the Masters and the assertion that humans were advancing towards becoming a new race of psychically superior beings.

By the time of Blavatsky's death in 1891, strains in the Theosophical Society had begun to show, and splinter groups and rival occult organizations were formed. The 'Blavatsky school' saw the only way to development as being through adherence to Eastern influence, while others sought a more Western-based esotericism. Another split was that between the occult work of the Theosophical Society and the progressive, educational and social welfare ethic that had sprung up in its midst. One of several Theosophical exponents of this latter trend was Blavatsky's eventual heir, Annie Besant, who ran a new-style Theosophical Society with Charles Webster Leadbeater (who invoked further controversy when accusations of his being a paedophile and homosexual were raised). Besant and Leadbeater made themselves more effectively the intermediaries between members of the Society and the Masters or Mahatmas ('Great Souls'). They identified an Indian boy, Jiddu Krishnamurti, as the physical vehicle of the coming World Teacher of the new age. In 1911 they founded the Order of the Star in the East, designed to facilitate this awesome incarnation. But further dissent broke out, resulting ultimately (in 1929) in Krishnamurti rejecting the role the Theosophical Society had thrust on him. There were various further defections, probably the most damaging being that of Rudolf Steiner, who took most of the German Theosophists with him to form the Anthroposophical Society.

The Theosophical Society thereafter declined, and some of its movers and shakers founded or joined other occult groups. But the influence of the Theosophical movement deeply affects New Age and earth mysteries concerns to this day. There is a continuing struggle within the more active research field of ancient earth mysteries interest to counter what scholar Joscelyn Godwin has referred to in *The Theosophical Enlightenment* (1994) as the 'deluded and deluding' tendencies of much Theosophical thought.

TIAHUANACO

The ruins of this ceremonial city and **pilgrimage** centre are situated several miles from the shores of Lake Titicaca, over 12,000ft (3700m) up in the Bolivian Andes, on the bleak, windswept altiplano. Tiahuanaco seems to have developed out of a religion that dominated the Titicaca basin as early as 1000 BC, and there is evidence that the site of Tiahuanaco was occupied by at least that date. But the city proper existed from *c*.250 BC to its abandonment *c*.AD 1000. At its height in the middle and second parts of that long period, the total area of Tiahuanaco may have covered some 1485 acres (595ha) with up to 40,000 inhabitants – a number that rose when accommodating pilgrims. The influence of Tiahuanaco extended great distances through the southern Andean region by means of religion, trade and, perhaps, a limited amount of military action.

At first glance, the location of the site appears so barren that it is impossible to think how a great centre like this could have supported itself, but recent archaeological research has revealed that the little-known people of Tiahuanaco had developed a raised field system, *waru waru*, which involved ridge-like earthen platforms built between a network of canals extending outwards for 9 miles (14km) from the shores of Lake Titicaca. To this would have been added the herding of llamas and alpacas and the exploitation of fish, birds and vegetation around the lake. Further, Tiahuanaco established enclaves in milder climatic areas of the southern Andes to help the supply of food in hard times.

Alan Kolata, an investigator of the site, points out that the positioning and structure of Tiahuanaco is an expression of sacred or **mythic geography**. Lake Titicaca was the mythological point of creation and emergence for Andean peoples from the earliest times – a mythology later appropriated by the Inca – and the sacred islands of the Sun and Moon in the lake contain Tiahuanaco shrines. The sacred, ceremonial core of Tiahuanaco is surrounded by a moat, thus creating a sacred island. The major ceremonial structures on this core island are oriented to the four cardinal directions, with the east–west axis being particularly important. The sun rises over the three snowy sacred peaks of Mount Illimani in Cordillera Real to the east, and sets over Lake Titicaca towards the west. Doorways and staircases in the temples and sacred edifices relate to both directions, but favour the east. To this day, as Kolata notes in *Valley of the Spirits* (1996), the Aymara Indians of the region (probably the descendants of the people of Tiahuanaco) continue mentally to shape the skies above them and the land around them in mythic, cosmographical ways.

The most dominant surviving monument at Tiahuanaco is the Akapana temple, a huge mound 56ft (17m) high, incised with seven stone terraces, some of which may have been faced with glittering gold sheet decoration. The centre of the ceremonial complex, it was long assumed to be a

Panoramic view of the ceremonial core of Tiahuanaco in the Andes. The Semi-subterranean Temple is in the foreground, with the Kalasasaya beyond. (*Klaus Aarsleff/ Fortean Picture Library*)

natural hill. The materials comprising the mound were transported to the site from other locations. The summit of this temple mound, which had originally been covered by a distinctive green gravel taken from stream beds in the Quimsachata mountains to the south, is the only place in Tiahuanaco from where Mount Illimani and Lake Titicaca are both visible. The cut stone terraces were punctuated with tenoned sculptures of human and puma heads, much like gargoyles on a cathedral façade.

Kolata's investigations revealed a complex and precision-built stone drainage system that carried the water that collected on the top of Akapana down through the mound, to a tunnel system that fed into the monumental sewer system deep underground beneath the entire core of Tiahuanaco and eventually drained into Lake Titicaca itself. Kolata notes that the drainage system is over-engineered, and was more than merely functional. The considerable volume of water that would have collected during the altiplano rains in the sunken court on the mound's summit was drained off by the system and carried down inside the mound, to reappear at the next terrace down where it would have gushed from a channel on to a drain on the terraces, there gurgling along before disappearing inside the mound once more, only to reappear at the next lower terrace. The water thus ran in both subterreanean and surface ways from the top of the mound, ultimately to replenish the waters of the valley, in the precise manner in which waters run down and through the nearby mountains to feed the rivers and the lake below. The green stream gravel reinforced this symbolism. Akapana was therefore an artificial holy mountain. Kolata also observes that during strong rainfall, the large drains inside the temple mound might have generated an acoustic effect, with the roar of rushing interior water causing a rumbling sound like the thunder in the mountains. Underneath a patio to one side of the sunken court on top of Akapana, Kolata and his team found a series of burials in which a row of seated adults were facing a seated male figure holding a puma-shaped incense burner. Perhaps these were the last priests of the temple.

Immediately below Akapana's north face lies a range of other ceremonial features. One is the so-called Semi-subterranean Temple, a sunken courtyard with a longer side of 95ft (29m). A carved sandstone slab 24ft (7m) tall, known as the Bennett stela, originally stood as the focal point of the temple but has been removed to La Paz. The complex carvings on this stone show a richly attired human form holding a ritual cup and ceremonial sceptre or staff, surrounded by an array of elaborate images, some of which have been interpreted as forming a calendar. Of special interest are depictions of the hallucinogenic San Pedro cactus. Along with snuff trays, inhalation tubes and other paraphenalia to do with the taking of mind-altering substances found at various Tiahuanaco sites, these carvings confirm that the religious phenomenon that provided Tiahuanaco with its mainstay of power was a shamanic one using **hallucinogens**, as was so often the case in prehistoric Native American religion.

Directly west of the Semi-subterranean Temple is the rectangular platform-temple of the Kalasasaya. This raised precinct area has a monumental entrance gateway and staircase and a sunken court. Viewed from the Semi-subterranean Temple, the gateway frames a tall sculpture known as the Ponce stela, depicting a figure carved with similar designs to the Bennett stela. This looks eastwards towards the Semi-subterranean Temple, where the Bennett stela had originally been placed facing west, as if the two were exchanging glances. The line of their mutual gaze marks a key astronomical orientation, because both the Kalasasaya and the Temple are aligned on the cardinal directions, and on the equinoxes the line of the rising sun bisects the Temple and the centre of the Kalasasaya's monumental staircase.

The most famous of Tiahuanaco's monuments is the Gateway of the Sun. This now stands in the northwest corner of the Kalasasaya, although it is thought it might originally have stood in a nearby complex. The gateway, which is 10ft (3m) high, was carved from a single block of andesite. Among the carvings on it is a long frieze of repetitive motifs, which may be a form of calendar.

The ceremonial structures of Tiahuanaco were built from red sandstone or andesite, and they were quarried at some distance and brought to the site. Not all the quarry sites have been located. Massive blocks like those used for the Gateway of the Sun must have entailed a colossal expenditure of labour. The masonry is remarkable, with stones sometimes being fitted so closely that a knife blade can barely be placed between them. The masons of Tiahuanaco found that if they chiselled out H- or I-shaped grooves in the sides of dressed stones and filled them with molten bronze, the metal would harden to form strong clamps that locked the stones together.

The adventurous Norwegian anthropologist Thor Heyerdahl has argued that the first inhabitants of **Easter Island** came from the Tiahuanaco area, but DNA tests on prehistoric skeletal remains from the island have revealed markers characteristic of Polynesian origins.

See also **Acoustics; Archaeoastronomy; Chavín de Huantar; Nazca Lines; Shaman; Shamanic Landscapes; Simulacra; Trance; World Navel**

TRANCE

This is a general term denoting an altered state of consciousness, especially a dreamlike or hypnotic state. It often involves dissociation – a condition in which the self feels divorced from the body. It can also denote a state of rapture and ecstasy – again, a sensation in which it feels as if the spirit has taken flight. Trance can be deliberately induced by many means, such as hyperventilation (rapid shallow breathing), chanting, drumming, dancing, whirling, sensory deprivation, lack of sleep, fasting, focusing on flickering light (such as flames) and meditation. All these and more have been used by those seeking religious, occult or transcendental experience. In particular, hallucinogenic drugs have been used, as these are a powerful if sometimes dangerous way to induce profound mind-altering, visionary states. Trance can also occur involuntarily, such as when driving a car at night (or any time) when drowsy, when just descending into or awakening from sleep (the hypnogogic and hypnopompic states respectively), on undergoing a physical or psychological shock or trauma, on becoming exhausted, as a result of a condition such as epilepsy, and so forth.

Trance holds an interest for students of ancient earth mysteries for two main reasons. One is that it was the focal experience involved in shamanism, that magico-religious practice that influenced so many of the cultures that built ancient monuments and left their marks on rocks or on the ground. Depending on the cultural context, the **shaman** would use a range of trance-inducing methods so that he could take an 'aerial journey' to the otherworlds inhabited by the gods, ancestors and spirits for various purposes. The idea of the spirit flight of the shaman is symbolized world-wide by bird, feather, arrow and similar imagery expressed in visual art, ritual gesture and costume. In classical Siberian shamanism, the shaman would use a drum which was supposedly made from a branch of the World Tree. This was the cosmic axis along which the shaman's spirit flew up to the heaven worlds or down to the underworld (*see* **World Navel**).

The other reason the subject of trance holds a place of interest in earth mysteries concerns is due to the matter of **entoptic patterns**. These are recognizable sets of 'form constants', which are produced in the human brain during certain stages of trance. Because they belong to the neuronal 'wiring' of all human beings, they occur in all societies and in all periods in which trance states have been induced. They are therefore cross-cultural. Although differing meanings may have been placed on these patterns by different societies in different places and times, the *forms* themselves remain recognizable. In relatively recent times, it has been claimed that entoptic imagery can be detected in **rock art** and the kinds of terrestrial markings forming **shamanic landscapes**.

See also **Chavín de Huantar; Effigy Mounds; Gavrinis; Hallucinogens; Hopewell Indians; Kivas; Leys/Leylines; Loughcrew; Nazca Lines; Newgrange; Tiahuanaco**

U V

UFOS

The subject of Unidentified Flying Objects or 'flying saucers' has rather surprisingly made contact with a number of ancient earth mysteries topics. The whole theme of 'ancient **astronauts**' relies on the idea of extraterrestrial craft, and this can be closely allied with modern New Age notions concerning **Atlantis** and the **Hollow Earth.** Those who cannot accept that **crop circles** are made by human hand often invoke the idea of UFOs descending over fields and making the markings. The great **ley** revival of the 1960s rode on the burgeoning interest in flying saucers during that period, and the idea that UFOs drew their energy from the supposed magnetism residing in the leys was promoted. A number of key 'ley hunters' came from the field of ufology.

On a quite different level, some earth mysteries researchers point to the acknowledged association of ancient sites and the appearance of unusual light phenomena (often comprehended as spirits or deities) in some ancient cultures, as well as anecdotal reports of such lights being seen at prehistoric monuments (*see* **Energies**). These researchers tend to dismiss the idea of such unusual skyborne lights being craft, extraterrestrial or otherwise, but see them as being exotic, little-understood forms of geophysical phenomena, perhaps loosely linked to earthquake lights and ball lightning (*see* **Earth Lights**).

VAMPIRES

The legend of the vampire, and its close cousin, the werewolf, belongs primarily (though not exclusively) to central and eastern Europe, especially the parts occupied by those who speak Slavonic languages, but extending to Russia and Greece. It goes back to very ancient beliefs in various kinds of blood-sucking ghosts and demons, and, as some earth mysteries investigators maintain, to garbled folk memories of shamanism.

An ellipsoid light form flying just above the treetops near the San Andreas fault, California, in the 1970s. It created shock waves as it flew, then stopped without deceleration, rotated and dissolved. Was it a craft or was it a mysterious natural phenomenon? (David Kubrin)

The word 'vampire' derives from a range of related old European words, such as the Magyar (Hungarian) *vampir*, which itself may have come from the Turkish *uber*, 'witch'. A related term, the Serbian *Vukodlak*, refers to both vampire and werewolf, and derives from roots meaning 'wolf' and 'wolfishness, mad rage'. It was popularly believed that a vampire was the re-animated corpse of a murderer, a suicide, an excommunicant, a witch or magician, or a person who in life suffered the misfortune of being bitten by a vampire. It was also believed that if an animal jumped or a bird flew over a corpse, it would become a vampire. To be on the safe side, it was a practice in Romania to thrust nine spindles into the grave of the deceased, so that if the corpse should become re-animated and attempt to rise, it would be pierced. Another Romanian way of destroying a corpse thought to be a vampire was to hack it into pieces that were then burned in a fire. Other methods generally employed in parts of Europe to prevent vampires from walking were to bury the corpse at a crossroads, exhume a body and pierce it with iron forks, hammer a nail through the head, drive a stake throught its heart or decapitate it. Garlic and silver were thought to be effective in warding off a vampire actually on the prowl.

There was a veritable epidemic of vampirism in southeast Europe in the seventeenth century, especially in Serbia, Hungary and Greece. News of wandering vampires eventually spread far afield, and in 1746 a French monk published a scholarly text on vampires. The legend became a Gothic element absorbed into late eighteenth-century romanticism, and by the following century had even become a theatrical theme. A tidied-up and dramatized version of vampire lore was brought into the twentieth century by Bram Stoker in his *Dracula* (1897), from which its great popularity has continued to develop.

The idea behind the werewolf ('man-wolf') also goes back into antiquity. In Roman times, for example, it was believed that powerful witches could turn themselves into animals, especially wolves. Such a process is known as lycanthropy, an infamous case of which occurred in sixteenth-century France, where one Gilles Garnier was accused of tearing apart children and eating them. He confessed under torture and was executed. The werewolf is, of course, considered today to be a mythical creature, but it is perhaps sobering to note that Brian Bates, a professor of psychology at Sussex University in England, states unequivocally that deep in an Austrian forest he actually witnessed the head of a woman turning into that of a wolf during a ritual. He saw her human features flicker as if with some form of energy during the transformation.

One earth mysteries scholar who has seen shamanic connections in the vampire/werewolf theme is Nigel Jackson. In *The Ley Hunter* journal ('Christmas As You Never Knew It', no. 120, 1993), he notes that a root term of Vukodlak was used in association with shaman-warriors in ancient Europe who could supposedly shape-shift and who identified themselves with the wandering spirits of the dead. In Norse tradition, Odin was accompanied by the warriors known as Ulfhedhnar, 'wolf-skins', on the Wutanes Her, the Furious Host, which rode the skies during the Twelve Nights of Yuletide. These warriors were said to take mind-altering mushrooms before battle to promote their fearsome shape-shifting. (It seems that there may have been wolf and bear martial clans in ancient northern Europe – the frenzied Berserkers were exemplars of the bear clan.) Tracing the deeper Indo-European roots of the theme to ancient Iran, there were the Haomavarka, 'Haoma-wolves'. Haoma was the name for soma, the sacred Indo-European hallucinogenic drink mentioned in the *Rig Veda*. In the entries on **Hallucinogens** and **Entoptic Patterns** it will be seen that one of the characteristics of hallucinogenic and other types of **trance** is the feeling that the entranced person's body-image is changing, typically into that of an animal. In South American shamanism, for instance, the **shaman** often transformed into a jaguar, as graphically portrayed in the ancient temple of **Chavín de Huantar**, where the hallucinogenic San Pedro cactus was the sacramental plant.

Interestingly, as Jackson relates, traditions in Prussia and Baltic countries claimed that werewolves roam through the land during the Twelve Nights of Christmas. During the same shadowy, **liminal** period of the year, hairy beings with animal attributes were said to rampage through Greece. Their attacks could be averted by the use of garlic. In Bulgaria it was said that anyone who was born or died during these 'unclean' Twelve Nights would become a vampire, and anyone born on Christmas Day in Naples was thought to be destined to become a vampire.

Further hints of a shamanic link with the vampire/werewolf theme were to be found in Russia, where it was said that anyone born with the caul (the foetal membrane) attached to their head would become a vampire, but in Hungary it marks the birth of a future Taltos, a folk-shaman said to be the result of a union between a woman and a wolf. Seventeenth-century sources also state that those born with a caul become either Vukodlaki or *chresnichi* – the *kresnik* is the traditional Slovenian shaman. There are also traditions of shamans drinking the blood of their animal familiars. The death association is present in classical

A World Centre scheme also infor
landscape of Ireland, which was divi
provinces – Ulster, Munster, Leinster
met in the centre, Mide, where stan
(now in the modern County Westr
boulder called Aill na Mireann, the
be found on the hill's slopes.

Jerusalem holds a special stat
Judaism, Islam and Christianity all
priate entry, the medieval Christia
in their *mappae mundi* – maps c
schematic religious diagrams s
centre.

In northern Europe, arctic Eu
Centre was often envisaged as
(*axis mundi*). The Yakuts of n
believed there was a tree with
'golden navel of the Earth'.
however, is surely the Norse
European **maypole** and the C
the *axis mundi* theme. Even i
present in the Lakota India
the Sun Pole at the centre
sage and buffalo hair are pl
top. A song accompanies
Earth/Stand looking arc
Stand looking around you
a representation of the V

Other cultures used
mountain. Indian (Hind
Meru (physically embo
Kailas) standing at the
only temples, were bui
symbolic representatio
as late as the eightee
dance with this tradi
Mountain can be tra
and moats of the ci
world surrounded b
ocean, and the tem
The whole of Tha
division into four
of which was the
centre of the wor
was built as a qu
palace in the ce
Malay Peninsu
Ribn, a huge r
summit a massive ...

shamanism in that it was assumed that while on his or her
entranced journey to the otherworlds, the shaman had
temporarily died.

It is in just such a dark jumble of **folklore** as this that earth
mysteries researchers feel they can trace the distant imprint
of shamanic traditions in the lore concerning vampires and
werewolves.

VARANASI (Benares)

Varanasi is the greatest focus of Hindu **pilgrimage**. It has 56
pilgrimage circuits, of which five are the most popular and
trace a sacred design or cosmogram on the landscape. The
circuits interconnect a variety of temples and shrines. Some
of these are sun shrines, *adityas*, and Indian scholar Rana
P. B. Singh claims that these form alignments to sunrise positions on symbolic days in the year. If so, the pilgrims thus
trace out a cosmically significant pattern during their devo-
tional visiting of the temples, and it is most telling that the
word for a cosmogram, *kashi*, was also the ancient name
for the city territory of Varanasi. Singh calls such symbolic
geography – strongly associated with pilgrimage centres in
India – 'faithscapes'.

See also **Archaeoastronomy; Mythic Geography**

VISION QUEST

This is a solitary sojourn in the wilderness in order to gain a
guiding vision or meaningful dream. Buddha, Christ and the
Prophet Muhammed all reportedly retreated alone into
nature to achieve spiritual orientation, but we know mostly
about the process of the vision quest from the archaic practices of Native Americans and palaeo-Siberian tribes. In
these contexts, the individual, often around the time of
puberty, goes alone into the wilderness, usually to some
special, sacred vision-questing site known to the tribe, and
there fasts, prays and goes without sleep for three or four days
and nights. During this time, a series of waking dreams or a
powerful vision – perhaps in the form of an animal that has
the power of speech – may be experienced, which can give
direction to the person's life. Such visions contain great

Pilgrims bathe in the sacred River Ganges at Varanasi in India.
(Dr Elmar R. Gruber/Fortean Picture Library)

'medicine-power', which can be embodied in the medicine-
bundle – a package of natural objects, such as feathers, stones
and crystals that was collected by the quester during the
vision-questing period.

The traditional vision quest is the celebration of **liminality**,
expressed in the wilderness location, its rite-of-passage status
and the altered mind states that occur during the experience.
The vision quest is the central foundation of all Native
American spirituality, originating in a remote period of
prehistory. Ancient vision-questing stone rings and 'beds' are
found in some areas. In earlier shamanic forms of vision
questing, plant **hallucinogens** were sometimes used to
enhance the experience. A modern form of vision-questing
activity is now called 'wilderness psychology'.

See also **Mythic Geography; Rock Art; Shaman; Trance**

The High Cross … mundus, marking … crossed at the c… in Bristol. (Rober…

The *axis mundi* was also imaged in the heavens. In many early societies, the canopy of the heavens was viewed as a roof or tent, the stars were holes or windows in the firmament, and the Milky Way the seam. The Pole Star, Polaris, which appears fixed, held the celestial tent like a tent pole, for the sky seems to rotate or pivot around that spot. Polaris happens to mark the north celestial pole – overhead at the North Pole and at an angle above the horizon equivalent to the angle of latitude it is viewed from further south. The Lapps and other arctic Europeans, as well as the Siberian reindeer-herder tribes, called the Pole Star the Nail Star. The Buryat of Siberia refer to it as the Pillar of the World. The Pole Star shines above the Hindu Mount Meru, further emphasizing the World Axis nature of the mythical mountain. The Omaha Indians of Nebraska had a myth in which figured a great, burning cedar tree to which the forest animals had worn four trails, one from each of the cardinal directions. In an annual ceremony, the Omaha people remembered this legendary burning cedar by setting up a sacred pole. But it was not erected vertically, because Omaha territory covered an area around latitude 42 degrees north, and to point at the Pole Star the sacred pole had to be angled accordingly.

The World Navel not only ordered the heavens and the land, it could also be incorporated into the structure of dwellings. The Siberian reindeer-herders, such as the Soyot and Buryat, saw their tent pole as the Sky Pillar. The pole itself was sacred, and offerings were placed on a small stone altar at its base. The central post is, or was, to be found in the structure of many tribal dwellings, including those of the Ainu of the north Japanese island of Hokkaido and of Sakhalin, many Native American peoples and the Khasi of northeast India (Assam). Everywhere it was common practice to place offerings at the foot of the post. The domestic fire, too, was considered to be the omphalos of dwellings in many ancient and traditional societies. The Latin for the hearth is *focus*, which the English language has adapted to mean *centre*. In the ancient Roman household the hearth was the seat of the **goddess** Vestia; in traditional Irish households it was associated with Brigit (a pagan goddess who was later Christianized).

The World Centre as a model for dwellings brings the image down to a more intimate, human scale. Yet even at this domestic level, it has not quite reached its deep roots, which lie directly in the human being – body and mind – for the image of the World Navel is essentially a projection of human physiology. The human being is an *axis* at the meeting point of the four bodily directions (front, back, left, right) extended to the cardinal directions. The World Centre is *here*, and 'here' is portable. This is literally the crux of the ancient, primordial

instinct of the World Centre, and why it could exist anywhere. 'Here' is always the centre; all the billions of human beings on this planet are at the centres of their worlds. The depth to which the perceptual and bodily Four Directions are unconsciously ingrained within us is indicated in C.G. Jung's identification of an archetype of quaternity. He commented on 'the centring process and a radial arrangement'.

The search for the Centre can go even deeper than the human body itself. The mysterious axis at the Centre of the World was a feature of shamanism, for it is a passage between this and other worlds or states of consciousness. The basic shamanic model is of three worlds connected by a 'vertical' axis: the underworld, the middle world of human existence and the upperworld of the gods, great spirits and celestial realms. (Depending on the cultural context, this basic three-world model can sometimes incorporate many more complex ideas, including the belief in there being seven or nine worlds along the axis.) The **shaman** would 'journey' to the otherworlds in trance, flying to the World Tree, Cosmic Mountain or whatever other form the *axis mundi* was culturally envisaged to be. The shaman went 'down' or 'up' this to enter the underworld or heaven world.

The wooden frame of a Siberian shaman's drum was said to have been fashioned from a branch of the World Tree, and perhaps an image of the primordial tree would be painted on the drumskin. The Goldi shaman's ceremonial robe had a depiction of the World Tree emblazoned on it. The Siberian Chukchee saw the Pole Star as a hole in the sky through which access to the spirit worlds is possible. The spirit of the Siberian shaman would float upwards with the smoke of the central fire through the smoke-hole, which was also associated by many tribes with the Pole Star. Sometimes the shaman would cut notches in a pole, perhaps the central tent pole, and climb it to symbolize his passage up the World Tree. This happened not only in Eurasia but around the world. The female shaman (*machi*) in Chile, for instance, would climb a notched pole 9ft (3m) tall called a *rewe*, at the top of which she would drum herself into **trance**. Shamans elsewhere might make a wing-flapping motion with their arms at the top of a pole to indicate spirit flight.

The World Centre at the intersection of the Four Directions is the crack between the worlds, the place where communication with the spirits and gods is possible, and where access to the spiritual otherworlds can take place. Projected outwards beyond mind and body, it is the reference point for ordering the earth and the heavens, and thus space and time.

See also **Borobudur; Cahokia; Chavín de Hunatar; Cuzco; Mecca; Tiahuanaco**

WUPATKI

The name is **Hopi** for 'tall house'. This complex of prehistoric pueblo buildings is situated north of Flagstaff, Arizona, near the Sunset Crater Volcano. The buildings are a mix of Sinagua and Kayenta **Anasazi** Indian work, and date to AD 1100–1225. Sunset Crater began erupting in AD 1064, and the layer of cinder and ash this produced, along with increased rainfall after the period of eruption, made the area suitable for settlement. The general district attracted not only the Singua ('without water') people and the Anasazi, but other groups as well. Hopi **rock art** motifs have been discovered on some of the rock surfaces in the region. It is not known what exactly the pre-eruption settlement pattern was like around the volcano, but an 11,000-year-old spear point has been discovered that indicates that some of America's earliest inhabitants roamed there.

The site has special interest for ancient **energies** aficiandos, because it is located over geological faulting, with some

One of the blowholes at Wupatki. These are openings to an estimated 7 billion cubic feet of subterranean caverns, fissures and faults. Factors such as changes in air pressure, thunderstorms and variations in surface temperature can affect the flow of air through these holes or vents, but usually air flows into the blowholes during the night and early morning, and out during the afternoon. Sometimes the air exits the vents at up to 30mph (48kph). Here we can see from the chiffon scarf that the blowhole is 'exhaling'. Some Hopi wind-god legends refer to these vents, but we do not know fully what they meant to the ancient Sinagua and Anasazi Indians who lived at Wupatki.

Part of the ruined Wupatki pueblo in Arizona. Note that the builders incorporated naturally outcropping rock into the fabric of the building.

buildings actually positioned directly on cracks in the Kaibab limestone beneath them, and the Indians incorporated vents in the complex to allow for exhalations of air issuing from the vast subterranean fault system.
See also **Chaco Canyon; Maya**

WYRD

This is the Old English spelling of the Norse Urdr, Fate. Wyrd was one of three sisters who wove the fates of human beings – the names of the other two sisters are unknown. An illustration in Holinshed's *Chronicles* (1577) shows them standing by a tree, probably the World Tree, and they are referred to in Shakespeare's *Macbeth*.
See also **Arthur; Yggdrasil**

Index